Stable Management
for the Owner-Groom

A

Stable Management
for the Owner-Groom

by **George Wheatley**

CASSELL

LONDON

To Pamela and Jennifer,
two enthusiastic ex-pupils, and their friends,
Lassie, Pickles and Playboy

Cassell & Company Ltd, 35 Red Lion Square, London WC1
MELBOURNE, SYDNEY, TORONTO, JOHANNESBURG, CAPE TOWN, AUCKLAND

© George Wheatley 1966
First published 1966

Phototypeset by BAS Printers Limited, Wallop, Hampshire
Printed by Ebenezer Baylis and Son, Limited,
The Trinity Press, Worcester, and London
F.566

INTRODUCTION

Unless he is wealthy, the horse-owner today must be his own groom and stable manager. A knowledge of these fields, apart from ensuring the health and happiness of the horse, can also reduce expense caused by needlessly heavy vet's bills or by waste. In short, no responsible owner should be without experience in the care of horses and stables.

Many people, particularly young people, are attracted by the idea of horses and riding. Their early enthusiasm is all too often damped, however, when they come to realize the work involved. Above all, they must learn to be unselfish: more suffering is caused by selfishness, ignorance and neglect than by calculated cruelty.

The real test of unselfishness comes in winter. While the horse is out at grass during the spring and summer months, it makes few demands on the owner's time and energy. But only true devotion will brave icy winds, snow and mud; or, worst of all, rise early on a freezing morning to attend to stable chores when the horse has been brought in at night.

So my advice to those anxious to acquire a horse or pony is this: go and learn stable management under proper supervision at a good riding school; you will find that no allowance is made for the severity of the weather. Then, and only then, if you are still keen—go ahead, by all means.

Hence the reason for this book is to provide a practical guide for those who have just acquired, or are about to acquire, their first horse or pony. And if one is a real horse-lover (as opposed to a mere horse-user), caring for one's horse and attending to the stable work that is always necessary can be as much a part of the pleasure of owning a horse as riding it. It must be remembered that the most important lesson to learn is that a horse is completely dependent upon its owner for everything.

CONTENTS

1 The Stable

Brick-built stables are ideally the best, but, unfortunately, the cost of building such stables today would be prohibitive. Those still in existence belong to old country houses, rectories, farms or a few old country inns, besides those specially built in more spacious days as hunt, racing stables or studs. Even these are rapidly disappearing, being converted into garages, storage places or even flats. One is indeed lucky if one can find an old stable intact with its stalls, loose-boxes, fitted mangers and partitions with rings for pillar reins, plus a tack-room.

Stabling. A modern range of loose boxes opening on to a yard
TAKEN AT THE RIDING SCHOOL OF MISS PETERS, REIGATE HEATH

The alternative then is the modern portable stable, often built of cedar wood or concrete blocks. A number of firms specialize in these and advertise regularly in *Horse and Hound*, *Riding School and Stable Management*, *Riding*, *Light Horse*, *Pony* and so on. These are built in units, from a single box, with or without an adjoining tack-room, to a whole range of boxes, to suit individual requirements. They have one advantage in that they can be added to, if one's string of ponies or horses increases in number.

If the choice of a site is not too restricted, choose a position on the top, rather than at the bottom, of a slight slope, and if possible on a light gravel or sandy soil rather than a cold, wet, clay subsoil. This will help drainage and reduce the amount of mud in winter. If possible, especially with a wet, clay soil, have the foundation dug out to eighteen inches or two feet and filled with rubble, topped with clinker or coarse ash, to help drainage. And have a good, firm path—not cement—laid down, and well rolled, leading to the stables. Do not use paving stones, as in time these become slippery and dangerous when wet. Use some material which provides a firm, rough surface, providing a good foothold.

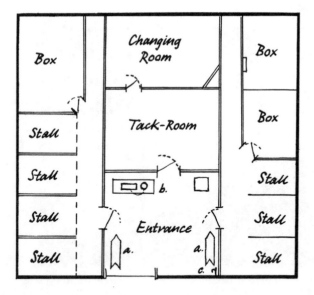

Sketch plan: Stables used by the author—the dotted line represents the barriers that enable the stalls to be used as temporary loose boxes when required
(a) Saddle horses
(b) Table with calor gas stove
(c) Water tap

The stables should face south and west, to protect them from north and east winds. If there are no trees already growing, plant some which grow quickly, to act as wind-breaks, on the north and east sides, but not close enough, when they grow, to make the stables dark or their roots interfere with the foundations. Stables of any size are frequently built to form two or more sides of a square, which can be used as an exercise yard. In any case, when planning, have the tack- and feed-room and storage space for hay and straw near at hand and easily accessible. Good planning can save hours of time and unnecessary extra work. It is quite a good idea to have the tack-room, feed-room, and hay-barn in the middle of the block of stables, so as to be approximately equidistant from all boxes and/or stalls.

The next choice is, stalls, boxes, or some of each. Stalls today are not greatly favoured, boxes being preferred. But they are useful for the temporary accommodation of ponies brought up from grass. Their use for this purpose saves messing up boxes, and therefore saves time and labour. Also more horses or ponies can be accommodated in less space. Personally, I would advocate having some stalls, especially for ponies, for this reason. Stalls should not be too narrow; if they are, moving about and handling a pony in them can be dangerous, especially for youngsters. They should be 6 feet wide, by 11 feet long from wall to centre of heel post. Such dimensions will give adequate room for safely handling a full-sized horse, and so give ample room for ponies. If wide enough, barriers can be put across as they can be used as temporary boxes for keeping ponies in at night in an emergency.

Partitions separating stalls should be high enough to prevent horses from putting their heads over the top and biting each other. They should be filled in at the head end so that horses cannot see each other when standing in the stalls or when feeding.

Loose-boxes can be 12 × 10 feet for a pony, or 14 × 12 feet for a horse. These are standard sizes; too large boxes are not recommended, as they use too much straw, and take more time and labour in mucking out. The horse or pony should have enough room to move around and lie down comfortably.

The height of the stables should be enough to give not less than 1,200 cu. ft. of air per horse, after subtracting the total dimensions of all fittings, such as manger, water-trough, and so on.

Stables should be both light and airy, with plenty of windows, which should be draught-proof. Windows should be sufficiently high to be out of reach if a horse puts its head up. The Sheringham type of window is the best as it prevents the air outside from blowing downwards on the animal's back. Cold never hurt a horse: a draught can kill. Avoid dark, damp, stuffy stables as they breed germs. In cold weather extra warmth can easily be provided, when necessary, by rugging up. There should also be some form of ventilation in the angle of the roof, to carry off the warm, stale air.

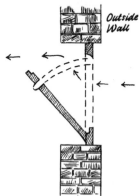

Sheringham-type stable window—opens inwards to prevent direct draught on the pony's back

All doors should open outwards, never inwards in case a pony gets cast in his box near the door. Doors of stalls and/or boxes can open onto a passage, which should be wide enough to allow a full-sized horse to be turned round easily and safely. Narrow passages are dangerous. The door to the entrance of the stables should be wide enough to allow the entry of a horse and man together. Narrow doors are dangerous and can cause accidents. They should also be high enough to allow for a horse suddenly throwing up its head. A bang on the top of the head can cause poll-evil.

Preferably, all doors of stalls and boxes should open direct onto the yard. The horse is an inquisitive creature and likes to be able to see what is going on in the outside world, and not spend all day staring blankly at a wall. Such doors should be divided in half, so that the upper half can be kept hooked back, permanently open. It should only be closed in bad weather conditions.

Bolts on doors should be of the type, and so placed, that the horse cannot undo them. There should be one at the bottom as well as at the top. I have known horses which were experts at undoing their bolts. The head of the bolt, when fastened home, should turn downwards, so that the horse cannot reach it over the top with his mouth.

Each stall or box should have its own drain, with a removable cover, and a trap to prevent straw and muck getting down, which can be taken out easily for cleaning and disinfecting. The floor should slope gently from all corners towards the central drain. The slope should be just enough to allow urine to flow easily down to the drain, and to allow water to flow away when boxes or stalls are washed out, as they should be periodically. The old-fashioned open channel, leading to a drain at the end, sometimes seen running along a row of stalls, is not to be recommended as it is difficult to keep clean.

Floors must be completely impervious to wet, non-slip, and durable. Wood floors absorb moisture and are unhygienic. They also rot and become very slippery when wet. Cement is impervious, but becomes slippery, if smooth. If used it should be deeply grooved in a herring-bone pattern before it sets. Cement slabs, even when roughened, wear smooth and become slippery. Any form of stone or cement floor is also very cold in winter. Cobblestones set in cement are uneven, and never give good, level standing; they also become very slippery. Ordinary bricks are not slippery, but are very porous and wear unevenly and quickly. Vitrified brick, such as the 'Blue Stafford', or 'Dutch', probably provides the best flooring. Such bricks have a grooved upper surface, with one or more lines. Their chamfered edges provide better foothold and facilitate drainage. They should be laid on edge. There are bricks or tiles specially manufactured for stable floors.

Tiles probably provide the best roofing, as they keep an even temperature and provide roof ventilation. But they can be easily broken or loosened, and then become untidy and leaky. Either flat tiles or pantiles can be used. Slates make excellent roofs, if kept repaired. They should have an under-roofing of boards. Slates are fastened to the woodwork of the roof by two nails driven through each, and if properly secured they are not easily dislodged by gales. Thatched and tarred-felt roofs should be avoided because of the risk of fire, though they are warm in cold weather, and noiseless. Galvanized iron is untidy. It is noisy in rain or hail, hot in summer, and cold in winter. Unless very securely fastened, it can be blown off in a gale. It has little to recommend it, except that it is cheap. Open roofs, without ceilings, should have louvre-board ventilation. The pitch or slope largely depends on the material used; thick tiles need more slope than slates. The maximum slope is about 45 degrees.

Stable fittings should be kept to a minimum: a corner manger saves space, and its interior should be of material which can easily be cleaned, preferably glazed. Some people like to have an automatic water supply, which certainly saves labour. Others prefer to keep a bucket of water in a corner of the box or stall. Avoid the old-fashioned hay rack. It is usually fastened too high up, so that hay-seeds can fall in the horse's eyes. Use a haynet instead. Mangers and other fittings should have smooth rounded edges. A manger should be boarded in underneath to prevent a horse from hitting its knee against it. Fitted mangers must be shallow in order that a pony cannot catch his jaw in them; they should be deep enough to prevent food being thrown out and broad enough so that they cannot be bitten. Some have a separate division for hay, but this is not advised as a pony often tosses its hay out onto the floor and wastes it. It will not eat hay which has been trampled on.

Some prefer to dispense with mangers and water-bowls altogether, which greatly facilitates cleaning the stable. Feeding is at ground-level, which is much more natural, using a moveable galvanized iron feed-tin, or a wooden feed-box. Either circular feed-tins, some 18 inches in diameter, or wooden boxes, about 15 inches high, with sloping sides, and about 18 inches square at the top, are long-lasting, easily cleaned and quite adequate. They are removed after feeding.

Pony secured by log and rope

There should be two firmly secured tie-rings: one high up for short-racking when grooming, and the other just below the manger for securing the pony. When tying a horse up to the latter use a heavy ball-weight or wooden block, to prevent the horse from putting its front leg, or legs, over the rope. This can cause a nasty accident. The log is fastened through the end of the rope and just touches the ground when the horse stands up to the manger, thus taking the slack out of the rope. Its use is essential in a stall if the horse is tied up the whole time.

Electric light switches must be well out of a horse's reach. A horse loves playing with anything moveable.

In case you ever get a crib-biter or a wind-sucker, do not have any bare wood in the box or stall. Cover it with zinc sheeting.

An adequate water-supply, with plenty of taps, is essential. Have a good pressure of water and freely-running taps. One tap outside each box, or between two boxes, is ideal, but expensive. There should be one at each end of a row of boxes, at any rate. Much time and labour can be spent in carrying water if there is only one tap. One tap, preferably near the centre of the stable-block, should have an attachment fitted for using a hosepipe, for cold hosing, and swilling down the stables and yard.

Have some means of providing hot water, either in the tack-room or entrance to the stables, for making bran mashes, hot fomentations, etc., when required, and for cleaning tack. A portable calor-gas stove is safe, efficient and economical to run.

If possible, have a separate loose-box well away from the main block as a 'sick bay' for isolating sick horses, especially in cases of contagion and/or infection.

2 Stable Equipment

In order to keep stables clean and tidy various, necessary stable tools are required. If there are youngsters working in stables, a zinc barrow is lighter, and therefore preferable to the old-fashioned wooden barrows which are heavy and cumbersome, even when empty. An extension can be fitted to the zinc barrow to increase its depth and carrying capacity. Zinc barrows are also easier to keep clean.

A sack is useful for carrying straw, to prevent scattering it all over the yard. In some stables sacks are cut open and used for carrying stable litter, but this is not recommended. The sacks become filthy and soil one's clothes, and are heavy to carry.

Wooden buckets, or zinc, plastic or vulcanized rubber buckets can be used. The old wooden buckets are very heavy to carry, and difficult to keep clean, though they are useful for water in a box as their weight makes them harder to upset. Zinc buckets are light and easily cleaned. They are strong and do not often upset if placed in a corner of the box. Plastic pails are also light and easily cleaned, but break easily if kicked or trodden on by a horse. They are, however, quite inexpensive and fairly durable, with reasonable care. Vulcanized rubber buckets are excellent but rather heavy; they wear well.

Also required are pitchforks, shovels, yard-brooms and skeps. Pitch- or hay-forks should be the ordinary two-pronged type used for tossing hay; the prongs should not be too long, or too wide apart; fairly short handles are best. Shovels should be large and broad, like snow-shovels. Yard-brooms should be the heavy duty variety, with fairly short handles. Handles invariably come off if the heads are nailed or screwed on. They are best secured by a metal attachment which clips onto the broom-head and handle, and is then screwed tight to both by wing-nuts. These attachments cost 7s 6d each and can be bought through an ironmonger. They have the advantage that a new broom-head or handle can be fitted quickly. A skep is a round, wicker basket used for picking up droppings. A bushel-sized potato basket serves the purpose perfectly well.

A long length of hosepipe is invaluable for washing down the stables and yard. Its length depends on the size of the stables and

A skep (for mucking out
and picking up droppings)

A tooth rasp, the use of which is
best left to the expert, for example,
a veterinary surgeon

yard, but should reach easily to the furthest end. Have a nozzle
which will give either a jet or a fine spray. A hose is also essential for
cold-hosing a horse's legs, and for bathing cuts (*q.v.*); also in case
of fire.

There is quite an art in mucking-out, for usually far too much straw
is thrown away. Beginners, particularly young pupils, are the worst
offenders because they will not take the time or trouble to shake out
the straw thoroughly. Requiring just that little extra time, effort and
concentration, they are often too lazy or slap-dash to do it, and good,
clean straw gets thrown out with the wet straw and muck as a result.
With the present cost of straw one cannot afford to be careless or
extravagant with bedding, especially with several stabled horses.
Another way to economize is to shake out and collect any cleaner,
drier straw on the manure heap, in dry weather. This can be collected
and spread out, preferably under cover in a good draught, to dry
and sweeten, when it can be re-used. It is surprising how much can
thus be saved.

Long wheat straw is undoubtedly the best bedding. Unfortunately,
as so much straw is 'combined' today, straw with long stalks is not

easily obtained. Wheat straw is the most attractive in appearance. Stalks should be as long as possible, and uncrushed, with the varnish unbroken. Being the most waterproof straw available it does not become sodden so easily, and is therefore more economical. Oat straw, being softer, becomes soggy easily. Also horses are inclined to eat it, which encourages them in the bad habit of eating their bedding. Never use barley straw; the awns irritate a horse's skin when it lies down; eating it may also cause colic.

Wood shavings are inexpensive and make excellent bedding. But they *must* be clean and free from foreign bodies such as pieces of paper, and chips of wood, which can become wedged in the horse's hoof. Take care there are no nails, screws or washers, etc., hidden among the shavings. Clean shavings make a warm, soft bedding. They are very absorbent and soak up urine, acting as a deodorant. Droppings also dry quickly on them. Give a fairly thick bed as they are apt to compress and pack solid under a horse's weight. When mucking out, first remove all loose droppings. Dig out wet, sodden shavings and remove them; if left down they can cause thrush, or other foot troubles. Finally sweep back the loose, top layer, adding fresh shavings as required.

Peat moss is often recommended, but is heavy to work with. Dig out and remove wet patches. Bracken can be used as bedding at a pinch, as in some parts of Scotland. Do not use when green, but collect it while green and dry it. It should not be collected when brown as it powders and crumbles to dust when dry.

The secret of good mucking out lies in thoroughly shaking out the bedding: the heavier wet straw and muck fall to the bottom, the lighter, cleaner straw remaining on top. Plan your work according to the size and shape of your box and the place where your horse will be tied up. Experiment, to find the quickest way for a particular box.

If mucking out a stall, remove the horse or pony and tie it up in an empty, preferably already used, box or stall which is unoccupied. In a box short-rack your horse so that he cannot move about and get in your way. Better still, remove him altogether out of the box. Horses can be most unco-operative and wrong-headed, standing precisely where you want to work. However, with patience, and always doing the box daily in the same way. the horse learns what is expected of it and can be trained to move over and stand where required. Eventually it does so automatically, or at a word of command.

Never leave any implements, especially a hay-fork, where a horse can knock them down and tread on them. This can cause a serious accident. Look after the sides and corners, and the middle of the box will look after itself. Start at one corner, picking up all loose droppings first, before disturbing any of the straw. Then shake out all clean, dry straw on top, putting it on one side. Keep shaking out the remaining straw, working it together into one pile, so that the rest of the floor can be swept clean. Eventually, only droppings, wet straw, or pieces too small to be of any use, are left. Surprisingly little straw need be thrown away if this is done thoroughly. Slightly damp, not sodden, straw can be left to dry and re-used at night. All droppings and sodden straw can then be collected into the wheel-barrow. The floor must be swept absolutely clean. A dirty floor can cause disease, particularly in dark corners, and can soon cause trouble to a horse's feet. If any droppings or straw are stuck to the floor scrape them off with the shovel or wooden edge of the brush. Once a week wash the floor with disinfectant such as Ibcol, or Jeyes Fluid.

Having cleaned and swept down one side pick up the clean straw which has been collected and stack it neatly along the side. Work round the sides of the box in this way. Having done one half, move the horse over to the clean side and tackle the other half in the same way. Stack clean straw neatly round two sides and the back of the box. Put the cleanest straw down where the horse's head usually faces. Work towards the door when sweeping. Then sweep any passages thoroughly. Finally sweep the entrance to the stables, the area of the stable-yard in front of the box-door, and keep the whole yard swept and tidy. Pick up any litter, rubbish, straw or leaves in the yard. An untidy stable-yard always gives a bad impression. If a stable manager keeps his yard neat, he is likely to be clean and tidy in other respects as well.

Leaving the floor bare during the day saves time, labour and straw, and gives it a chance to dry and air thoroughly. If the horse has to be kept standing in all day, put down only a thin layer of straw to prevent slipping. Droppings can easily be swept up and it is better for a horse's feet than standing all day on a thick layer of wet, dirty straw. If the bedding is put down again during the day, it necessitates mucking out again at evening stables.

When setting the box fair for the night, first remove all droppings and wet straw and sweep the floor clean. When putting down the straw from the sides of the box, toss it into the air with the hay-fork so that the stalks criss-cross and make a firm, yet elastic, bedding. There is a knack in doing this. Put the less clean straw down first, with the cleanest on top. Clean, fresh straw can be stacked around the sides, making a support for the horse to lean against when he lies down, and helping to prevent him from becoming cast.

A good thick bedding at night is more economical as the straw becomes less soiled. It is also warmer and more comfortable and encourages a horse to lie down. This saves his legs, which is important as a horse stands so much. Within reason, the heavier the horse, the thicker the bed should be. Lying on a thin bed, on a hard, stone floor can easily cause a capped hock or elbow. Furthermore, a horse feels the cold and damp, and any draught, much more if he has too little straw to lie or stand on.

Do not bring the bed too far forward towards the front of the box; leave about four or five feet from the door, with another space in the corner for the water bucket, which should not be stood on the straw. To make a neat finish lay the broom-handle on the floor and plait the straw neatly along it, across the width of the box, facing the door.

Used straw bedding can be a source of income, which helps to buy fresh straw. Nurseries, strawberry- and mushroom-growers are glad to have a steady supply of good wheat-straw horse-manure. If several horses are stabled it can be arranged to have the manure collected periodically—weekly or monthly, according to the number of horses. Sometimes, instead of selling the manure, fresh, clean straw can be supplied in exchange. Prices vary according to locality. Some firms advertise regularly in *Horse and Hound*. Sawdust is useless for this purpose. In fact, nurseries and mushroom-growers will not accept straw manure if there is any sawdust mixed with it. So, when mucking out boxes bedded with sawdust or shavings, keep the refuse separate from the manure heap used for straw bedding.

The muck heap should be accessible yet sufficiently far away to prevent the stables becoming infested with the flies and midges which congregate around the manure. Spraying the muck heap periodically with paraffin or disinfectant helps to keep down flies and midges in summer.

The best way to build a manure heap is to build a three-sided brick receptacle, about 4 feet 6 inches high at the back, and to collect the refuse in this. It should be kept tidy and muck should always be emptied at the back, so that it slopes towards the front. It should never be tipped untidily in the front. Periodically it should be piled up towards the back with a fork and shovel and the front swept clean. Use a wide wooden board for running up the wheelbarrow to tip the muck at the back. As already mentioned, any fairly clean straw can be collected and dried, thus helping to economize in straw.

Fire precautions are very important in a stable. There should be easy entrances and exits from all stalls and boxes. All latches and fastenings on doors should work well and quickly, and passages should be completely free from any obstructions. Keep pails of water always filled in passages and at strategic points. No smoking should be allowed, especially cigarettes, in boxes or stalls, or near where hay and straw are stored. One spark is enough to start a blaze, especially in hot, dry, summer weather.

Fire extinguishers should be placed at strategic points near boxes and stalls, in the tack-room, and in the hay- and store-room and the feed-room. These should be the pistol-grip type and the conical foam extinguishers. They should be regularly inspected to see that they are filled and in working order, ready for instant use. A supply of refills should be stored nearby in a cool, dry place. Everyone who uses the stables should know exactly where all extinguishers are, and the drill necessary for getting horses out and extinguishing the blaze.

Fire in a stable is a terrible thing, but one must never panic for the horses will panic quickly enough. First get the horses out. Try to be quiet and calm and unhurried. If there is much smoke and the fire is near the boxes, put a wet cloth round your nose and bandage the horses' eyes. If they panic and will not be led out, open the doors and drive them out, well away from the stables. They can be rounded up again afterwards. See that they do not break back again into the stables. Panic-stricken horses will often try to run back into their boxes in a blazing stable. Meanwhile other people should be using the extinguishers. Use the hose if it is long enough to reach and the water-pressure is sufficient to give a powerful jet, but do not use water on blazing paraffin, petrol or oil. Saturate as much of the buildings near the blaze as possible to prevent the fire from spreading, and soak any stored hay or straw.

It is a good plan to have a fire drill periodically, so that in an emergency everyone has a specified job and knows exactly what to do. The horses should also be trained and accustomed to being blind-folded and led out with their heads covered.

3 Stable Routine

Early morning stables: 6.30 a.m. in summer.
7 to 7.30 a.m. in winter.

Inspect your horse for any injury incurred during the night. Remove and fold up any night rug or rugs. If the weather is cold, put on a day rug. Do not leave the horse standing unrugged in cold weather if it has been rugged-up all night. If no day rug is available, replace the night rug inside-out.

Night stains and compressed state of bedding will show whether the horse has been lying down. If so look for signs of capped hocks or elbows, caused by lying on insufficient bedding, and for swollen legs, or any other possible injuries. Remove and roll up any leg-bandages put on overnight; massage the leg or legs briskly to restore circulation.

Remove the water-bucket, clean, refill and replace it so that the horse can drink before feeding. Give it its first 'short' feed of oats, bran, pony cubes, or whatever it has, while folding and putting away rugs and bandages; fill haynet and prepare to muck out. When the horse has finished eating, put on its head-collar and tie it up ready to muck out. Hang the refilled haynet up within reach so that the horse can amuse itself while being mucked out. If any horses or ponies kept in during the night are going to be turned out, give them their short feed (if any) and turn them out before starting to muck out. And then muck out as already described.

Having mucked out, short-rack and groom the horse. Early morning grooming in stable parlance is called quartering, or 'knocking-on'. Its object is to remove night stains, dust and scurf and make the horse presentable before taking it out to exercise. The methods of grooming a stabled horse and a pony kept out at grass, respectively, are dealt with later in Chapter 6.

In cold weather, if the horse is rugged-up do not remove the rug before quartering. Turn the front half of the rug back onto the horse's back and groom its forehand, then replace the rug, and throw the back of the rug forwards towards its head, in order to groom its hindquarters.

After quartering untie the horse from being short-racked and tie it to the ring below the manger. Tie its haynet up to the short-racking ring, so that it can eat its hay while you have your own breakfast.

After breakfast pick up any droppings, sweep the box tidy and tack up, ready to exercise the horse. The amount of exercise, type of work done and its duration, depend on the horse's condition and its purpose. If simply hacking for pleasure and exercise, then walking and trotting uphill, with perhaps a short, fairly slow, canter on any available grass, will be sufficient. It should take about $1\frac{1}{2}$ to 2 hours.

On returning, put on its head-collar. If the weather is cold, or the horse is at all warm, do not take off the saddle immediately. Loosen the girths, raise the saddle up and put it down again and leave it on for about ten to fifteen minutes. If the horse shows signs of sweating, remove the saddle, smack briskly the part where it rested and where the girths were, to restore the circulation, and then give a brisk rub down with straw or a stable-rubber. Then put on a light rug until it has dried off and cooled down. Never leave a warm horse, especially if sweating, standing unattended, especially in a draught. The loins are the most vulnerable part. Also dry thoroughly between the front and back legs, the flanks and between the ears.

If it is raining, bring a wet horse in warm, and having rubbed it down, cover it with straw, under a rug with a surcingle round to keep it on. A wet horse brought in warm dries more quickly than one which is cool. Never let a horse drink when warm or sweating.

Midday stables: pick up any droppings. Refill water bucket and haynet. Give any midday 'short' feed. Tidy and sweep box and yard. If not riding again, clean tack. Mix any short feeds required for evening stables. Groom thoroughly when the horse is cool and dry.

Evening stables: pick up droppings. Set the bed fair. Sweep and tidy box, stables and yard. Give evening 'short' feed. Fill water bucket and haynet. Put on head-collar, short-rack and lightly groom the horse. Put on night rug and any stable bandages required. Remove head-collar. If the horse was ridden again in the afternoon, clean tack, including head-collar. Bring up any ponies or horses out at grass which are stabled at night, having prepared their boxes. Brush off any dry mud if they have been rolling. Clean their head-collars. A good horseman will inspect stabled horses last thing at night to see that haynets and water-buckets are filled, and that rugs and leg-bandages have not shifted or come undone.

To take off a rug, first undo the surcingle, take it off and either hang it over your arm, or fold it neatly and put it in a corner of the box. Next undo the breast-buckles and fold the rug neatly over the horse's back, so that the edges coincide. Next, with the left hand holding the upper part and the right hand the part over the horse's croup, sweep the rug off in the direction of the hair, backwards over the horse's tail. The rug as it comes off automatically folds into four.

To rug-up, gather up the rug (or sheet) and throw it well forward over the horse's back. Then smooth out the front part and fasten the buckle. Next, walk behind the horse and pull the rug into position with both hands. See that the centre of the rug runs along the horse's spine, so that it hangs evenly on either side. This is one of the few occasions when one should stand directly behind a horse. Next place the surcingle (or roller) in position, so that it comes underneath in the girth groove, just behind the wither and elbow, with the buckle on the near-side. If using a roller pad, place it under the roller, behind the withers. Then from the off-side see that the roller hangs well forward, where the girth goes, to prevent it from slipping forward and working loose when the horse moves. Buckle the roller on the near side, firmly but not tightly. Smooth the rug down on both sides below the surcingle, or roller, running the fingers between it and the rug. At the same time pull the rug slightly forward in front of each elbow, so that it does not drag on the points of the shoulders or on the withers. Fasten the breast strap which should lie loosely above the points of the shoulders. A breast strap is not required when the surcingle is sewn onto the rug. The rug must not press round the neck and shoulder, but should fit the horse or pony, being neither too large nor too small. Both may cause sore withers, besides other discomfort.

When using a blanket under the rug put it on first, in the same way. Place it well up on the neck and see that the back of the blanket does not hang over the root of the tail. Place the rug on top and, having fastened the roller or surcingle, fold back the part of the blanket lying on the neck, as an added safeguard against its slipping.

When tying up a haynet, whether in the stable or outside on a fence, pull the draw-string tight. Then slip it through the tie-ring, or round the top of the fence, and pull the draw-string through one of the meshes of the haynet, fairly low down, and pull it up strongly; this prevents the haynet from sagging as the horse eats the hay. It is especially important when tying it to a fence, as otherwise the haynet can sag right down and a horse can get its foot caught in the meshes and cause an accident. Then, having pulled the draw-string tight, so as to pull the haynet up tightly, loop it, using a simple quick-release knot. Never tie it in a knot that is difficult to undo. As the horse eats he will naturally tighten the knot, and probably twist the haynet round as well. Nothing is more annoying than a haynet with a knot which is difficult to unfasten, especially when one is in a hurry.

4 Handling

The first thing anyone who is going to handle horses must learn, is to be quiet and gentle, both in voice and movement. There is no place in the stable for a boisterous, loud-voiced, rough groom. Approach quietly, speak quietly and handle gently, yet firmly. Horses and ponies are naturally timid and easily frightened. Also they resent noisy treatment, and, having very good memories, never forget it. Nor do they ever forget a person who handles them roughly and will show their dislike, which originates through fear, with teeth and heels.

Always warn your horse of your approach. Speak cheerfully, and talk to your horse constantly. Horses quickly learn to understand simple words and commands such as, 'Whoa', 'Stand', 'Walk' and 'Trot', 'Move Over', and so on. They also go largely by the tone of voice. One's voice can soothe or frighten, scold or praise. It is not so much the actual words as the tone of the voice.

While handling gently, be firm. Horses quickly recognize a person who is accustomed to handling horses and knows his job. They hate a 'fumbler'. Also, like dogs, horses know at once if a person is timid or afraid, and will take advantage and play up accordingly. So, never let a horse see that you are afraid of it, even if you are. And never be sudden or undecided in your movements. If a pony turns its head or moves towards you, do not jump away suddenly. A sudden movement not only tells a horse that you are frightened, but also startles it. If, for instance, while being groomed, it turns its head round suddenly and makes a snatch at you, or kicks out with its hindleg, stand your ground and speak to it, firmly but quietly. 'Now then, old fellow. What's up with you? Stop that!' And never hit a pony on the head, or when in a temper. Scold it with your voice, and if it has to be punished give it a hard slap on its rump, at once. It is no use hitting it even two minutes after it has done wrong. It will not understand why it is being punished and will resent it, and become afraid. Many a horse has been made permanently head-shy, through being hit on the head, or even banged accidentally while being groomed by a rough, heavy-handed groom.

Patience is essential always when handling horses. They may not understand what you want; shouting and rough handling only make them bewildered. The more highly-bred, the more sensitive, highly strung and 'nervy' (or temperamental) a horse or pony is. Native ponies are far more placid than, say, thoroughbred racehorses.

Many a horse has been ruined by mishandling when young. It is then accused of vice, when really the original cause was fear, through rough handling as a colt.

To put on a head-collar always speak first and then approach from the front. Have the head-collar hung ready over your left forearm, and hold a tit-bit out in your left hand. As the pony or horse stretches its head forward to take the tit-bit, stand by its shoulder on the near (left) side, with your right shoulder towards it, facing its front. Slip the head-collar over its nose while it is eating; at the same time quickly slip the neck-strap over its neck and buckle it. If the horse is in a stall with its hindquarters towards you, speak first as you approach, then put your hand on its hindquarters, holding its tail just below the root and walk quietly but boldly in, at the same time running your right hand gently along its croup and back until you are standing level with its shoulder. Then proceed as before.

To lead a pony in hand, lead from the near-side, especially with a strange pony. Most horses are accustomed to being handled from the near-side. Later, when you know a pony well, train it to lead equally easily from either the near- or off-side. Speak to the pony and walk forward, but do not look at it. Many ponies will stop and refuse to move if stared at. Hold the leading rope about 8 or 10 inches from the head-collar in the right hand, with the other end of the rope in the left hand. Many horses, particularly thoroughbreds, hate being held too close to the head-collar, or too tightly. If you wish to turn the pony, always push it away from you. Never pull it towards you.

If a pony is restive and plays up while being led, slightly shorten your right-hand hold on the rope and push your elbow up into its neck. This helps to give you more control.

When tying up a horse, whether in a loose-box, outside in a field, or in a horse-box, always use a quick-release knot. This can be undone instantly by a quick jerk on the end, yet the more the pony pulls, the tighter the knot becomes.

To tie a quick-release knot, slip the rope-end through the tie-ring, or loop it round the object to which the pony is to be tied.

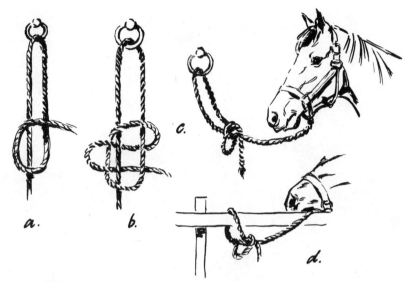

Quick-release knot: always use when tying a pony in the stable, outside, or when travelling
(a) First stage
(b) Second stage
(c) Completed knot
(d) Used for tying to a fence

Bring the end under the rope with the right hand. Hold the part which is under in the left hand and give it a twist, then with the right hand put a loop, not the end, of the rope through the twisted part and pull tight. This will leave the end dangling. Once learnt, this is very simply and easily tied, yet can be undone instantly in an emergency. A few ponies learn to undo a quick-release knot. In this case pass the end of the rope through the loop after tying and pulling tight.

When turning a pony round in a box or stall, again turn it away from, and not towards, you.

Always look over your shoulder and watch your pony when leading out of the stable or through any doorway, to see that it does not knock its hip against the doorpost, or its head against the lintel, if the door is low. The hip joint can be seriously damaged by knocking it, and poll evil can result from a blow on the head between the ears, if it throws up its head.

 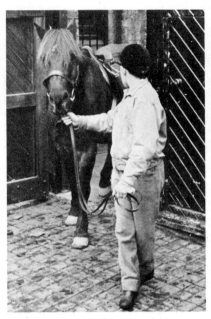

Left Leading a pony through a door. Incorrect. 'Johnny head-in-the-air' is not paying attention or looking where the pony is going. It will bang its hip against the door while rounding the corner, with possible serious injury

Right Leading a pony through a door. Correct. The rider is looking back over his shoulder, watching to see that the pony does not damage itself by hitting the door as it emerges

Speak first always and approach a stabled horse from the front. Walk up to its near-side shoulder. Avoid sudden movements when handling a stabled horse, and never rush round behind one which is tied up, without warning. One is asking to be kicked, and some ponies will readily oblige. Incidentally, mares are more likely to kick out than geldings. To walk round a stabled horse when tied up, put your right hand on its head-collar, speak, and then walk round or duck underneath its neck, holding the head-collar. If it is necessary to walk round behind, face the horse's tail, speak, put your hand on its croup, and run it down to its tail. Hold its tail just below the root and walk round, keeping as close to its hindlegs as possible. The closer you are, the safer you are; if the horse kicks, you will simply be pushed away if you are close to its leg, whereas if you walk round some distance away you will receive the full force of the blow—and probably get a broken leg. Holding the horse's tail makes it tend to walk forwards, rather than to kick out backwards. Also, it warns the horse of your intentions. If you are going to walk round behind a horse without holding its tail, then keep right away out of kicking distance.

A horse must be taught good stable manners. Teach it to obey simple commands, such as 'move over' (or 'get over'), 'foot' when you want to pick up a foot, or 'stand' when you want it to stand still, while grooming, and so on. If the same command is always used for the same movement, and is part of its daily routine, a horse soon learns to understand and obey.

If a tethered horse tries to turn its head and nip, for instance, while being groomed, immediately rap it smartly on the nose with the palm of your hand, and say 'No', or 'Naughty', sharply, in a scolding tone of voice. Never let it get away with nipping, as this can develop into serious biting. A horse which is inclined to turn its head and try to nip, soon learns not to after a few attempts, if promptly checked and scolded each time. Hold its hock while grooming its hindleg. This will give you warning if it intends to kick out, as you can feel the muscles tighten. If it tries to do so, again rap it sharply on its hindquarters with your hand and scold it.

Such things as lifting its feet when asked, standing still, moving over, or forwards or backwards when told, or putting its head down, are all part of good stable manners. Never let a horse get away with disobedience.

A horse which has formed the vice of kicking or biting can be cured, given time and patience. In the case of a really bad kicker, have someone to hold up its front leg on the side on which you are grooming. A bad biter can be controlled by fastening a length of stick to its head-collar, to lie flat against its neck, so that it cannot turn its head, or by fitting a muzzle. As biting and kicking were probably initially originated through fear, they can be cured if one has the time and patience by spending several hours daily in the horse's box. Tie it up and then sit down by its head and read. From time to time speak to it and offer it a tit-bit, until eventually the horse will begin to realize that you do not intend to harm it. Usually, once one has gained a horse's confidence it can be handled perfectly safely, both in and out of the stable.

C

5 Watering and Feeding

As regards the daily routine the golden rule is always water a horse *before* feeding; water should not be given until at least an hour after a full meal. The reason is that a large drink immediately after a heavy meal washes the food out of the stomach and frequently causes colic. The exception to this rule is when water is left all the time in the box, so that the horse can help itself whenever it likes. This is the more natural method of watering, and the horse, while eating may take a few sips; this does no harm. But if this method of watering is not used, water should be offered about half-an-hour before feeding; the bucket is then removed until at least an hour has elapsed after feeding. A horse should be watered thrice daily: at early morning stables, midday, and at evening stables. It normally drinks from about 8 to 15 gallons a day, according to its size and the time of year. Very cold water does no harm, provided a horse is not hot or sweating. In bitterly cold weather the chill can be taken off, or a filled bucket can be left standing until the water is the same temperature as the air in the stable.

As already stated (Chapter 1) hay is given in a haynet, tied with a quick-release knot.

Types of hay are Mixture, Meadow, Clover and Sainfoin. Mixture hay is an excellent feed, consisting of rye-grass and clovers. It comes from re-seeded land. Meadow hay varies considerably in food-value. It comes from permanent pasture land. That from upland meadows provides the best hay. Lowland and water meadows are liable to flood and may contain coarse-stemmed water plants, of little or no feeding value. Good meadow hay smells sweet and feels hard and crisp. It is greenish to brownish in colour—yellow or dark-brown shows deterioration, dark-brown sometimes being due to the stacked hay overheating and becoming mowburnt. Clover hay is rich in food-value, but difficult to save well. It easily becomes mouldy, and is often very dusty. Good, well-harvested clover hay is golden in colour. It is inclined to be wasteful as it falls through the haynet and much is lost in transporting it. Sainfoin is very nutritious, and probably the best. It is also golden coloured, and its stalks are rather coarse.

Hay varies considerably in quality. Soft hay has less feeding value than hard, crisp hay. Some horses will apparently enjoy hay which is slightly mowburnt. Musty hay can be detected by its smell, for it is usually hay which has not been properly dried and has been baled and stacked while damp. Mouldy hay has whitish spots on it and a sour, dank smell. Both are quite unfit as food. New hay, less than six months old, can be indigestible and may cause colic. Old seed hay should be about a year old and meadow hay should have been stacked about eighteen months. Hay over eighteen months to two years old is inclined to be dusty and brittle and its food-value has begun to deteriorate.

The quantity of hay eaten depends upon the size of the horse or pony. A hunter eats about 20 to 24 lbs. per day; a cob or pony between 14 and 16 lbs.; a small pony, up to about 12·2 hands, between 6 and 9 lbs. The total amount of hay for a stabled horse or pony should be divided into three, or preferably more feeds; four feeds a day are better than three, and five are even better than four. The smallest hay-feed should be given at early morning stables, and the largest at evening stables, to last throughout the night. If possible haynets are best weighed. One used to be able to buy haynets in three sizes: hunter (approx. 10 to 12 lbs. when stuffed completely full), cob or pony (7 to 8 lbs., stuffed completely full), small pony (up to 3 lbs., stuffed completely full). Unfortunately, nowadays haynets only seem to be obtainable in two sizes, known as 'single' or 'two-horse' nets, which is misleading and conveys little regarding the quantity or weight of hay each contains.

When purchasing hay it is not a good idea to buy it in a stack. The outside may be very weatherbeaten, and the inside mowburnt, and altogether there may be considerable waste. Hay is generally bought in trusses or bales. The trade weight for a truss of 'old' hay is 56 lbs. and 60 lbs. for 'new' hay. Bales usually average about 1 cwt. in weight, but may vary considerably.

The approximate weight in tons of a stack of hay can be found by dividing the contents (or volume) in cubic yards, by 11 (for straw divide by 16). The formulae for rectangular stacks are:

$$\text{Hay} \quad \frac{\text{Height} \times \text{Breadth} \times \text{Length}}{11} = \text{tons of hay}$$

$$\text{Straw} \frac{\text{Height} \times \text{Breadth} \times \text{Length}}{16} = \text{tons of straw}$$

All dimensions are in yards. The height = distance from ground to eaves, plus half distance from eaves to ridge.

For a circular stack:

$$\frac{3^1/_7 \times \text{radius}^2 \times \text{height}}{11} = \text{tons of hay}$$

$$\frac{3^1/_7 \times \text{radius}^2 \times \text{height}}{16} = \text{tons of straw}$$

When inspecting, ask for one bale (or truss) to be opened and inspect inside for signs of mould, or being mowburnt. The hay should be free from dust and have a good 'nose', i.e., be sweet smelling. Pull out a handful and smell it. The sweet smell so characteristic of hay is chiefly due to the presence of sweet vernal.

In summer, ponies and horses can be turned out to eat their natural food—grass. But in winter when there is no grass, they need some form of 'green meat', and as a substitute for grass, cabbage or cauliflower leaves or any other winter greens can be used. The leaves should be cut into small pieces, and stalks can also be used, provided they are cut up really small.

When turning ponies and horses out to grass in spring do not turn them out suddenly on lush, rich young grass for the whole day, especially if they are not being used, otherwise they will almost certainly contract laminitis. Small ponies are more susceptible to it than larger ponies or horses, though the latter can get it. If they have been stabled during the winter, accustom them gradually to the change of diet. Otherwise they may also go down with grass colic. Gradually cut down on the amount and number of short feeds, and at first turn them out only for about an hour daily. Over a period of about three weeks gradually lengthen the grazing time, until ultimately they can safely be left out all day. But even so, unless regularly ridden and exercised they tend to get very fat, and it is inadvisable to leave them out for the whole twenty-four hours. During the summer it is a good plan to let them out early for an hour or so; then bring them in during the day, and turn them out at night to graze. They will graze all night. This method also prevents them from being pestered by flies during the day. According to the weather they can start going out about the end of March. If very cold, thoroughbreds may not be able to start living out until well into mid-April.

In winter short feeds may be given in addition to hay. The contents, number of feeds per day and the size of each depends on the size of the horse or pony, condition, amount of work being done, age, and so on.

Some horses are good doers, and seem to thrive on whatever is given them. Others are bad doers, lose condition easily, and never seem to put on flesh whatever food, or how much, one gives them. Some horses are shy feeders, while others are dainty, finicky eaters, whose appetite constantly needs tempting. Feeding is largely a matter of observation and knowing one's horse individually. A diet which suits one horse, may not suit another. Therefore experiment until you find the diet which suits your horse. If a horse leaves food in the manger, try cutting down the amount, until everything given is cleared up at each meal. Do not leave stale food in the manger.

An old horse may need more food than a younger one. Extra food may be necessary in very cold weather—'a hungry pony is a cold pony'. More food and energy are used up in just keeping warm in bitterly cold weather. Also, the amount of work done affects the amount and kind of food required. If a horse is doing little or no work it may not need any 'short' feeds, but will do well on only hay, or maybe one small 'short' feed a day.

Oats are the best and most nutritious of the grain foods but the amount given should be regulated by the nature and amount of work done, and the size of the horse or pony. Oats have a very stimulating effect and too many may make a horse over-fresh and unmanageable. This again depends on individual temperament, and to some extent on age. A placid horse can safely carry more oats than an excitable 'hot' one. A racehorse in training, or a hunter being hard hunted may need up to 14 or 16 lbs. of oats daily. Racehorses, even when not in training, are given about 10 lbs. of oats daily, to keep them in condition. Small ponies should never be given oats, except for an occasional handful as a treat, especially when ridden by children. Ponies generally tend to be more excited by oats than large horses, and as a rule, the smaller the pony the more this tends to be the case. There are two varieties of oats, the black and the white. Whichever is given, they should be fat, plump and clean, and feel hard. They should have no smell, and should break sharply across when bitten, tasting like oatmeal. Any discoloration shows that the grain has suffered from damp. New oats are softer and heavier than old and are indigestible.

Oats should be bruised before being given. Crushing them tends to cause waste owing to loss of their floury content. 'Rolled' oats—crushed very fine—should not be used. Whole oats may pass undigested through the horse, whole grains being found in the droppings. 'Foxy' oats have a peculiar acrid smell, hence the term. They have been stored in bulk before being sufficiently dried, and have become 'heated'; sometimes they may be actually steaming. Their colour deepens.

Do not buy kiln-dried oats; they are usually dried in a kiln because they were previously damp or foxy. Kiln-drying eliminates the foxy smell, and restores the hardness, but deepens the colour. To restore their original colour, kiln-dried oats may then be bleached by exposure to sulphur fumes. Musty or mouldy oats are caused by the grain having been wetted by rain before harvesting, or accidentally after being stored. Affected grain smells musty, even if the mould is not visible, and it feels soft and spongy. Grain stored in a place infested by rats can become so tainted that horses refuse to eat it. This can be detected by the presence of nibbled oats and by the characteristic smell of rats, and by their droppings. Sprouting oats which have already germinated are quite unfit for consumption. Other grains can be given but are inferior in nutritional value.

Barley can be boiled and added to tempt the appetite of a 'faddy' horse, or to add variety when a horse is jaded and overworked.

Maize is the staple grain in South Africa, where it is called 'mealies'; also in North and South America, where it is known as 'corn'. It is also used in India and Egypt. It is deficient in protein, and should be given with a nitrogenous diet such as clover hay, alfalfa, or beans. A recommended mixture is one part of beans to two of maize—$7\frac{1}{2}$ lbs. of this mixture are said to equal 10 lbs. of oats in food value. Maize should be a bright colour, hard, dry and free from dirt and weevils, not at all brown. It should have no smell, and taste sweet when bitten.

Rye is inferior to oats, but forms a large part of the ration in Belgium, Denmark and Sweden. It is said to cause diarrhoea if fed in large amounts. In Russia, horses are fed on rye-flour; it is also used in America in smaller quantities.

Rice is used in Burma and in the Indian rice-growing districts of Assam and Bengal. It is very indigestible if horses are not accustomed to it. It can be used boiled or crushed, but the husk should not be removed.

Wheat is regarded as most unsuitable for horses in England.

Other foods are bran, a by-product of wheat, after the flour has been extracted by milling. Its food-value depends on the amount of flour present, and upon its containing vitamins B and E. There are several grades of bran: broad or flaked; medium; fine; and No. 2 Bran. The writer usually uses No. 2 Bran. Bran should be perfectly dry and free from any lumps, which are a sign of dampness. If the hand is plunged into a bran sack it should come out floury. Damp bran has a musty smell. It is an excellent food, particularly when mixed with other foods, in a 'short' feed, as it helps to provide bulk. Dry bran has a binding effect, while a bran mash has a slightly laxative effect. A hot bran mash is excellent for a horse which comes in cold or tired, say after a long day's hunting. Scald 2 to 3 lbs. of bran with boiling water in a bucket; add a pinch of salt to make it more palatable, cover and allow to stand until cool enough to eat.

Beans are very nutritious, but also very heating, so should only be given in small quantities. A double handful, mixed with other food twice daily, is sufficient for ponies. They are a useful winter food, especially in cold weather, for ponies living out and also for horses doing a considerable amount of hard work. Bruise or split them with a hammer before use. Beans should be hard and dry, sweet tasting, a light brown colour and free from weevil. English beans are better than imported varieties; their skins are thinner and they are smaller, rounder and more plump. Those from the Dutch Indies are poisonous.

Linseed is a useful addition to the diet for thin horses as it is fattening. It also helps to make their coats glossy, and is therefore used for about three or four weeks before a show. Linseed is either boiled or fed as linseed cake, as used for cattle. Linseed cake is the residue left after the linseed oil has been extracted. Never give unboiled seeds; when moist and warm they contain prussic acid.

Boil the seeds (about a $\frac{1}{2}$ pint) in a saucepan with water, all night. Add a little more water in the morning, bring to the boil and then simmer for two to three hours. It becomes a jelly when cool, which can be added to the feed. It is especially good in a bran mash (*q.v.*). Linseed is sometimes given when the coat is being changed. It is valuable for tempting a sick horse's appetite, or if it has an inflamed digestive tract, and also during convalescence. Linseed oil is less easily digested and disliked by some horses. One or two tablespoonfuls can be mixed daily with other foods. It helps to improve condition, and in cases of slight colic forms a mild laxative.

Malt grains, or Brewers' grains, also called 'draff' are the malt refuse left over from brewing. They are obtainable either dried (desiccated) or fresh. They can be fed occasionally and horses greatly enjoy them, either as a change of diet or to whet their appetite. They quickly become sour if kept, so should be fed immediately while fresh. They are unsuitable for horses doing severe, fast work.

Dried sugar beet is an excellent addition to a 'short' feed and is liked because it is sweet. As it swells considerably it should first be soaked overnight before using.

Peas, like beans, are nutritious but heating. Only give small quantities. Bruise or split them before using. Varieties are the blue, grey or white. They should be dry, sound, free from weevil, and at least a year old.

Potatoes are not recommended, and are indigestible when raw. Horses are fed on them in Ireland and people used them during World War II, when food was scarce and rationed. The skins should not be given.

Chaff is chopped hay. It is useful for mixing with all feeds and prevents a greedy horse from bolting its food. It can either be bought, or one can make one's own if one has a chaff-cutting machine.

Oatmeal gruel is a valuable restorative for a tired horse after a very long, hard day. If a horse is overtired its digestion is impaired, and the normal feed should not be given. Pour boiling water onto a double handful of oatmeal in a bucket, and stir well. Make it thin enough to drink, and give when cool.

Apples are an appetising and useful addition to a feed, and horses love them. Too many can cause colic.

Root vegetables are especially valuable after Christmas. They include carrots (which can be given at any time when obtainable), swedes, mangels, and turnips. All these can be given chopped up fine in the short feeds. Carrots should always be cut lengthwise; if diced they may get stuck across the horse's gullet, and choke it. Swedes, mangels and turnips can be boiled.

Pony cubes and horse nuts are now manufactured. The makers claim that they form a completely balanced diet and that horses and ponies fed on them do not require anything else; also that the hay ration can be considerably reduced. This would seem to be rather a monotonous diet, and somewhat expensive. A better plan is to use them with other feeds to add variety and interest.

Small quantities of salt are essential. This can be added to the short feeds, or a salt lick given in a container fixed to the stable wall. Ponies and horses when living out can be given a lump of rock salt; rock salt can also be put in a stabled horse's manger. A teaspoonful of table salt can be added to a feed, once daily.

The writer gives his own horses and ponies a mixture of bran, oats, pony cubes, a slice of white or (preferably) brown bread; to which is added one apple, a chopped carrot, any turnips or swedes available (about one large slice chopped up), and some leaves of green vegetables, chopped up fine. They start with one feed per day, increasing to two as winter sets in, and three feeds in the depth of winter; the feeds similarly gradually decrease in number as spring and better weather approach. The amounts of each ingredient vary according to the horse or pony's size; for example, a 12·2 hand pony: 5 handfuls of bran, 2 of oats, 2 of pony cubes, plus an apple, carrot, slice of bread and a small slice of swede, if available; a 13·2 hand: 6 handsful of bran, 3 of oats and 3 of pony cubes; a 14·2 hand: 7 of bran, 6 of oats and 3 of pony cubes; a 15·2 hand: 8 bran, 8 oats, 4 pony cubes. The rest of the mixture as before, with slightly more for the 15·2 hands horse.

The ponies enjoy this mixture and have always come through the winter in excellent condition on it. In addition, they get a haynet in the morning and another at night. The 15·2 hand has two haynets at night.

Grasses which form good food, either as green pasture or hay, are the meadow grasses, in four varieties, the fescues, especially meadow fescue, meadow fox tail, timothy (or meadow cat's tail), crested dog's tail, both types of rye grasses, yellow cat grass, cock's foot and sweet vernal.

Grasses which are useless as food are: barren fescue, couch grass or twitch, darnel, slender fox tail, tufted hair or tussock grass, soft brome, quaking grass, Yorkshire fog, meadow and wall barley, sedges and rushes.

The best clover is red clover, of which there are three varieties: broad red clover is biennial, the other two, Alsike or Swedish clover and white or Dutch clover, are perennial. Valerian (Italian or crimson clover) is an annual, commonly called trefoilium. There are three small clovers: birdsfoot trefoil, yellow suckling clover, nonsuch or hop trefoil. All clovers are valuable food, as pasture or hay. Vetches also are good.

Lucerne or alfalfa and sainfoin both form good hay.

Weeds such as coltsfoot, goose grass, docks, sorrel, knap weed, plantain, cat's ear, yellow rattle, buttercups, ox-eye daisy, nettles, thistles and dandelions should not be present in pasture or hay, being useless as food, though horses eat (and apparently relish) dandelion flowers and leaves in spring. They will also eat nettles.

They like hog-weed leaves and flowers.

6 Grooming

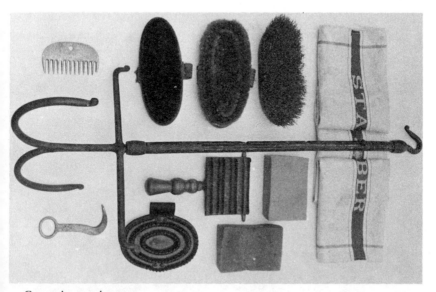

Grooming equipment
Top row (left to right) Mane comb (only used for pulling or trimming mane or tail). Water brush. Body brush. Dandy brush
Centre Bridle hook (for handing bridles on when cleaning, suspended from ceiling
Bottom row Hoof-pick. Rubber curry comb (for removing dried mud and loose hairs). Metal curry comb for cleaning body and dandy brush (not to be used on the horse). Sponges for cleaning eyes and nose, and one for cleaning the dock. Stable rubber for putting a final polish on a groomed horse's coat

The essential articles required for grooming are: dandy brush, rubber curry comb, metal curry comb, body brush, water brush, hoof-pick, two sponges, wisp, stable rubber, mane comb, sweat scraper.

The rubber curry is invaluable for removing encrusted mud and loose hairs when moulting. If used vigorously on the coat it acts as a form of massage, toning up the circulation. The dandy brush brushes out mud and dust, and removes scurf. The body brush is used after all mud has been removed, and on a stabled horse's coat. Its bristles are too soft to remove mud. It should be used on the head, mane and tail. The dandy brush bristles tend to pull out mane and tail hairs. The water brush can be used for putting a final polish on the coat of a stabled horse. Its main use is for damping the hairs of mane and tail. Do not make it too wet. The hoof-pick is for picking out a horse's feet in the stables. A small, folding type should be

Picking out feet. Running hand down pony's hindquarters before picking up the off-hindfoot. Hoof-pick in right hand
Continuing the movement, hand sweeping down from hindquarters over hock towards fetlock

carried when riding, in case a horse picks up a stone in its foot. Two sponges, one for washing eyes and nostrils; the other for washing the dock and sheath. A wisp is made from straw, a rope of plaited straw about 8 feet long should be made. It is folded over to about 2 feet long and securely fastened. It is used to tone up the circulation and improve a stabled horse's coat, by banging it down smartly in the direction of the hair. Avoid the head and other sensitive parts. This part of grooming is known as strapping. Most horses enjoy it. A stable rubber is a linen cloth about two feet square. It is used for removing dust from, and putting a final polish onto a groomed coat. A mane comb is chiefly used for pulling, trimming and thinning a mane or tail. A sweat scraper is used on a sweating horse, and also for scraping off rain or after washing.

The object of grooming a stabled horse is to remove all scurf and grease, and to improve the coat by forcing the oil up from the oil sacs or glands to the base of the hair roots. Grooming acts as massage and improves the circulation. By opening the pores of the skin it enables the horse's skin to breathe, which is very important for its health.

Thorough grooming (strapping) should be given after exercise, when the pores of the skin are open. It is then easier to remove all scurf and grease. A horse is 'knocked-over' or quartered before exercise to remove night stains and dust, and to make it look respectable to go out. Quartering takes about ten to fifteen minutes, thorough grooming between forty and forty-five minutes. Strapping is hard work and tiring if properly done.

To groom, always short-rack first, especially with an unknown horse or pony. If left on a long rope it can turn its head round and nip. Then, unbuckle and turn back any rugs off the forehand, but do not completely remove them in cold weather. Start on the near- (left-hand) side. With the body brush, groom the horse's head gently, brushing its poll, between the ears, and its forelock. Be especially careful not to knock the horse's head or face with the brush. Then with the dandy brush work from the neck to the wither; hold the head-collar with the left hand and work with the right. Next work down the shoulder and elbow, and down the outside and inside of the front leg. Hold the leg with the other hand, opposite to where you are brushing. Change hands when grooming the inside of the leg. Some grooms do the inside of the opposite leg at the same time. Brush right down the leg to the coronet, not forgetting the heels; neglect of this may cause chapped or greasy heels, or mud-fever. Also groom the chest and underneath and between the front legs, especially where the girth lies.

Having groomed the forehand, turn the rugs forward and turn back the back of the rug to expose the horse's back, ribs, belly and hindquarters. Start from the wither and brush along the back and croup to the root of the tail. Then brush the ribs and underneath

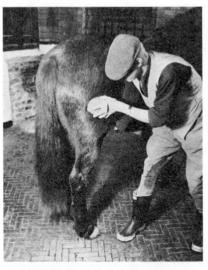

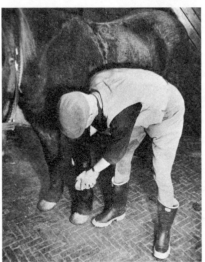

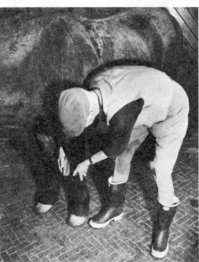

Top left Grooming offside hindquarters. Note how brush is held in the left hand, in order to face the tail and not stand behind the pony. The right hand supports the leg on the inside

Top right Grooming offside hindleg. Stoop—never squat or kneel. Note brush in left hand. Right hand supporting pony's leg from the inside

Bottom left Grooming nearside foreleg. Facing pony's forehand, with right hand supporting leg inside

Bottom right Grooming inside of nearside foreleg. Left hand supporting leg opposite the right hand

 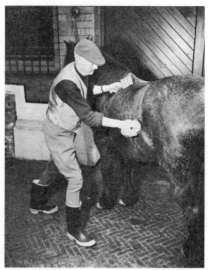

Left Grooming the near-side. Note position of groom's body with weight taken on right leg. Curry comb in left hand for getting rid of dust out of brush

Right Grooming underneath the pony. Again note the groom's stance with his weight driving the body brush through the pony's coat. Metal curry comb in left hand, taking particular care not to knock it against the pony

the belly. Next groom the loins, flanks, hip and thigh, facing the hindquarters. When grooming the hindleg, hold the inside of the leg with the left hand while brushing the thigh and second thigh (or gaskin). While brushing the lower part of the hindleg, hold the hock. Change hands to do the inside of the leg. Always stand facing the tail. Never stand behind a horse when grooming its hindquarters or hindleg; if you stand facing its tail you are out of danger if the horse kicks. Holding the leg with the other hand gives warning of any intention to kick, by a slight preliminary tightening of the muscles.

Having gone thoroughly all over the horse with the dandy brush repeat the process with the body brush. Bring the brush down firmly, but without banging; lean your body weight on the brush, driving its bristles through the coat with long, sweeping semi-circular strokes.

When grooming the off-side (right hand) in the same way, use both dandy and body brush in your left hand so that you are again facing the horse's tail when brushing its hindquarters. This also enables one to hold the head-collar with one's right hand when grooming the neck, shoulder and elbow.

To brush the mane, use the body brush—the dandy brush pulls out the hair. Brush the hair out in strands from underneath, working from the wither towards the head, until all hairs are separated and free from tangles. Most scurf accumulates on top at the roots of the mane. While grooming brush and train the hair to fall over. Most manes fall naturally on the off-side; some fall on the near-side, while a few awkward ones have a double parting and fall on both sides. In this case gradually try to train the mane to fall over on one side, usually the off-side. Do not wet the mane in winter. It can be slightly damped when the weather is warm enough. In very obstinate cases clip a mane board onto the mane, leaving it on for about three hours.

Pick up the tail in the left hand. If the horse is uncertain stand

Left Grooming tail. Brush from underneath separating the hairs. Use the body brush

Right Grooming tail. Brushing out tangles at the end of the tail

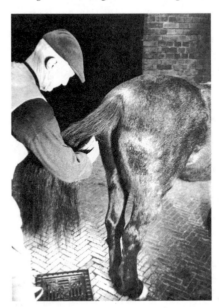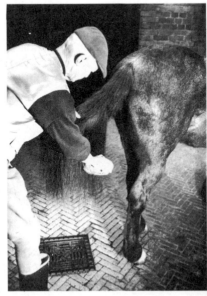

slightly to one side; not directly behind it. Using the body brush again, brush the tail out in strands from underneath until all the hairs are separate, then brush the top of the tail from the root, right down, and on either side to help keep it in shape. If the tail has been 'pulled' (*q.v.*) slightly damp it and put on a tail bandage to shape it, from the root to just below the end of the tail-bone.

Next go all over the horse's body with the wisp. Bring it down smartly in the direction of the hair, avoiding the head and all sensitive parts. A thorough strapping puts a wonderful shine on a stabled horse's coat.

With a damp (not wet) water brush, go all over the coat to give a final polish. Lastly, use a folded stable rubber to remove any specks of dust. Sponge eyes, nostrils and dock with the appropriate sponges.

The feet should be picked up and cleaned out with the hoof-pick. When picking up a foot on the near-side face the horse's tail, with your shoulder against his. To pick up the forefoot run your hand down with a sweeping movement from the shoulder to the fetlock, at the same time saying 'Foot'. Never grab the fetlock suddenly without making this preliminary warning movement, especially with a young horse, as it will startle it. If the horse refuses to pick up its foot immediately, pinch the tendons, just above the fetlock, gently between your finger and thumb, at the same time again saying 'Foot', and pressing against it with your shoulder to unbalance it, and make it take its weight off its foot. Having picked up its foot rest the hoof in the palm of your hand. Stoop and do not lift the foot up too high. With the hoof-pick, first work round the outside, nearest the shoe, working from the heel towards the toe. Never work towards the heel until the frog can clearly be seen; otherwise one may accidentally dig the hoof-pick into the frog and cause lameness.

Do the same with the hindleg, running your left hand down the hindquarters from the hip to the fetlock. Push with your shoulder against the horse's thigh. Do not pull the hindleg out too far or lift it too high.

When working on the off-side, use your right hand to pick up the foot, transferring the hoof to the left hand when lifted. Use the hoof-pick in the right hand, again working outwards round the outside, nearest the shoe, from heel to toe.

When grooming is finished replace the day rug, or a linen sheet in summer to prevent the horse from getting dirty and dusty again.

D

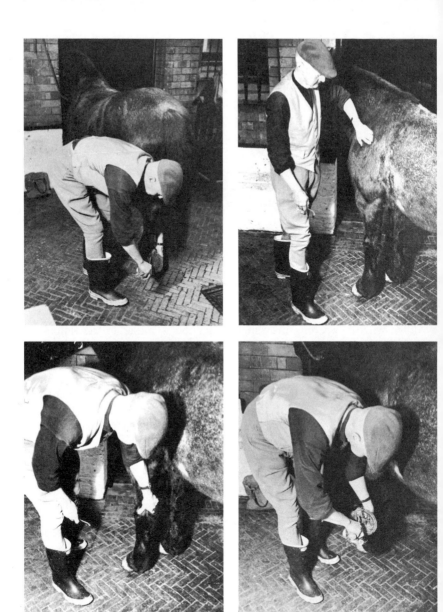

Top left **Picking out the foot. Always work round the edge from heel to toe,** *away* **from the frog—***never* **work towards it. The pony's hoof rests comfortably in the right hand, not too high off the ground. Note position of groom's body, near to pony**

Top right **Picking up the near forefoot, warning the pony by running the hand down from the shoulder with a semi-circular sweeping movement**

Bottom left **Picking up the near forefoot and continuing the movement**

Bottom right **Picking up the near forefoot. Hoof-pick working outwards away from the frog. Groom's body is again close to the pony**

Hooves can be oiled with hoof or neatsfoot oil; if black they can be polished with boot-blacking for special occasions, such as shows. Having groomed, sweep up all dust and dirt from the feet off the floor of the box (or stall). Or stand a skep underneath each foot while cleaning it.

The purpose of grooming a pony kept out at grass is to make it presentable to ride. In winter, it also helps to keep its thick coat free from lice. The object is not to remove all the scurf and grease from its coat, as this helps to keep it warm and dry, protecting it from the weather. Regular grooming is important as brushing off dried mud helps to prevent mud-fever.

Do not attempt to remove wet mud off a pony. It is inadvisable to wash the legs in winter. If absolutely necessary use cold water, and afterwards dry thoroughly, especially the heels, to prevent chapped heels, and to avoid risk of a chill. Use the rubber curry comb first to loosen and remove dried, caked mud and loose hairs, especially when moulting. Then groom thoroughly with the dandy brush; if mane and tail are very dirty and tangled, and caked with mud, it may be necessary to use the dandy brush on these as well; the body brush hairs will be too soft for grooming a dirty pony. If the coat is full of dust, smack it gently all over with both hands, or with the wisp, to bring the dust to the surface. Then brush out the dust with the dandy brush. It may be necessary to do this several times, on both sides of the pony.

Stand in exactly the same position as when grooming a stabled horse and work in the same way. It will not of course be necessary to keep a rug on a pony with a thick winter coat, which is living out. When picking out the feet, remove all mud and especially look for stones which may have become wedged between the bar of the foot and the frog (in the 'seat of corn'), also look for signs of any possible punctures in the soles of the feet, by nails, or broken glass, and so on.

Cleanliness of stable equipment (mucking-out tools, etc.) and of grooming kit is essential. Pick any accumulated straw off the prongs of the pitch-fork, keep the shovel and wheelbarrow clean. Keep all grooming brushes free from dust and entangled hairs. While grooming scrape the brush frequently against the metal curry comb, while turning away to prevent the dust from flying back onto the pony. Periodically knock the dust out of the curry comb on the floor, in a corner of the box.

Ideally each horse should have its own special grooming kit which should not be used on another. Infection, especially skin diseases (for example, eczema, sweet-itch, and so on), can very easily be spread by careless use of dirty grooming kit belonging to one pony on another. In case of any illness always use the same grooming kit on the patient. Keep it well away from other grooming kits and wash all brushes in strong disinfectant every time after use.

All grooming brushes should be frequently washed with carbolic soap and warm water. Do not wet the roots of the bristles where they are fastened into the wooden handle of the brush. Stand them on end in a warm place to dry, but not too near direct heat from a fire or stove. Do not wash brushes in any detergent washing powders, which might have a bad effect on a horse's skin. Also wash regularly all stable rubbers and cloths used for drying wet ponies. Sponges used for eyes and dock should also frequently be washed in soapy water, then rinsed thoroughly and left to air.

Tack-cleaning sponges should be boiled periodically. Also wash the polishing cloths at the same time.

Stand yard and stable brooms with their heads uppermost, not with the bristles on the floor.

7 Horses and Ponies at Grass

There are six types of fencing which can be used: iron railing, post and rail, pig-wire or sheep-wire mesh, plain wire and barbed wire. Iron railing is very expensive, but will last indefinitely and is unbreakable. It will eventually rust, but even that can be prevented if it is painted periodically. Post and rail is excellent. Although expensive both in material and cost of erection, it is very strong and will last for years, especially if treated with creosote. Posts should be of oak, with sycamore rails. The top rail should be 4 ft 6 in to 5 ft high. Three rails are best, but two are adequate to save expense, provided the inner one is so spaced that a small pony cannot squeeze between them. It is surprising what a narrow gap a small pony can squeeze through if it makes up its mind to escape. One solution is to have a rather wide second, lower rail. Pig- or sheep-wire mesh is quite effective. The danger is if a pony gets its hoof caught in the mesh. For large hunters it is perfectly safe, especially if a small mesh is used. Plain wire is reasonably effective provided it is kept really taut. If it stretches and becomes loose it is dangerous, and quite useless as ponies can squeeze between the strands, and in the process get the wire entangled round their legs. And if wire gets wound tightly round a pony's leg it can almost sever it. There should be at least three strands: four are better. Posts should be fairly near together so that the wire can be strained really tight. At intervals, especially at the corners, there should be two buttress posts on either side of the upright post, to help take the strain. Galvanized wire is rather soft and stretches considerably. Being soft it is also apt to snap when stapled tightly, or with constant friction. Barbed wire is about the commonest type of fencing, unfortunately, because it is one of the cheapest. Personally, I loathe it, having known of some horrible accidents caused through its use. If it must be used for reasons of economy, the posts must be driven in at least two feet deep, and be absolutely firm and immovable. The wire must also be strained as taut as possible. Loose, sagging barbed wire is very dangerous. If a horse kicks out and catches its leg in it and pulls it, barbed wire can inflict a horrible wound. Corner posts must be well buttressed, with the intermediate posts fairly close together, not more than about 15 feet apart, to take the strain. Have two, preferably three, strands. Barbed wire rusts fairly quickly, and old, rusty wire is dangerous and should be replaced at once. When erecting a plain, or barbed, wire fence, use a strainer, as otherwise it cannot be pulled tight enough.

Where pasture is limited and it is necessary to economize and make the most use of the land by strip grazing, an electric fence is effective. After the initial capital outlay for the battery and special posts, it is cheap to run, easy to erect and move, and efficient. Horses quickly learn to respect it. With cattle, once they know it is there it can be switched off periodically to save the battery; horses soon get wise to this. A battery in continuous use lasts about eight or nine months. The apparatus costs about £12 plus the posts. Only one strand of wire, between 2 ft 6 ins and 3 ft high, is necessary. The posts must be completely insulated, otherwise in wet weather the current leaks to earth and there is no shock felt on touching the wire. Check periodically for any breaks in the wire. An electric fence is only recommended for dividing a field and not for fencing off the whole area.

If there is no natural water supply, some form must be provided. If main water is available an automatic water trough is the best. It is labour-saving and automatically ensures a fresh supply every time a horse drinks. The ball-cock apparatus is totally enclosed, and there are no projections on which a horse can injure itself. If a tap is used it must be so placed that a pony cannot interfere with it, and there must be no projecting inlet tap on which it can become caught up.

Old baths are often seen but are thoroughly bad. A horse can injure its knee on the sharp projecting rim. If a projecting tap is used this also can be dangerous.

If the main water supply is unavailable, then any receptacle must be hand-filled, at least once daily, preferably twice according to its size and the number of animals using it. A horse drinks about 8 gallons of water a day. Failing anything else a round zinc or plastic dustbin makes quite a good receptacle and will probably need filling twice daily. Zinc is more durable; frost will crack a plastic receptacle.

All artificial receptacles must be cleaned out periodically and kept free from dead leaves or other rubbish. If near a public footpath see that passers-by, especially children, do not throw in any poisonous leaves. This is usually due to well-meaning ignorance. One of my ponies once had a bad attack of colic and was very ill, due to some

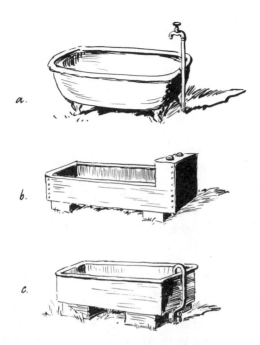

(a) Bad. A pony can injure its leg on the sharp rim, or on the tap
(b) The best type—fully enclosed automatic trough
(c) Also good—tap placed underneath where pony cannot interfere
with it. No projecting inlet tap to cause injury

laurel leaves being thrown into the water receptacle.

The best natural supply is a fairly swift flowing stream with a clean, gravelly bottom. A stagnant pond with a muddy bottom is not recommended. See that any pond or stream has a flat, level place from where the water is easily accessible. It should also have a firm bottom. It can be dangerous if a pony has to reach down from a bank to drink.

When inspecting prospective pasture there are a number of possible snags and pitfalls to look for. The fencing must be safe and secure. If a thick hedge forms part of the boundary, it must be thick and stout enough so that a horse cannot break its way through, particularly if adjoining the road. If at all thin in places, the possible gaps should be filled with stout poles placed lengthways and securely fastened, or posts should be firmly driven in and strands of wire placed across, or a length of post and rail fence inserted. The best type of natural boundary is something thick-set and prickly, such as blackthorn. The hedging should be regularly cut and laid by an expert hedger, so that it grows really thick and compact. But a hedge alone never seems completely safe. Ponies especially will worry away at a weak spot if they find one, until they have forced a way through.

Look at all wire fences—and in particular barbed fences—with a careful eye. Replace loose or rotted uprights, and renew any rusty wire. Tighten loose, sagging wire until absolutely taut again. Wire fences are too often seen in a deplorable condition, and then owners wonder why their ponies escape onto the road and are killed. Besides the risk of the pony being killed or injured, the owner is liable in the event of an accident for any damage or injury to a third party. The onus is on him to see that his livestock cannot escape. He can be heavily fined, and the police can impound any animal found straying on the highway. Even post and rail or iron fencing should not be taken for granted, but be carefully examined periodically.

See that the hinges of all gates are in good condition, so that they are properly hung and open and close easily. Nothing is more maddening than wrestling one-handed with a refractory gate which will not open or close properly, while trying to hold a restless or unco-operative pony. If other horses are in the field they will probably escape while you struggle to get yours in, or out. Latches should work properly and be so placed that a pony cannot undo them. Some ponies become very expert at this, as I know from practical experience. Farm gates are the worst offenders and seldom work efficiently. Wooden gates should be in good condition and painted. Tubular iron gates are cheaper and better than wooden ones for they are stronger and more durable, and usually hang well. Keep them painted to prevent rust. Avoid any kind of latch which a pony can push down with its nose.

All rabbit holes, mole-hills or other holes in the ground are potentially dangerous and must be filled in—a galloping pony can easily break a leg in one.

Rubbish and litter such as old tin cans, broken crockery or china, broken bottles, old iron, pieces of wire and so on can all cause injury, besides looking unsightly and untidy: they must be removed.

Poisonous plants are another possible danger: these are yew, laburnum, deadly nightshade, 'lords and ladies' (wild arum), ragwort, laurel, foxglove, autumn crocus, acorns and green oak leaves (in spring), green bracken, some species of vetch and privet. Ragwort should not be cut and left in the field as it is more poisonous when dead than alive.

Antidotes for poisonous plants depend on the nature of the poison and its effect on the horse. If the particular plant is not known a good, safe, general antidote is powdered charcoal—4 pints; magnesium cabonate levis—1 pint; tannic acid—1 pint (recommended by Hungerford).

The effects of eating various poisonous plants and specific antidotes are as follows:

Yew: Generally the horse or pony is found dead; if still alive symptoms are difficult breathing, collapse, and trembling. Yew poison is alkaloid taxine. Death can occur within five minutes, or the animal may survive for several hours. The effect largely depends on whether the stomach is empty at the time of eating, and upon the amount eaten. Immediate treatment is essential. As taxine has a depressing action, stimulants should be given such as alcohol or caffeine, and frequent large doses of strong coffee or tea. Also give purgatives such as eserine or arecoline with a hypodermic to ensure that they act quickly. Inject adrenalin to help the action of the heart. If colicky (abdominal) pains persist chloral hydrate should be given.

Ragwort: In acute poisoning when a large quantity has been eaten there are symptoms of colic. Death may occur within a few days or may take longer. Cases may occur when ragwort has been harvested with hay. In chronic poisoning, symptoms are loss of condition and appetite, lethargy, staggering walk, constipation, sometimes diarrhoea. A purgative should be given, followed by arsenic and strychnine tonics. Glucose may also be beneficial. If a large amount has been eaten, treatment usually proves useless.

Acorns: These are more poisonous than the green oak leaves, especially unripe acorns. Both acorns and green leaves contain a large quantity of tannic acid, and a small amount of volatile oil. Large doses of liquid paraffin should be given, and stimulants administered by stomach tube.

Bracken: This contains an enzyme which destroys vitamin B_1. The symptoms are identical with those of vitamin B_1 deficiency— slow pulse, loss of appetite, poor condition—but the appetite remains fairly good. Later symptoms are a tacked-up appearance and hollow flanks, owing to wastage of the muscles on the hindquarters, an unsteady, reeling walk and possible difficulty in turning, a weak fast pulse, trembling and exhaustion follow even light exercise. In severe cases if a horse lies down it may not be able to get up again unassisted. 50 to 100 mg. of aneurin hydrochloride B.P.C. (vitamin B_1) should be administered, and repeated injections given subcutaneously. This is claimed to be successful if treatment is given before the poisoning is too far advanced.

Horse tail: This is found growing in wet, marshy soil. It produces similar symptoms, and requires the same treatment as for bracken poisoning.

Privet: This contains a glycoside called legustrin. The symptoms are that hindquarters lose the power of movement, the pupils of the eyes dilate, mucous membranes swell slightly and the walk is unsteady. Death may occur within four to forty-eight hours. There appears to be no treatment.

The best 'treatment' is in prevention. All fields and surrounding hedges should be very carefully examined for any known poisonous plants which should be uprooted bodily before turning any animals out to grass. Do not merely cut off the stems, but remove the roots of any poisonous plants so that there is no danger of their growing again.

It is usual to estimate at least an acre per pony for grazing. If land is constantly grazed without rest it becomes horse-sick. Rest the land periodically and in winter or early spring give it a top dressing of lime to sweeten the soil and encourage growth of new grass. Chain-harrowing, to distribute the droppings, is also good. Horses are wasteful feeders. They roam about the field and their droppings if left on the ground make the grass coarse. They refuse to eat this coarse grass, and so the amount of grazing gradually decreases. Hence the value of strip grazing with an electric fence, when grazing is limited. While resting a field, allow cattle and/or sheep to graze on it. If the ground is soft and wet horses also poach it with their hooves and, by killing the grass, help to make it muddy.

Inspect paddocks and horses daily when they are out at grass. If possible take a wheelbarrow and collect the droppings every day, if time allows. If not take a rake and scatter them.

When inspecting horses catch them daily. This helps to make them easy to catch, if they are frequently handled. When caught tie up and examine for any cuts, kicks or other injuries. Look at their legs for signs of over-reach or kicks, and their feet to see that they have not picked up any stones in their hooves, also that no nails or glass have punctured the sole of the foot. Tetanus (lockjaw) is very easily caused by an unsuspected and neglected injury. Tetanus bacteria can lie dormant in the ground for a long time, especially in a field much used by horses. While tied up, groom the ponies to remove caked mud, particularly from their bellies and legs, and, especially in spring, when they are moulting, to remove loose hair. If left on, a horse can eat the hair which can cause an obstruction in the bowels with serious consequences. Ungroomed ponies can also harbour lice.

If horses are going to be left out unused for any length of time, remove their shoes, especially the hind ones, to prevent injury by kicking. Fit grass-tips to prevent the toe growing too long and the wall of the hoof from cracking. Feet should be trimmed every five or six weeks to prevent them growing too long.

The winter care of ponies and horses at grass is especially important. Feed hay as soon as the grass begins to lose its keep and the weather grows cold. This is usually between the middle and end of October, and after a very hot, dry summer, when the grass has become scorched and dried up, it may even be the middle of September. After a wet summer, followed by a fine mild autumn, it could be as late as the beginning of November. Start with one hay-feed, increasing to two as it grows colder. In very cold weather it may be necessary to supplement the hay ration with one, or more, short feeds daily. One must use one's own judgement by observing the condition of the ponies. If they remain fat and lively and appear healthy and happy, short feeds may be unnecessary.

In frosty weather keep the ice broken on their water supply. This may be necessary twice a day, or even more frequently in very severe weather. Ponies can suffer greatly from thirst due to frozen water supply. People do not seem to think of this. The poor brutes will even vainly try to get water by licking the ice, and in very arctic weather their tongues may become frozen and frost-bitten, causing much suffering.

Mus is another frequent cause of trouble, often resulting in mud-fever. Scatter ashes on the ground and try to make a place free from mud where the hay is fed. Also change the place where they are fed to prevent it from becoming too poached.

Ponies grow thick winter coats and do not appear to mind cold or even snow. But they do need some sort of protection from biting winds and freezing rain. The danger lies in rain followed by severe frost. Their soaking wet coats become frozen and they could be frozen to death—not a pretty sight. Therefore some sort of shelter is necessary. A tall, thick hedge on the north and east sides may form an adequate wind-break and protection. But, better still, provide some form of shed or shelter into which they can go. This also protects them from sun and flies in summer. The shelter should be large enough to accommodate all occupants of the field at once, without risk of injury from kicking. It should have a wide, not a narrow, opening. In fact a three-sided shelter open in the front, is perfectly adequate, provided it protects from the north and east winds. Encourage the ponies to use it by feeding them in it frequently (provided it is big enough to do so with safety), and by putting down a good, thick straw bed. Pick up droppings and keep the floor of the shed clean.

An open field shelter PHOTO SUPPLIED BY EDWARDS & SON (MALMESBURY) LTD.

In very cold, snowy weather, it is wiser and kinder to bring them in at night, even though it gives much extra stable work. They can be turned out in the morning for the day.

Thoroughbred horses are thin-skinned and feel the cold, so should never be left out in winter. They can, however, be safely turned out during the day to exercise themselves if they wear a New Zealand rug. This is waterproof, and windproof, and is so designed that it cannot shift or become displaced, even if the horse rolls. The best type is the Emston New Zealand rug. It is made of waterproof

New Zealand rug for turning a clipped horse out by day in winter

canvas partly lined with wool. A surcingle is sewn on with the ends passing through the rug and fastening at the girth. It buckles in front like an ordinary stable rug. Fillet straps are fastened to the rug, which pass round on the inside of the horse's legs and buckle at the back—they help to prevent the rug from shifting when the horse rolls. They should be buckled fairly loosely. A clipped-out, or trace-clipped horse or pony can be turned out by day during the winter in a New Zealand rug. A horse needs accustoming to a New Zealand rug before being turned out. Some horses or ponies do not take too kindly to it at first. If at all nervous, the rubbing of the leg-straps and the stiff canvas upsets them. Let them first wear it several times in the stable for short periods until accustomed to it. A horse turned out in one needs attention to see that the rug has not slipped back onto the wither and that the leg-straps are not chafing the insides of the thighs. They also become very muddy and should be cleaned frequently. If one's purse allows, it is best to have two, so that one can be washed and dried while the other is in use.

While it is true that people do hunt horses and ponies off grass, it is unfair to expect them to be able to do such hard or fast work as a clipped, stabled horse. Owing to their thick winter coats fast work makes them sweat profusely, and causes them to lose condition. Fast work may break their wind as they are not in hard condition.

Hunters which have been turned out at grass all the summer to rest are in soft condition and fat, with a 'grass belly'. If they are to be hunted during the winter they must be brought into condition and made 'hunting fit'. The fat must gradually be turned into muscle, and the 'grass belly' must disappear. This is accomplished by slow, steady regular work, gradually increasing, over several weeks. Walking up and down hill, with an occasional trot, is the best exercise to give. Walking and then trotting uphill helps muscular development. Start with about two hours' exercise, gradually increasing to about four hours daily (two in the morning, and two hours after tea, with a rest after lunch from 12 to 2 p.m.). Hunters are usually brought in to start conditioning in mid-August, and should be fairly fit by the time cub-hunting starts at the end of August or beginning of September.

The change-over from grass to a corn-fed diet must also be gradual. Some people give a mild purge to empty the stomach of grass when their horse first comes up from grass, and give them a worm powder as a precautionary measure. The latter is not essential unless the horse has been running out with a number of others. Personally, I am not very keen on the idea of giving even a mild purge, and interfering with the natural process of digestion. It does not seem necessary if the change in diet is accomplished slowly, and more naturally. Gradually reduce the number of hours the horse is out at grass, and simultaneously increase the hay ration. Start by giving a small corn-feed daily and increase the amount, as the amount of work done increases. Mix the oats with bran or chaff, using crushed—not whole—oats. As the horse hardens up introduce a short, slow canter; gradually increase in distance and speed, until one can safely give an occasional short, sharp burst, say once a week, to clear the wind without fear of making the horse broken-winded. A grass-fed horse will probably sweat profusely, but this will decrease as it becomes fit. Like a trained athlete a really healthy conditioned horse should not have an ounce of fat or surplus flesh on it; muscles should be hardened up and the bloom on its coat and bright, alert eyes should give evidence of perfect health. Remember that a stabled horse is living an artificial, unnatural existence.

Roughing off, preparatory to turning out to grass, is the reverse process. A fit horse must gradually be let down and 'unwound' as it were. If abruptly turned out in spring to grass, it will probably develop grass colic, or laminitis—or both. A sudden change of diet upsets the digestion. Gradually cut down the amount of oats and number of daily short feeds, and the amount of hay. Turn out at first for about an hour a day, increasing the length of time until the horse can be left out half the day, and eventually all day. It can then be left out all night and brought in during the heat of the day, to protect it from the sun, and from flies. Also gradually reduce the grooming from a thorough daily strapping to just lightly quartering. Leave it ungroomed a couple of days before it is finally turned out the whole time to allow its coat to collect some protective scurf and natural grease. Hunting usually ends on the 1st May, and hunters can then start being roughed off. The same principle applies to letting race-horses go out of training and the process should be gradual.

The more highly-bred the horse the more gradual the processes of conditioning or roughing off should be. Native breeds of British ponies, being hardy and accustomed to sudden changes of climate, need a shorter period of time for roughing off, though conditioning will still take time.

Catching a pony out at grass is quite an art. Accustom your pony to come to call, by going down daily at the same time and giving it a tit-bit. When doing so always call it at the same time so that it eventually associates your visits and the sound of your voice with food. When the pony begins to come when called take a head-collar down and gently slip it on. When the pony allows this make much of it and give it a further tit-bit. Eventually there will be no difficulty in catching a pony thus trained. Never wave your arms about or shout at the pony. If it turns away and refuses to be caught, never chase after it. It will only think it is a game, and being able to run faster than you can, it soon learns that it can win every time. A pony which has been chased will always be difficult to catch. Let the pony come to you and as it comes near have the head-collar hanging ready on your outstretched left arm, with the tit-bit on the palm of your left hand. As the pony takes the tit-bit, turn slowly round facing in the same direction and catch its forelock from the near-side. Never snatch suddenly at it as this will only startle the pony. Most ponies will submit once one has them firmly grasped by the forelock. Alternatively slide your right arm gently under its neck and hold its nose with your hand. The head-collar can then be slipped quietly over its nose with the left hand, while the right is ready to help throw the strap over its neck to be buckled.

Always approach from the front to the pony's shoulder, and never from behind it. A pony can swing round so quickly and let out with its heels. Be careful in approaching a pony in a field containing other ponies. They are jealous creatures, and if the others think one is receiving too much attention, they may either attack with outstretched neck and teeth bared, or turn round and kick out. You may suddenly find yourself the centre target of a kicking match between two ponies. Mares are more prone to jealousy, usually, than geldings.

When turning a horse or pony out, lead it into the field and shut the gate. Then lead it several yards forward and turn it round to face the gate. Having done so make it stand still for a few moments before unfastening the head-collar. While standing still make much of it and give it a tit-bit. Then quietly undo the head-collar and walk slowly away. The object of turning the pony to face the gate is to give you time to move away, as many ponies will give a buck, fling up their heels and gallop away directly they are released, with the consequent danger that one may get kicked. Never unfasten the head-collar and give the pony a slap on the rump, or flourish your arms, to make it gallop off. The last impression left on its mind may influence whether it is going to be easy or difficult to catch next time it is wanted.

If turning out a pony with others keep them well apart, and arrange to release them simultaneously.

When two or three people are catching ponies at the same time, those who are ready first should wait until all the ponies have been caught before moving off. Meanwhile they should stand still and not let their ponies roam about or fidget. If one person moves off the other ponies will try to follow and if any have not been caught they may play up and refuse to be caught.

8 The Tack-Room

A well-arranged, well-organized tack-room saves time and work, thus making for general efficiency. The tack-room reflects the owner's mentality. A neat, well-arranged tack-room generally indicates a methodical, careful and efficient stable manager. An untidy one with dirty tack strewn about anywhere, anyhow, usually denotes a slack, slovenly, inefficient stable manager, whose horses also will probably be neglected.

Saddles, bridles and head-collars should be put up on their respective racks and/or hooks. There are several alternative ways of organizing tack. Some saddle-racks are made with hooks underneath for bridles and head-collars. All saddles can be grouped together in one place, all bridles in another (preferably hung up in a glass-fronted cupboard) and all head-collars together in a third place. Or they can be arranged in sets, with the saddle, bridle and head-collar belonging to each horse being put up together, with the horse's name above.

The last is probably the simplest and quickest way, especially for young pupils who are not very familiar with the tack; it prevents the wrong saddle, bridle or head-collar being used on the wrong horse or pony.

Metal saddle-racks are expensive to buy. Efficient substitutes can very easily be made with pieces of wood about 12 ins long by 3 ins wide and about $1\frac{1}{2}$ to 2 ins thick, rounded on top and screwed onto large iron right-angle brackets, screwed into the wall.

Similarly, efficient bridle-racks can be made with a round cocoa tin or piece of wood, fastened to a bracket screwed onto the wall. They are much cheaper than the bought article.

If the bought saddle-racks have no bridle-hook or -hooks underneath, or home-made ones are used, bridles and head-collars are hung up below or alongside the respective saddles with which they form a set.

There should be proper bridle-hooks suspended from the ceiling for cleaning bridles and head-collars. These hooks are adjustable in length, but one can pinch oneself badly when altering the length of one. They should be securely screwed in one of the cross beams of the

E

ceiling, and not merely into the plaster; otherwise the weight of several bridles will pull them down and may hurt someone. They have either two or three prongs, and are a necessity in a well-planned tack-room. It is difficult to clean bridles quickly and efficiently without a bridle-hook.

A wooden saddle-horse, on which to rest saddles for cleaning, is also invaluable, though again new ones are expensive, but one can sometimes pick up a secondhand one quite cheaply at one of the many horse and tack sales. It is also possible to make one at home. If the tack-room is fairly small, keep the saddle-horses, and bridle-hooks just outside if possible. Otherwise, if several people are trying to clean tack simultaneously, the place becomes rather congested, and tempers become somewhat frayed. The ideal is to have a small, adjacent tack-cleaning room, with a cold tap, and some source of hot water.

There should be a cupboard or large chest for storing unused day and night rugs, New Zealand rugs, or summer sheets, also rest- and exercise-bandages, knee-pads, Yorkshire, sausage and brushing boots, and other items. Have another cupboard for hanging spare tack, bridles, spare reins, lunging reins, leading-reins, riding whips and so on, with a bottom shelf or other space for riding or jodhpur boots. Riding boots should always be kept stored with trees inside them. Otherwise they sag and wrinkle horribly.

Sets of grooming kit can be hung on the tack-room wall. Each bag should be numbered, with the same number on each article of grooming kit inside it. With young pupils this makes it easy to check quickly that each set of grooming kit is complete. Youngsters are notoriously careless about leaving brushes, curry combs, or hoof-picks lying about in mangers.

Alternatively, each horse can have its own grooming kit, with its name on the bag and on each item inside. This is the most hygienic method, and helps to lessen the risk of spreading any infection.

Medicines and first-aid essentials should be in a locked cupboard. They should only be used by the owner, or person in charge, or under the strictest supervision. The medicine chest should contain the following: 1 pair blunt-pointed surgical scissors; a clinical thermometer; 1 lb. roll of cotton wool; small packets of lint; 3- and 4-inch wide calico bandages; safety pins (assorted sizes, fairly large to large); roll of gauze; medium-sized needles; reel of strong cotton;

reel of thread; roll of adhesive plaster, 2 to 3 inches wide; disinfectant (Dettol, T.C.P.); permanganate of potash crystals; jar of Boots' Pink Healing ointment; sulphanilamide powder; tincture of iodine; lead lotion; colic drink and drenching bottle; cough electuary; boracic powder; Kaolin paste; small hypodermic syringe.

The medicine cupboard must be air-tight and dust-free so that all contents can be kept surgically clean.

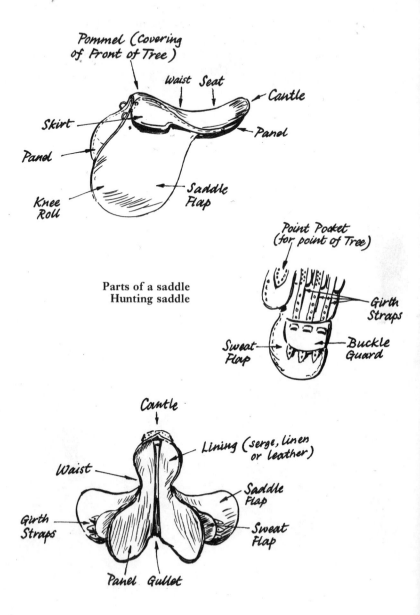

Pommel (covering of Front of Tree)

Waist   Seat

Cantle

Skirt

Panel

Panel

Knee Roll

Saddle Flap

**Parts of a saddle
Hunting saddle**

Point Pocket (for point of Tree)

Girth Straps

Sweat Flap

Buckle Guard

Cantle

Lining (serge, linen or leather)

Waist

Girth Straps

Saddle Flap

Sweat Flap

Panel   Gullet

Parts of the saddle are: pommel, skirt, waist, seat, cantle, flap, stirrup-bar, point-pocket, sweat-flap, girth straps, panel and gullet. A saddle is built on a tree or frame, of which the pommel forms the front arch and the cantle the back. Ribs run lengthwise. Lining may

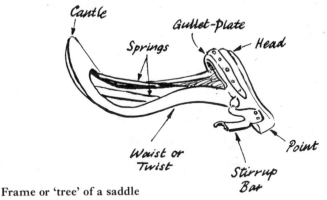

Frame or 'tree' of a saddle

be linen, serge or leather. The latter is the most durable, but apt to be rather cold in winter, especially for a horse with a 'cold back'. Unless kept scrupulously clean a leather lining can become encrusted with grease and dirt and can cause a sore back. Serge linings should be kept well brushed. Linen linings can be sponged periodically, if thoroughly dried after, but not directly in front of a fire or stove.

There are seven types of saddle, shaped according to their specific use: the army, from which originally developed the colonial and western saddles; the hunting (or general purpose) saddle, most widely used; show-jumping, dressage and racing saddles.

The modern hunting or general purpose saddle is the forward-cut pattern, to give the now generally accepted forward seat. The army, colonial and western saddles have very high pommels and cantles, so that the rider sits very deep in the saddle, with very long stirrup-leathers and almost straight legs. He does not 'post' or rise in the saddle when trotting, but does the sitting trot. A show-jumping saddle has a much more forward-cut flap with much thicker knee and thigh rolls to provide extra grip for the knees when jumping. A dressage saddle has a straight-cut flap, with little or no knee roll; it may also have a half instead of a full panel, in order to bring the rider's knees and legs into as close contact as possible with his horse. The racing saddle is as small and light as possible with very forward

Military saddle—note the
high pommel and cantle and
long stirrup-leathers

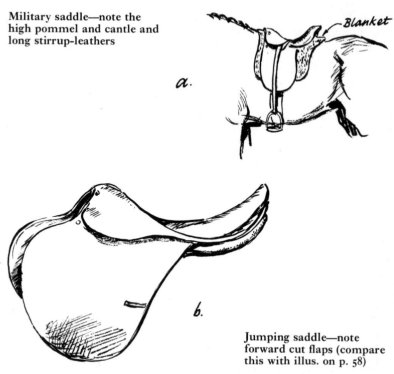

a.

Blanket

b.

Jumping saddle—note
forward cut flaps (compare
this with illus. on p. 58)

cut flaps. The jockey rides with very short stirrup-leathers, with his
seat right off the saddle and his weight on his knees, taken on the
forward-cut flaps. A weight-cloth, with pockets to contain lead
weights, is used.

Parts of a single bridle are: the brow-band, head-band or head-stall
to which are buckled the cheek-straps. The bit is fastened to these
with buckles or billets, or is sewn on. The throat-lash (or latch)
comes from the head-stall on the off-side, under the horse's jaw and
is buckled on the near-side. The nose-band has its own separate
head-stall and cheek-straps, and again buckles on the near-side. The
cheek-straps supporting the bit, and those for the nose-band, are
adjustable in length. The reins are either stitched onto the bit, or
fastened with buckles or billets; buckles fasten on the outside, billets
on the inside. Reins and cheek-straps stitched to the bit (or bits)
look neatest on a show bridle, but have the disadvantage that they
cannot be taken off for cleaning. A double bridle has two separate

head-stalls, one for the bridoon or snaffle bit, the other for the curb bit. The curb bit is lower in the horse's mouth than the snaffle.

There are three main types of bit, the snaffle, curb and pelham,

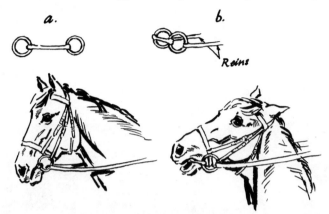

Straight-barred snaffle—the mildest form of bit
(a) Correct position—bit acts on bars of pony's mouth
(b) Wrong position—bit slides up, acts on corner of mouth

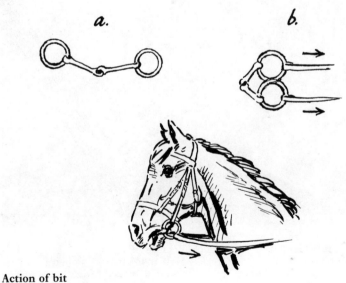

Action of bit
(a) Jointed snaffle
(b) Nut-cracker action

with numerous varieties of each. It is said that there is a key to every horse's mouth. But ultimately the real key is 'good' (light) hands. However, it is a fact that some horses will go better in one kind of bit than another. This does not mean that a rider should keep experimenting and changing the bit. When a horse pulls, the usual mistake is to try a more severe bit. A horse usually pulls through fear of the bit, or pain caused by it. Therefore a more severe bit will only make it pull harder and try more evasions to escape from pain. The answer lies in using a milder bit in most cases.

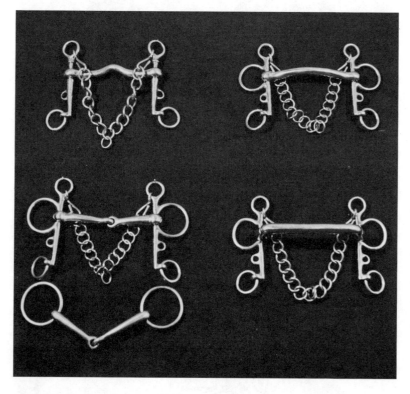

Double bridle bits (*left*)
Weymouth curb bit
Ward Union curb bit and
bridoon (or snaffle) bit

Pelham bits (*right*)
Half-moon (metal) pelham
Straight-barred (metal) pelham

EQUIPMENT KINDLY SUPPLIED BY MOSS BROS.

Snaffle bits
Plain jointed snaffle
Egg-butt jointed snaffle
Egg-butt twisted snaffle

EQUIPMENT KINDLY SUPPLIED BY
MOSS BROS.

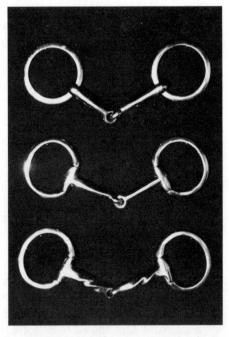

Snaffles are either straight or jointed (i.e. 'broken'). They are the mildest form of bit, but vary in degrees of severity. The straight vulcanite rubber snaffle is the mildest form of all. It is useful for making a young horse's mouth, for a horse with a very soft mouth, or for restoring confidence in the bit and remaking a hard mouth which has been ruined through bad riding and heavy hands. A straight metal snaffle is also mild (a little more severe than a rubber snaffle). It is a safe bit for a beginner to use on a quiet, well-mannered horse. The advantage of a 'broken' or jointed snaffle is that one rein can act on one side of the mouth, without pulling the bit through it and affecting the other side. All jointed snaffles have a 'nutcracker' action on the corners of the mouth. The ordinary snaffle bit is safe for an inexperienced rider to use for hacking and learning to jump, as it is mild. Yet it will hold most horses or ponies in the hands of an experienced rider with good hands, provided they are not hard pullers. It should also be used by an experienced rider for making a young horse's mouth, and on a horse with a soft mouth. The egg-butt snaffle is another mild jointed bit. Owing to the 'egg' shaped portion of the ring through which the bit passes, there is less likelihood of it pinching the corners of the horse's lips, or of making them sore, and is thus a little milder than the ordinary jointed snaffle. These two bits also vary in severity according to their thickness; the thicker the bit, the milder it is. The twisted snaffle, whether straight or jointed, is a powerful bit which should only be used by an experienced rider with light hands. The gag snaffle is a very severe bit acting on the corners of the mouth; it is only suitable for very experienced riders.

Some types of snaffle bits have straight cheek-pieces instead of cheek-rings. Their severity depends on the length of the cheek-pieces; the longer they are the more severe the bit. The bridoon (snaffle) bit of a double bridle has a thinner mouthpiece than that of the ordinary jointed snaffle. The curb bit has a straight mouthpiece, with fixed or moveable cheek-pieces, and a curb-chain, usually with a lip-strap, though it can be worn without. The mouthpiece of the curb bit acts on the mouth and tongue. The cheeks of the bit form a lever giving increased pressure on the bars; the longer the cheeks the more severe is the bit. A high port (arch) on the mouthpiece also adds to the severity of the bit by pressing against the roof of the mouth, and there is downward pressure on the top of the head from the head-band. One should mostly use the bridoon; continuous use of the curb bit alone, without the bridoon, eventually deadens all feeling through constant pressure on the lower jaw. The curb-chain acts as a fulcrum, but without causing any pain; it has seventeen or nineteen links and a lip-strap link. The lip-strap is in two parts, each being fastened to the 'D' on the cheek of the bit. The bridoon (snaffle) makes the horse flex or give to the bit, by raising its head. The curb bit lowers the horse's head, arching its neck so that its muzzle is held inwards towards its chest. It cannot raise its head or 'stargaze', or throw it up preparatory to bolting.

The long cheeks of the long-cheeked curb bit with straight mouthpiece increase the bit's severity by greater leverage. The short-cheeked curb has a central port (arch) fitting over the tongue, and pressing on the roof of the mouth; the higher the port the more severe the bit. The Weymouth and Ward Union are two of the more usual types of curb bit. The Ward Union has moveable pieces which slide up and down on the cheeks; the Weymouth cheeks are fixed. In a Banbury bit the cheeks can revolve round the mouthpiece.

A pelham bit is really an attempt to combine the functions of a

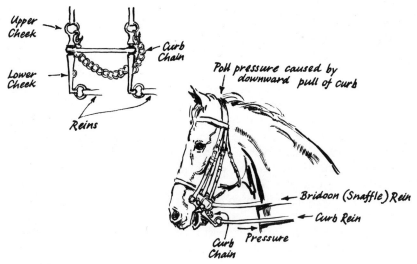

Curb bit
Action of curb bit

Action of pelham bit
(a) Top snaffle rein in action
(b) Lower curb rein in action
(c) Jointed pelham

snaffle and a curb bit in one bit. The bridoon and curb reins are both attached to the one mouthpiece, the snaffle rein to a ring at the end of the mouthpiece and the curb (or bit) rein to the ring of the lower cheek. There is a small 'D' on the lower cheek for the lip-strap, with a hook for the curb-chain on the upper cheek. One rein only can be used on a pelham bit by attaching it to leather 'D's which fasten to the rings on the upper and lower cheeks. It is then used as an ordinary snaffle bridle, but this is not recommended.

When using two reins, by riding with the lower rein the pelham acts like a curb, and when using the upper rein it acts like a snaffle bit. Although the pelham is in a way really a makeshift, trying to make one bit perform the functions of two separate bits, some horses, curiously enough, seem to go better in a pelham than in other kinds of bit.

A quiet horse can be ridden perfectly well in a snaffle bridle without a nose-band, but it has become the accepted fashion to wear one, and many people consider that a horse does not look properly dressed without one. A cavesson nose-band is necessary if a martingale is used.

Girths can either be string, nylon, web or leather. String and nylon girths are less likely to cause a girth gall as the air can circulate freely and so the pony is less likely to perspire so much underneath them. A string girth is less durable than nylon. Nylon girths are easily washed in warm soapy water and are very strong and hard-wearing. They are, in my opinion, the best type of girth and are very popular. Web girths are liable to snap. If used two should be worn as a precaution. Narrow web girths are liable to chafe and can slip if the horse is wet or perspiring. Personally, I do not recommend them. Some people like a leather girth best. They are certainly strong, durable and unlikely to break, but unless frequently cleaned and always kept soft, they are very liable to gall. Also, they are inclined to slip round on a wet or sweating horse. To keep a folded leather girth soft, cut a strip of woollen cloth the same length and width as the girth, soak it in neatsfoot oil and keep it folded inside the girth. Renew the oil as soon as it dries out. Many riders prefer a Balding to a folded leather girth as it is less cumbersome and allows air to circulate underneath. It also must be kept soft, and regularly cleaned after being used.

The dropped nose-band should only be used with a snaffle bit. It must be very carefully fitted with the front well above the nostrils and the back in the chin-groove. It must be tight enough to prevent a horse from opening its mouth wide or crossing its jaw, but not tightly enough to stop the jaw flexing.

The cavesson nose-band is used with a single (snaffle), or a double bridle, or a pelham. It should be loose enough to allow the mouth to open and the jaw to flex. It should fit half-way between the projecting cheek-bone and the corners of the mouth. It should be possible to put the breadth of two fingers between the nose-band and the front of the face. Its main use is for attaching a martingale or a leading-rein.

Types of martingale are standing, running and Irish. The standing martingale has one end attached to the cavesson nose-band, the other end passing through a neck-strap, down between the horse's legs, and fastened to the girth, underneath the belly. To test for correct length, the martingale strap when raised should just come up to the top of the horse's neck. The object is to prevent the horse from throwing up its head higher than its normally correct position. A martingale should never be used to force a horse to keep its head down. A badly-trained, excitable, or young horse will throw its head about and be inclined to bolt. The standing martingale helps to prevent this. It is never attached to a dropped nose-band, but only to a cavesson. A running martingale is attached to the girth at one end, under the horse's belly; the other end divides into two straps, each having a ring at the end, through which the reins pass. It is also supported by a neck-strap. When using it on the curb reins take care that the martingale rings are smaller than those on the curb bit. If they were larger and slipped over those on the curb bit, it could cause a bad accident. A running martingale can also be used on the bridoon rein, or with a snaffle bridle. It has little practical use, because if adjusted tightly enough to have any effect it would interfere with the action of the reins; if fitted longer it has little or no effect. The Irish martingale is a strap about 4 to 6 inches long with a ring at each end. The snaffle reins pass through these rings below the horse's neck. It merely stops the horse throwing the reins over its head, and does not prevent it from throwing up its head.

A breastplate is used on a horse with a high wither and rather low croup, to stop the saddle from sliding too far back. This is due to faulty conformation. The breastplate consists of a strap fastened to the 'D's on the pommel of the saddle, with the other end fastened to a metal ring on each side of the horse. Another strap joins these rings across the neck, just below the wither. A third strap comes from each ring and joins into one strap which passes underneath between the horse's legs, being fastened to the girth like a standing martingale.

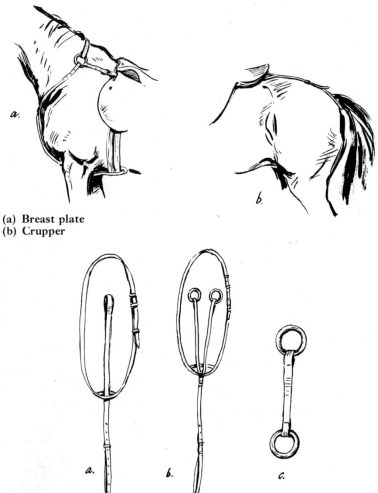

(a) Breast plate
(b) Crupper

Martingales
(a) Standing martingale
(b) Running martingale
(c) Irish martingale

The opposite type of faulty conformation is a low wither and a rather high croup. This gives the saddle a tendency to slide too far forward, necessitating the use of a crupper. This is a strap attached to the 'D's on the cantle of the saddle. The tail passes through a loop at the other end of the strap, which is adjusted to fit just below the root of the tail. It is more often necessary to use a crupper on small ponies than on horses.

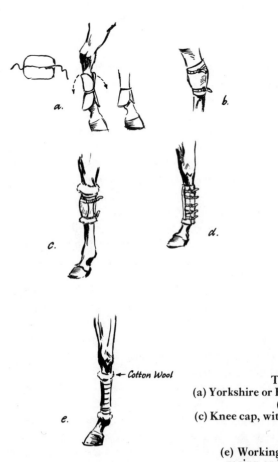

Types of boots
(a) Yorkshire or Brushing boot
(b) Hock boot
(c) Knee cap, with cotton wool underneath
(d) Boots
(e) Working bandage for racing or hunting, with gamgee or cotton wool underneath. They do not cover the fetlock joint

Brushing is caused through faulty conformation, fatigue, poor condition; also a risen clench or a bad shoe with a projecting edge. A brushing boot is used when the cause is bad action (resulting from faulty conformation), fatigue or poor condition. The horse knocks its legs together while moving, cutting itself on the coronet, or on the inside of the fetlock. Speedy cutting is caused when a fast-moving horse knocks itself just under the knee with the opposite toe. A Yorkshire or brushing boot is made of felt; a tape is sewn across the middle and is tied on just above the fetlock joint, and then folded over. An over-reach is most often caused by jumping, when uncollected, galloping through soft wet ground, jumping on and off a bank, especially when the going is soft. The horse hits the back of the forefoot, usually the heel, with the inner edge of the hindfoot toe. A rubber over-reach boot covering the heel can be worn though it is not always an effective remedy. A sausage boot is a small sausage-shaped pillow which fits like a ring round the pastern. It is used to prevent a capped elbow or capped hock. These are swellings often caused by lying on hard ground or (in the case of a capped elbow), on the heel of the shoe. Hock boots are used to prevent a horse from injuring its hocks when lying down at night, especially likely to happen if stabled on insufficient bedding.

Knee caps are used for protection when travelling, or as a precaution when riding over very rough, uneven ground, especially if a horse is prone to stumbling. The lower strap should always be loosely fastened.

Boots are worn on the front legs to prevent a horse knocking itself when jumping or schooling. They should not be worn out hunting or when riding over muddy ground, because the mud gets inside and may cause a rub. For hunting or racing working bandages are used instead of boots. These have cotton wool or gamgee underneath to allow for the wet bandages shrinking.

A hunting crop should only be carried when hunting. It has a crook at the top end, for opening gates, and should never be carried without a thong and lash. To carry a crop without a thong is a *faux pas* often made by would-be 'horsey' weekend riders. Always carry a crop head downwards walking, or riding, with the thong looped in the hand when riding.

A schooling whip is longer than the ordinary cutting or riding whip carried for hacking. As its name implies its purpose is for use when schooling a young, green horse. It should be about 3 feet long with a leather keeper at the end. A cutting whip for hacking is about 2 ft to 2 ft 6 ins long. It is a mistake to have one which is too short. It is advisable for it to have a wrist-strap which loops over the wrist to prevent dropping it. The best ones are made of whale-bone, but these are expensive. Cheaper ones are wire or even wood, covered with very tightly twisted twine. I prefer a leather-covered whip as it lasts longer. A racing whip is very similar but has a very broad leather keeper. If the horse is hit with it it makes considerable noise without cutting or marking the horse.

A leather-covered riding cane is often carried instead of a riding whip for hacking. This should be held in the middle at the point of

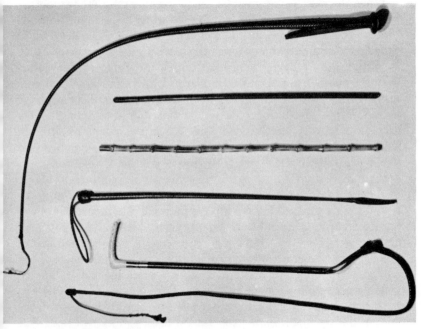

Types of riding whips (*top to bottom*)
Rawhide whip. Leather-covered riding cane. Plain rattan riding cane. Schooling whip—an ordinary riding whip for hacking is similar but shorter. Hunting crop—this should never be carried without a lash, and strictly speaking it should only be carried out hunting, when it should be held with the crook pointing downwards towards the rider's elbow and the lash looped in his hand. The crook is for opening gates.
EQUIPMENT KINDLY SUPPLIED BY MOSS BROS.

F

balance, with the head of the stick pointing diagonally across towards the horse's left ear.

A plain riding cane is also popular for hacking and should also be held in the middle, with the head pointing across to the horse's left ear.

A blackthorn riding cane is beloved by all real horsemen and horsewomen. It is carried in the same way as above when riding.

When fitting a saddle the arch at the pommel must be the correct width so that the rider's weight is taken on the muscles covering the horse's ribs, just behind the wither. If the arch is too wide the pommel will press down on the wither and cause a saddle gall; if too narrow it will pinch the withers.

When the rider is mounted he should be able to insert two fingers between the pommel and the wither even when he leans forward and throws all his weight onto the front of the saddle. On no account should the saddle rest on or touch the horse's spine anywhere. There should always be daylight visible through the gullet of the saddle, from the pommel to the cantle. Similarly, if the rider leans backwards in the saddle the cantle should not press down on the top of the horse's back. The fitting of a saddle can vary quite considerably according to the horse's condition. When the horse is fatter in summer there will often be more space between the pommel and wither than in winter, or when the horse is in hard condition.

If the saddle sinks down onto the wither, either through widening of the arch, or the horse becoming thinner, it should be taken to be restuffed by the saddler. With continuous use the stuffing will harden and cause the saddle to sink down, and it should be restuffed about every two years. A temporary expedient, until the saddle can be restuffed, is to use a wither pad. This is a knitted woollen oval bag stuffed with soft material, or it may be a piece of foam rubber of suitable size; a folded stable rubber can also be used. The wither pad must not be flat on the withers but must be pulled well up into the arch of the pommel. Some people use a foam rubber pad under the saddle. A sheepskin numnah is also used, particularly for jumping. But it is very hot and smells vile if not kept clean.

When trying on a new saddle, put on a blanket underneath. Then ride the horse for about an hour. On dismounting and removing the saddle an exact impression of where it rested, and where the pressure came, can be seen on the blanket. Remember that a new saddle will

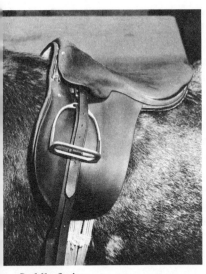

Saddle fitting
Left Correctly fitting saddle. Front arch well clear of withers, weight taken on pony's muscles and ribs

Right Incorrectly fitting saddle. Arch too wide. Saddle too low on withers and spine

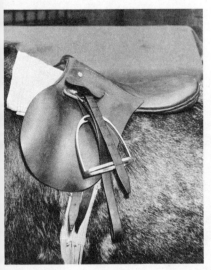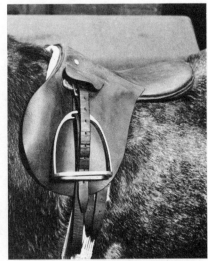

Left Wither pad incorrectly placed. It does not prevent saddle pressing on the wither

Right Correctly placed wither pad pushed well under the arch so that the pommel does not press on the pony's wither. This is only a temporary expedient until the saddle can be restuffed and made to fit correctly

widen slightly and settle down, often quite appreciably as it gets 'ridden-in'. A cut-back head at the pommel obviates the risk of pressure on the wither.

The important points when trying on and fitting a new bridle are that the brow-band should be sufficiently long so as to fit comfortably without causing pressure or rubbing at the base of the ears. When adjusting the cheek-straps, a snaffle bit should be at the corners of the lips without wrinkling them; conversely it should not be too low in the horse's mouth, so that it can get its tongue over the bit. If very low the horse could even manage to spit it out. In a double bridle the cheek-straps supporting the curb bit should allow it to be below the snaffle bit, midway between the corner teeth and corners of the mouth, and level on both sides. The nose-band should hang about two fingers' breadth below the cheek-bone. Cheek-pieces should be in line with and behind the cheek-bones. With a double bridle or a pelham the curb-chain should lie snugly in the chin- or curb-groove, without being tight.

10 Tack Cleaning

Tack cleaning is important for several reasons and should be done daily after riding. A good horseman takes a pride in the appearance of his tack. If slovenly over his tack the owner will probably be slipshod over the care of his horse and in his general stable management. It is no use being smartly dressed, with one's horse well-groomed, if one's tack is dirty. Unfortunately some people only clean their tack once a week, or even only before a show, but it is much harder work and takes far longer than if it is given a rub over daily after use. Also it cannot be checked so easily for wear and tear.

Quite apart from appearance, regular cleaning preserves the leather and keeps it supple—this especially applies to reins and stirrup leathers. Nothing is more unpleasant or more conducive to heavy hands than hard, unyielding, dirty reins. If inspected and cleaned daily any wear can be detected immediately and repaired. More accidents when riding are directly caused by neglected tack than anything else. Girth-straps should be inspected for wear under the saddle flaps. Stirrup-leathers wear at the buckles and stitching, and where the rider's weight bears on the stirrup-iron. Also inspect all metal studs and stitching on the saddle. And on the bridle inspect all buckles and billets and all stitching, on cheek-pieces, head-stall and reins. Girths need regular frequent inspection, particularly string, web and leather girths, especially at the buckles. At Pony Club mounted rallies there is usually an inspection and this frequently reveals tack in a parlous condition, often positively unsafe.

Materials required for tack cleaning are: a bucket of cold or lukewarm water (in winter), two sponges, a chamois leather, bar of glycerine saddle soap, tin of Duraglit and two polishing cloths.

In bygone days bits and stirrup-irons were made of iron or steel and had to be cleaned with emery cloth, or fine sandpaper, silver sand, jeweller's rouge, and 'elbow grease'. Modern bits are either stainless steel, nickel or even chromium plated, and only need polishing with Duraglit and a rub over with a polishing cloth.

If a saddle is not going to be used for some time, before being stored it should be rubbed all over with either castor oil, neatsfoot oil, dubbin, olive oil or glycerine. The same applies to all the leatherwork of a bridle before storing it. Never use linseed or mineral oil as it hardens leather.

To clean a saddle, place it on a saddle-horse and strip it, removing the girths and stirrup-leathers. Take the irons off the leathers and place them in the bucket of water. Sponge off all mud, dirt and dried sweat. If the saddle has a serge or linen lining brush thoroughly with a new stiff dandy brush kept for this purpose, to remove hairs and dust. A leather lining should be thoroughly sponged; if any grease or dirt are left on, it can give the horse a sore back, as the leather hardens. After removing all dirt apply glycerine saddle soap with a nearly dry sponge. If the sponge is too wet the soap merely lathers instead of being rubbed into the leather. Use two sponges, for removing dirt and soaping the leather. Soap under the skirt, the underside of the flap, the sweat-flap, and the panel; also the girth-straps. All black, greasy 'jockey' marks should be removed from the leather. Also wash and soap the stirrup leathers thoroughly. Dry the stirrup-irons, apply Duraglit and polish. Hold the iron with a cloth in one hand while polishing with the other, with a second cloth, to avoid getting finger marks on it. If any holes in the girth straps or stirrup leathers become filled with soap, either blow it out or remove with a match-stick. Leather girths must also be thoroughly cleaned, soaped and oiled if of the folded variety. Nylon girths can be rinsed and scrubbed in warm, soapy water or with soap powder.

Having reassembled the saddle, fold the girth over the top and place it on the saddle-rack. Alternatively the girth, leathers and irons can be hung up separately below the saddle.

To clean a bridle hang it up on the bridle-hook and undo all buckles, noting which holes they go in, especially on the cheek-straps. Put the buckles into the lowest holes. Then wash, dry and soap all the leather-work, especially the under-sides. Wash and dry the bit and then polish all metalwork (buckles and bit). Replace all buckles in their correct holes, and run strap ends into their respective keepers and runners.

The procedure is the same for a pelham or double bridle, except that the curb-chain is removed and placed in the bucket. When dry a curb-chain can be polished by placing it in a bag with other curb-chains and swinging it round, or by rubbing it between one's hands.

Before 'putting up' the bridle on the bridle-rack, run the throat-lash through the ends of the reins and put the nose-band right round the outside of the cheek-pieces. Hook the curb-chain of a pelham or double bridle in front of the bit.

Alternatively a bridle can be taken completely to pieces and each part cleaned and soaped separately, and the bit or bits polished, before reassembling. It is good practice to do this, say, once a month if time allows. All leatherwork can then be thoroughly oiled with neatsfoot before being put together again. This gives an opportunity to clean the insides of billets or buckles and to check for wear where they are fastened to the bits.

To undo a billet, push the leather forward from the end where it is fastened to the rein or cheek-strap, so that the slot slides down off the hook. If there is any difficulty slide a pencil underneath, between the end and the hook and lever forwards and upwards.

The best way to clean reins and all straps is to fold the sponge round them and rub vigorously up and down several times. This cleans both inside and outside of the leather simultaneously; the same applies to stirrup-leathers.

Many people advocate the use of 'Flexolan'. This is applied to all leatherwork of saddles and bridles after it has been thoroughly cleaned. It is supposed to keep the leather supple and reduce labour by obviating the necessity for soaping it each time. The dirty saddle or bridle is simply washed and dried after use and the metalwork polished.

Head-collars are all too frequently neglected, but should be regularly cleaned and inspected with the rest of the tack. Those with white brow-bands should be pipe-clayed daily.

It is advisable to give whips a wipe over, especially leather-covered ones.

If a saddle is stood on the ground it should always be placed upright on its pommel, with the girth under it to protect the leather. If thrown down with the flaps and panels spreadeagled it can easily cause a broken tree. It costs almost as much to repair a broken tree as to buy another saddle.

Well-kept tack will last for years. When visiting the Mounted Police stables in Stafford I saw a saddle dating back to the Boer War period. It was still regularly used, and in showroom condition.

For very special occasions brown boot polish can be applied to the tack, which, after being cleaned and soaped, must first be allowed to dry thoroughly. It is impossible to polish while damp. Do not polish the seat of the saddle; it makes it too slippery. Mounted Police tack is always kept polished.

It is advisable to oil tack periodically. Neatsfoot oil is excellent for this purpose; Mars oil is also made especially for this. Take the tack completely to pieces, wash and saddle-soap it thoroughly and rub the oil well in with the finger-tips, then reassemble. It is necessary particularly to oil the insides of all billets and stitching round buckles.

Do not oil too much or too frequently, otherwise it will 'kill' the leather and rot the stitching. New leather should be oiled two or three times consecutively after being used and cleaned, to make it supple. Oil before the warm weather begins, as in a hot, dry spell the leather will dry and harden, and then crack.

Before storing tack for any length of time, take it to pieces, clean thoroughly and then oil it. Castor oil or dubbin may be used instead of Mars or neatsfoot oil. Polishing with boot polish helps to prevent tack becoming mouldy when not in use.

11 Horse Clothing

Bandages include woollen stable- or rest-bandages, exercising and working bandages, which have already been mentioned (Chapter 9), and tail-bandages and a tail-guard.

Stable- or rest-bandages are used in very cold weather for warmth, if a horse is unwell, after hunting or other hard exercise, and when travelling to protect the legs. They are about 7 feet long, and about 4 inches broad.

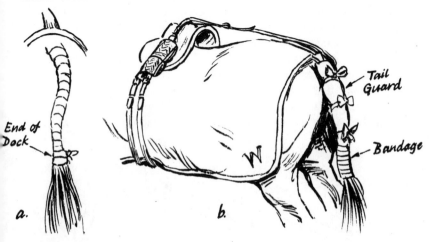

Bandages
(a) Tail bandage
(b) Tail guard

Tail-bandages are used to keep a pulled tail in shape. They should be long enough to extend from right under the root to the end of the tail bone, and should be about 2 to 3 inches wide. An ordinary wide bandage is adequate if long enough. A crepe, elastic bandage is not recommended as it stretches while being put on and is then inclined to shrink, becoming too tight. Tapes should be sewn on at one end for tying.

A tail-guard is worn over a tail-bandage when travelling to prevent the tail being rubbed. Made of wool or leather, it has a strap at one end which fastens to the roller to keep it in position.

To roll a bandage, fold in the tapes on the side to which they are sewn. Start rolling from this end, holding the other end between the knees. Pull the bandage tight and roll evenly between both hands, keeping it level and the tension even. The more tightly it is rolled the more easily it can be put on.

When applying a bandage never squat or kneel near a horse's legs, always stoop. Hold the tightly rolled bandage in the right hand with the rolled part on top. Take one turn round the horse's leg, with the end of the bandage sticking out at the top, using the left hand to hold it in position under the knee. Do not bandage over the knee-joint. Then, with as few turns as possible bandage downwards over the fetlock to the pastern. Follow the shape of the horse's leg and make each turn tight enough to keep the bandage firm and prevent it from slipping. When going round the pastern joint follow the contour of the leg so that there are no bulges. Then wind up again to the top, turn the flap over and tie the end with a bow on the outside of the leg. Do not tie the bow on the front or at the back of the leg as this can cause pain and stop the circulation, and do not tie it on the inside as the horse can untie the bow by rubbing one leg against the other.

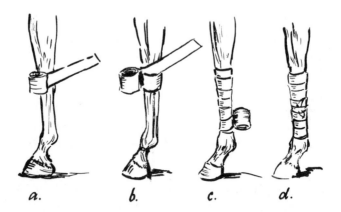

a. b. c. d.

Exercise bandage
(a) First stage
(b) Second stage
(c) Third stage—bandage smooth, closely following contours of leg
(d) Complete bandage. Top of bandage, left protruding, is neatly folded over. Bandage is always tied with a bow on the *outside* of the leg

Never use a knot, but always fasten with a firm bow which can easily
be undone. Tuck in the ends of the tapes.

When unrolling a leg-bandage pass it quickly from hand to hand.
Never attempt to roll it up while taking it off, but get it off as quickly
as possible.

Woollen stable- or rest-bandages are made in sets of four. Bandage
so that the bandage covers as much leg as possible from knee or hock
(on a hindleg), downwards. If applied too tightly it will stop the
circulation, should the horse's legs swell.

If cotton wool, or preferably gamgee, is applied under an exercise
bandage see that there are no wrinkles; it must be absolutely smooth,
otherwise it may cause a rub.

When applying a tail-bandage first damp the hairs thoroughly with
the water brush so that they lie quite flat. Never wet the bandage as it
will shrink, causing the horse considerable pain and stopping the
circulation, which will produce white hairs in the tail. Start the
bandage as high up as possible underneath the root of the tail. Let

Correctly rugged-up horse

each new turn of the bandage slightly overlap the one above, and continue down to the end of the tail-bone. Tie the tapes in front in a bow, just below the end of the tail-bone. Never unwind a tail-bandage to take it off. Simply slide the bandage downwards off the tail with both hands.

To prepare a horse for a journey put on a rug with a surcingle and roller. In warm weather it need only be a light cotton summer sheet. Bandage the tail and put on the tail-guard and fasten it to the roller. Finally, put woollen rest-bandages on the legs, with knee-caps on the front legs. The upper strap of the knee-cap should only be just tight enough to stop it sliding down over the knee, and the lower strap should be fastened loosely.

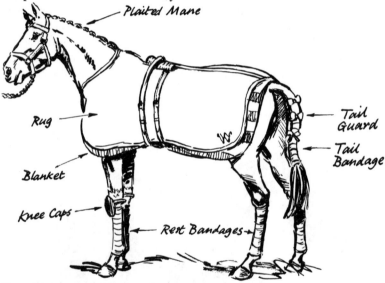

Travelling—preparing for a journey

At one time one's horse was considered improperly dressed if one took it out hunting with its mane unplaited. Nowadays one sees quite a number out with unplaited manes. It is not correct to plait the mane for cub-hunting. Manes of show horses and ponies are always plaited, but it is optional for show-jumpers at smaller shows; at Windsor, the Royal and Horse of the Year Show one sees them plaited for show-jumping. Mane-plaiting takes considerable time—and patience. To make neat, even plaits which will not work loose is a real art.

The number of plaits varies from six to eight according to the length of the horse's neck. Seven plaits was the normal, conventional number. Nowadays the Continental fashion, which seems to be spreading in this country also, is to have as many small, tight plaits as possible—sixteen or so for a neck of normal length. I personally prefer the conventional British seven plaits—to me the other looks fussy.

To plait one needs a water brush, cotton to match the colour of the mane, brown for a bay or a chestnut, white for a white or grey, and black for a black, brown or blue roan; also a blunt needle with a large eye and a pair of scissors. Having very thoroughly groomed the mane, damp well with the water brush. Without actually soaking it, with water dripping off, see that all hairs are thoroughly damp underneath and on top. Then divide the mane from just behind the ears to just in front of the wither into seven equal parts. Start from the ears and plait the first strand, right down to the end of the hair. Make the plait tight and pull it right up to the root of the mane to start it. When plaited turn under and sew it, twisting the cotton round tightly to keep it firm. Fold and sew again. Finally turn under again and sew. The finished plait should hang down about $1\frac{1}{2}$ inches, and be firm and not too large. Repeat in turn with each of the seven strands down to the wither. Plaits for hunting or shows should always be sewn. Some people use elastic bands to match the mane. But they snap easily, do not always remain done up and look amateurish.

Tails are not plaited for hunting, but they are plaited for show classes, though not for show jumping, usually. Plaiting a tail is even harder than a mane, especially with a fidgety horse or pony. If inclined to be a bit free with its heels and 'light behind', have a helper to stand at its head and hold up a foreleg to prevent it kicking. As with the mane, thoroughly damp the tail with the water brush after it is perfectly groomed. Starting from about six inches below the root of the tail, take strands of hair from each side and plait them in very fine plaits straight down the middle to the end of the dock. A beautifully plaited, shaped tail is a real work of art and a joy to behold, but one badly done with thick, clumsy plaits, looks horrible. Coarse hair cannot be plaited really neatly. The hair must be severely thinned out before attempting to plait.

12 Conformation

The main sections of a horse are the forehand, midriff and hind-quarters. The forehand, controlled by the rider's hands through the bit, consists of the head, neck, forelegs and shoulders, to the wither. The midriff is the back, true and false ribs and the belly. The hind-quarters comprise the loins, croup, thigh, dock and hindlegs.

The points or parts of a horse in detail are shown in the accompanying diagram.

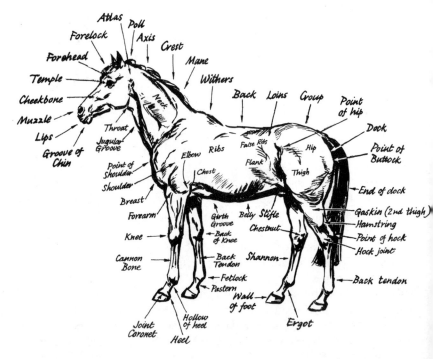

Points of a horse

Those who have been brought up with horses all their lives, develop an instinctive 'eye' for a horse. But any observant person who knows the different points of a horse thoroughly, can develop one as he gains experience.

See and handle as many different horses and ponies as possible, good, bad and indifferent. Note where the conformation of the bad and indifferent ones differs from the mental picture which you have of an ideal horse. Go to as many horse shows as possible and watch the show hack and pony classes. Pick out those which you think have

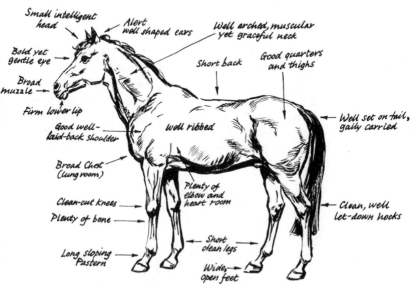

Points of good conformation

the best conformation. Try to place those which you think will be the first three in winning order, and then see where the judge's eventual choice differs from yours. If his choice differs try to find what good points he has seen, which you have overlooked. Possibly it may be that the winner may not have quite such perfect conformation, but it may be better schooled, have better manners and be a better, more comfortable ride. The judge has the advantage of riding the exhibits —you cannot. If possible take an expert horseman with you and see which he picks out, and how his choice differs from yours and the judge's.

Good conformation in a horse is the sum total of the following: a well-shaped head, small, intelligent-looking and rather lean, with well-shaped, rather small ears pricked alertly forward; eyes set well apart, rather large and prominent, bold, yet gentle; a broad, soft muzzle with a firm lower lip; a graceful, well-arched neck, muscular when seen from the saddle, yet not too thick when viewed sideways from the ground. A riding horse should have a sloping shoulder; an upright shoulder gives a rather jolting, jerky action for riding, but is not a disadvantage for a horse used in harness, as it gives plenty of power for collar-work, especially if combined with a short rather thick neck. The elbow should stand well out, with ample room to put one's fist between it and the body. The chest, viewed from the front, should be broad. Regarded sideways it should be deep from the wither to the girth-groove just behind the elbow, giving plenty of heart and lung room. The forearm to the knee should be long, with good bone below the knee. Short, clean legs with short cannon bones; from the front they should appear perpendicular to the ground, with knees looking as if cleanly chiselled out of wood. Pasterns should be long and rather sloping; if too upright they give a jolty action, while if too sloping they may be weak, especially for jumping. Feet should

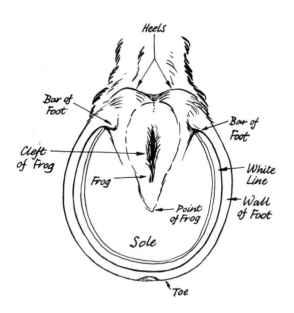

A well shaped, open foot

be of equal size, wide and open; avoid rather small, narrow, 'boxy' feet like those of a donkey or mule. They will give a 'pottery' action and be prone to foot troubles. From the wither, which should be fairly prominent, but not too high, the back should be short, broad and level. The spinal vertebrae should not protrude, and the back should rise very slightly to the loin. Ribs must be well-sprung and rounded, giving plenty of support for the muscles which carry the saddle. Quarters should look broad, well-rounded and powerful, with good thighs; the hip bone should not be too prominent. Hocks, 'well let down', with a good sweep to the stifle joint. A perpendicular line dropped from the point of the buttock should pass through the point of the hock and the fetlock to the back of the heel, coinciding with the back of the shannon bone. Hocks should be parallel, viewed

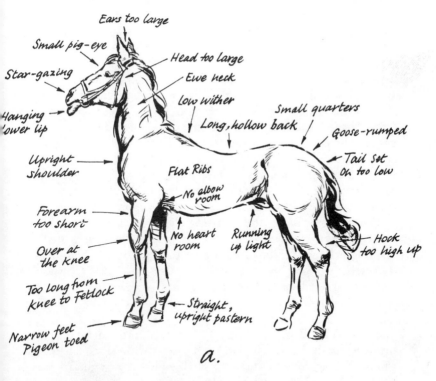

Points of a horse—everything that a horse should *not* be
(a) Bad conformation

from the back, with all four legs perpendicular to the ground. The tail, well set on, high up, and carried well out, not drooping or tucked in between the hindlegs.

Bad conformation shows lack of quality and breeding. The following should be avoided: small 'piggy' eyes set too close together. They often indicate bad temper and a poor field of vision; a horse or pony with a small pig-eye, close set, shies easily. A wall-eye is bluish in colour and frequently indicates defective sight, or possibly blindness in that eye. A large heavy 'fiddle' head often denotes stupidity, obstinacy and wilfulness. A very long, large head is called a 'coffin head'. A short, thick, heavy neck often means a horse that 'pulls' and therefore a bad ride, although useful for harness work. A horse with a ewe-neck cannot bridle properly and therefore may be difficult to control. As the neck curves the wrong way the horse cannot flex its jaw properly, it 'pokes its nose' and 'star gazes' and is liable to stumble through not looking where it is going. A horse with a thin, scrawny neck like a chicken's is called 'cock-throttled' or 'swan-necked'; besides lacking in good looks it is difficult to ride. A heavy, upright shoulder gives a draught horse power for pulling against the collar, but gives a jolting action and an uncomfortable ride as the front legs move up and down too perpendicularly. Badly-shaped knees are called 'over at the knee'. Straight, upright pasterns cause a jerky, pottery action. Faults in foot conformation are: a shallow, brittle hoof; narrow, 'boxy' or 'mule' foot, 'down at heel' and heel too narrow. All these can lead to foot troubles and un-soundness. 'Tied in at the elbow' means that the leg is too close to the body at the elbow and prevents a free action. Insufficient heart and lung room, is due to a narrow chest and lack of depth from wither to girth-groove. 'Tucked up', 'waspy', 'herring gutted' and 'like a greyhound' means running up too light to the hindquarters. 'Grass belly', 'pot belly' or 'cow belly' means a large, pendulous stomach. A weak back is often long from withers to croup, and is frequently combined with weak loins and shallow false (back) ribs. The curve from withers to croup may be exaggerated, forming a hollow back. Back curving up with a prominent backbone, forms a 'roach' back. The tail set on too low down is called 'goose rumped'. Poor hindquarters are small and narrow and lack power. Flat ribs and sides cause trouble in saddle fitting and give rise to saddle galls. Withers may be too high or low. Very high withers are usually too narrow, again causing trouble with saddle fitting, and are therefore liable to be rubbed, and the saddle slips too far back, necessitating the wearing of a breastplate. When the wither is too low, especially combined with a rather high croup, the saddle slides too far forward, making it necessary to use a crupper (*vide* Chapter 9).

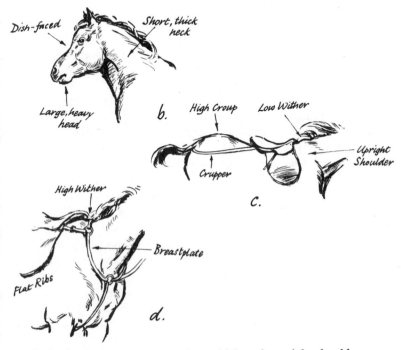

(b) **Dish face, large heavy head, short, thick neck, upright shoulder**
(c) **Croup higher than wither. Crupper to stop saddle slipping forward**
(d) **Breastplate to stop saddle slipping back**

'Cow' hocks slope inwards, instead of being parallel to each other when viewed from behind. 'Sickle' hocks are less obvious and harder to detect; they stand too far back and curve too much when viewed sideways. Cannon bones (front) and shannon bones (hind) may be too long. Bad conformation such as being 'tied in at the knees', 'calf' knees and pigeon-toe causes faulty action. A horse with good conformation and therefore good action moves straight with its hind feet following in the tracks of the front. 'Dishing' means that the leg is thrown out sideways when walking or trotting.

'Plaiting' means that a horse puts one leg across in front of the other. It causes stumbling and can be dangerous when moving fast. 'Winding the clock' means that both front legs are thrown out sideways with a circular movement.

Unless one's purse is very deep one can seldom hope to buy a horse with perfect conformation. If it has excellent conformation yet is going cheap, there is probably some other snag: a mean, vicious temperament, unsafe in traffic, 'nappy', liable to rear or bolt or maybe bad stable manners, and so on. A horse that shows the whites of its eyes and tucks its tail in between its legs, is generally 'light behind' and free with its heels.

A working compromise must usually be made, and that is where experience counts, to know which faults in conformation will rule a horse out, and which can be tolerated. Personally, for instance, I would never buy a horse with a ewe-neck, or goose rump, or one without much heart and lung room; I would also avoid one with poor quarters or badly shaped legs or feet, especially one that plaited its front legs. Other people might assess points of conformation differently. If a horse is well-mannered in and out of the stable, has a good, kind temperament and is traffic-proof, sound and easy to catch, many small imperfections in conformation might be overlooked. A horse that would never win a prize in the show-ring may be a good, honest worker, with a charming disposition and give excellent service. Many a horse with no looks has been a brilliant performer, though naturally it makes one feel good to ride a good-looking horse. But frequently some very good-lookers have been the biggest frauds that ever looked through a bridle.

Apart from bad conformation, blemishes may cause unsoundness and be due to accidents or injuries. Carelessness or bad riding may have been the cause. Broken knees, due to a fall, may have resulted from slovenly, careless riding, poor condition, overwork or rough ground. Curb is caused by sprained ligaments at the back of the hock. Splints may have resulted from a knock or jar (too much trotting on hard roads, or jumping on hard ground), overwork when young, or carrying too much weight; splint and cannon bones become fused together by a long growth of lime deposit, which helps to strengthen the splint bone. It may cause unsoundness while forming, but is harmless once formed, though incurable. Capped hock is probably due to lying on a hard stable floor with insufficient bedding, or to getting cast. Capped elbow is usually the result of a hindfoot iron shoe pressing against a foreleg elbow while lying down.

It is said that 'a good horse is never a bad colour'. Nevertheless while all colours and shades are found, experts usually tend to avoid pale, indeterminate, 'washy' colours, believing that horses so coloured seem rather nondescript in appearance and lacking in character. It is also said that colour gives some indication of character; for instance, a bright chestnut (like a red-haired person) is said to have rather a fiery, excitable temperament; a grey is generally reputed to be temperamentally uncertain, high spirited and rather a handful; a bay is generally considered to be hardy, placid, with a good disposition and an honest, hard worker. There seemed at one time to be a prejudice against black horses, possibly because they were always associated with funerals. A white foot and hoof are considered to be less hardy than a black.

Colours found are: Bay, bright, light or dark; Black; Brown; Chestnut, bright, dark or liver; Cream; Dun; Grey, plain, dappled, flea-bitten, iron; Blue Roan, Strawberry Roan, Red Roan or Sorrel. There are also Piebald and Skewbald, Palomino ('golden' horse or pony), Appaloosa (spotted horse), Odd Coloured.

Bays vary from very dark, rich mahogany, merging through bright bay to a light golden or yellowish colour, almost a dun. A bright, blood bay looks like polished mahogany. Browns vary from almost a bay to nearly black. A brown shading into black towards the legs and feet is favoured. White markings are permissible, particularly on the face and sometimes on the legs. Black is not so frequent nor as greatly favoured as a bay or brown. Blacks are common in Belgium. Thoroughbreds are frequently black. Chestnuts vary from a bright, almost copper, colour and dark liver chestnut to a pale, washy, nondescript colour, which should be avoided. Except for Suffolk Punch Shire horses, plain chestnut with no white markings is uncommon. There may be exaggerated white markings on the face and legs. A chestnut may have a black mane, tail and feet (or 'points'). Dun varies from a nondescript mouse colour to a golden dun which is very attractive. Pronounced zebra markings are common in India, but are infrequently found in England. A dun, especially with black points, is usually considered a good, honest worker and hardy. Creams, usually with a silvery mane and tail, can be very attractive, though they seem more associated with the circus and are not much

Bad conformation
(a) **Calf knees**
(b) **Cow hocks**
(c) **Sickle hocks, too curved**

a

b

c

favoured for ordinary riding. Greys when young are nearly black, but become lighter as they grow older. An old grey is nearly white. Dappled greys have circles of black hair all over the body, being especially prominent on the hindquarters, reminiscent of a child's rocking-horse. Flea-bitten greys are attractive, with black specks of hair all over the body, which account for the descriptive name. Markings may occur on the face, with white or black points, and an almost white mane and tail. Iron grey is very dark, sometimes nearly black. There is no definite marking, but there is a fair amount of black hair distributed all over the body. A Blue Roan's coat is a mixture of black, white and yellow hair. The mane may have streaks

A golden Palomino. PHOTO BY JOHN NESTLE

of chestnut in it, and the tail black. The coat changes tone, becoming much darker in winter and a light, smoky grey in summer. A Strawberry Roan has a mixture of bay, white and yellow hairs all over its body. This also becomes lighter in colour in summer. A Red Roan (Sorrel) similarly has a mixture of black and chestnut (reddish) hairs. (The Strawberry roan is probably the most often seen.) Piebalds have bold black and white markings varying in size and irregular in shape. Skewbalds have similar white and bay,

Example of a spotted horse. This is not an Appaloosa but comes from Denmark. The Appaloosa from the U.S.A. is very similar in markings
PHOTO BY JOHN NESTLE

chestnut or brown, irregular markings. A Palomino is best described as the 'golden' horse or pony. It frequently has a flaxen or cream mane and tail. Its golden colour deepens as it warms up with exercise. Palominos are very beautiful and attractive, but the colour is uncertain to produce. If one parent is a chestnut, the offspring may be a

Palomino. Two Palominos will not necessarily beget a Palomino. It is not a particular breed, and the colour occurs in both horses and ponies. The Appaloosa is the true original breed of 'spotted horse'. It originated in America in the Palouse territory, being bred by the Nez-Percé Indian tribe. Other kinds of spotted horse are also found in Europe, for example, the Danish Knabstrup.

This is a good example of an Appaloosa. PHOTO BY E. R. MORRIS

If the colour of a horse or pony is doubtful it is determined by the colour of the points, viz. muzzle, mane, tail, extremities of the legs and tips of the ears.

Odd-coloured horses are of no fixed colour. They may be similar to a piebald or skewbald, but with patches of more than two colours. They are usually rather too striking in appearance for most people's taste for ordinary riding, but for this reason are in demand for circus acts.

Markings

Star

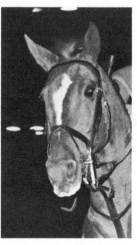

Star, running into blaze

Star, running into stripe

White face

Snip into right nostril

Star, stripe and snip

White pastern

White sock

White stocking

White leg

Facial markings are a star, blaze, stripe, white face and snip.

Star: a white, generally more or less round, mark in the centre of the forehead. Can be large or small.

Blaze: a fairly wide white marking, almost covering the whole forehead between the eyes; extends down the front of the face covering the width of the nasal bones.

Stripe: a narrow white marking, which may be narrow, straight or irregular; it may form a continuation of the star.

White Face: an exaggerated blaze, covering all the forehead and front of the face. It extends laterally to the mouth.

Snip: a white mark between the nostrils, which may be central, or may run into one or both nostrils.

Upper lip: Underlip; white skin at the edges of lips.

White Muzzle: nostrils and both lips are white.

Leg markings: white feet; white heel; white coronet; white pastern (with or without ermine markings); white fetlock(s); sock; stocking.

Only one front or hindleg may have white on it, or both front or both hind, or all four legs. One may have very little white while the other or others may have a sock or stocking, or a white leg.

A sock extends to just above the fetlock, while a stocking or white leg reaches nearly to the knee. The other terms are self-explanatory. Ermine markings on a white pastern or a sock are small black tufts of hair round the coronet resembling the black markings on ermine fur.

Body markings: list; ray; dark lines along the backs of all donkeys, many mules and some horses.

Zebra markings: stripes on the neck, withers, limbs or quarters; seldom seen on horses, and more frequently on mules and donkeys. Also seen on spotted horses.

White markings can result from injury, or from constant pressure by the saddle, bridle, girth or collar (on a harness horse); they may also be caused by bandages, firing (legs) or hair which has regrown over an old scar. Sometimes tick bites produce small white patches all over the body, particularly in the tropics. Flesh marks are colourless patches of skin. Whole coloured means that there are no white markings at all.

When describing a horse or pony the height, colour and age must be given, together with an accurate description of any markings which are not of natural origin, scars, brand marks or any other characteristic feature. For example, '14·2 hand bright bay pony.

Age: 6 yrs. rising 7. Small star with stripe, leading to snip into near nostril; white underlip. Near foreleg has white coronet with ermine marks. White stocking on off hindleg. Small white saddle patch just behind wither on near side. Brand mark, "G.W." just behind shoulder, under saddle. Black mane and tail with some white hairs near upper part of dock. Small scar on off-side buttock.'

Horses are any height over 14·2 hands; ponies 14·2 hands and under. An Arab is always called a horse—never a pony—even if only 14 hands high. A polo pony is still a 'pony', even if it is 16 hands.

A horse or pony is always measured in hands—1 hand=4 inches —originating from the average breadth of a man's hand across the broadest part of the palm. A horse is measured from its wither at its highest point. Shetland ponies on account of their small size are never measured in hands, but always in inches.

When measuring for showing purposes an allowance of half an inch, either way, is always made for shoes; the difference between a new and an old, worn shoe can amount to that. For show classes a life certificate of measurement can be obtained through the British Horse Society (16, Bedford Square, London, W.C.1) or through the Pony Club from the same address, from whom the address of the local District Commissioner or Branch Secretary can be obtained. The fee for a life certificate is one guinea. The possession of a life certificate has obvious advantages if one is showing a horse or pony: it saves the trouble of having it measured every time on the show-ground. And obviously a much more accurate measurement can be obtained by measuring a calm pony in its own familiar surroundings, than by trying to measure an excited one amid all the noise and distractions of the show-ground.

'Ageing a horse', or estimating its age is done by the appearance of the mouth and its teeth, though even experts may sometimes be mistaken. Unlike human teeth, a horse's teeth are always growing as they are worn down. They also lengthen with age (hence the expression, 'long in the tooth'). A young horse's incisors (front teeth) meet almost vertically; with increasing age, both top and bottom incisors not only grow longer, but gradually slope and protrude outwards. This sloping angle is very marked in old horses. Another way of assessing a horse's age is by the Galvayne groove, or mark on the corner incisor. It was named after the famous veterinary surgeon who first noticed it. It is a brown mark which first appears at the top of the tooth at ten years old: it reaches half way down at fifteen years, reaches the bottom at twenty years, is half grown out at twenty-five years and disappears at thirty years. Hence, if the mark is just beginning to appear the horse is ten years old; if it is about half-way down it is about twelve to fifteen years, while if there is no Galvayne groove visible and the teeth are long and very sloping, the horse is over thirty.

Another way of estimating the approximate age is by the tushes. These teeth develop just behind the incisors in the upper and lower jaws in a horse, as opposed to a mare, at the age of about four to five years. So if a stallion or young gelding has tushes which are just beginning to appear, it is about four or five years old. Mares sometimes grow tushes when they are older; there is a saying that mares

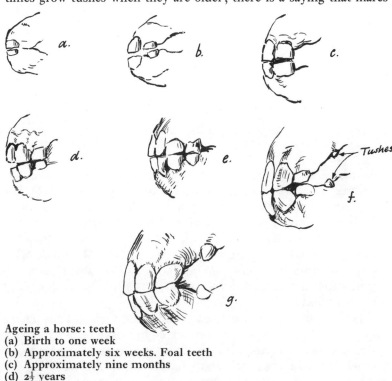

Ageing a horse: teeth
(a) Birth to one week
(b) Approximately six weeks. Foal teeth
(c) Approximately nine months
(d) 2½ years
(e) 3 years
(f) 4 years. Tushes just beginning to appear
(g) 5 years. Tushes through

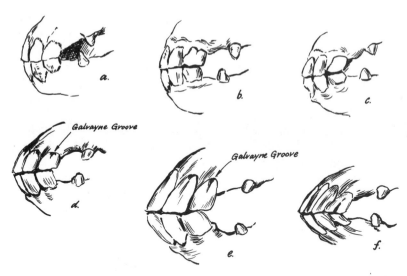

(a) Approximately 6 years
(b) 7 years
(c) 8 years (aged)
(d) 10 years. Length and slope increasing. Galvayne groove starting to appear at the top
(e) 15 years. Galvayne groove half way down
(f) 25 years. Galvayne groove down to the bottom, starting to disappear

with tushes become barren, but its truth cannot be vouched for.

Horses have two complete sets of teeth, temporary milk or foal and permanent or horse teeth. Temporary teeth are small and white; they have a distinct neck and a short fang. The latter almost disappears as the teeth grow older owing to upward pressure from the growing permanent teeth underneath in the gum. The temporary tooth is eventually pushed out of the jaw. Permanent teeth are larger, stronger and more brown in colour, with a long, stout fang and no marked neck.

The table of the tooth is the wearing surface which bites on the opposite tooth in the lower jaw, and on food. It has a black depression called the mark, surrounded by a distinct, narrow, pearly-white enamel ring, standing a little above the rest of the surface level. The mark is very broad and deep in a new tooth; it becomes smaller and more shallow with age and wear, finally disappearing completely. The black colour of the mark is caused by discoloration from food which is masticated and is absent in a new tooth. The neck is the point where the gum and tooth meet; the crown is the part appearing above the gum. The fang is in the jaw and is hollow. The fang-hole or cavity contains the nerves and blood vessels which nourish the tooth and make it sensitive. The fang-hole becomes filled in with lighter coloured dentine as the tooth grows upward; eventually this appears as a small white spot in the centre of the tooth's table; if the mark has not already disappeared the white spot is in front of it.

Each jaw has six incisor teeth, first milk and then permanent. In the centre are the two central teeth; the next tooth on each side is the lateral; the outside teeth on each side of the jaw are the corner teeth. There are six molar teeth on each side of each jaw. The gaps of sensitive gum between the incisor and molar teeth are called the bars of the mouth, and is where the bit or bits rest. The jawbone is very near the surface here, only being covered by a thin layer of sensitive skin. The 1st, 2nd and 3rd molars are first temporary, and then permanent; the 4th, 5th and 6th are only permanent teeth.

A foal has only the two central temporary incisors in each jaw at birth. The lateral temporary teeth appear at about one month old; the corner temporary incisors appear at the age of six to eight months. A yearling has all its temporary incisors; the inner side of the corner tooth has not yet grown up level with the front and the tooth looks 'shelly' and is little worn. Between two and two and a quarter years permanent teeth begin to replace the central temporary teeth; the tooth becomes loose and the gum red and swollen. A two-year-old mouth has often been mistaken for a six-year-old mouth, due to unfamiliarity with the different appearance of temporary and permanent teeth. At two and a half years the central permanent incisors appear. At three years they are in use. At three and a half years the lateral permanent incisors appear and are in use at four years. The corner permanent teeth appear at four and a half years, but are not in full use at five years. Tushes appear in males between four and five years. At six years the horse has a 'full' mouth, with corner teeth in full wear over their whole surface. The marks are broad; those of the centrals, which appeared first, are smaller and more worn than those of the laterals; the laterals show more wear than the corner teeth which appeared last.

After six years old the marks grow smaller and rounder; they may disappear at about ten years. They may last much longer in some

H

teeth depending on the depth of the mark and thickness of the enamel lining; it also depends upon how the upper and lower incisors meet. The marks may last for a long time in an undershot mouth.

At about eight years old the fang-hole appears on the central teeth's wearing surface as a transverse line in front of the mark. As the horse grows older the line becomes a spot in the centre of the table as the mark disappears. Over eight years a horse is said to be 'aged'; this does not mean 'old'.

The wearing surface changes from oval to triangular shape; the top of the triangle is at the back of the tooth.

With increasing age the teeth elongate and project forward instead of meeting nearly perpendicularly.

A thoroughbred's age is calculated from the 1st January; native British ponies and others from the 1st May.

The term 'rising' means nearly; for example, rising six means nearly six; 'off' means past; for example, eight off means past eight but not yet rising nine.

Other signs indicating old age are a deepening of the hollow in the temple, above the eye. A very deep hollow is usually a sign of old age. But this is not entirely reliable, as even some quite young horses have somewhat pronounced hollows, while comparatively old ones may have quite a shallow depression. With advancing age the back tends to become hollowed. Though again this is not entirely reliable, as some horses, owing to conformation, may have a 'dipped' back; some may be quite pronounced.

But these signs, taken in conjunction with the teeth, help one in forming an estimate regarding a horse's age.

When the upper teeth protrude over the lower incisors it is called a 'parrot mouth'. It becomes increasingly noticeable with advancing age and interferes with digestion as a parrot-mouthed horse cannot masticate its food properly.

In the old days of unscrupulous horse dealers ('The Mustard Brigade') various tricks were used to make a horse look younger than it was. To make a colt look older than its age, its temporary teeth were extracted. 'Bishoping', called after an unscrupulous dealer named Bishop, who reduced it to a fine art, consisted of digging out the crowns of the corner incisors and plugging them with a black composition, to look like the original tables of the teeth.

Sometimes the long teeth of a very old horse were cut and filed down before bishoping.

Other tricks were: 'setting' the wind of a broken-winded horse; 'puffing the glims' meant introducing a fine tube into the hollow above the eye, blowing it out to make it look round and full, as in a young horse; 'Figging' was the introduction of ginger into the rectum before showing the horse, to make it appear to carry its tail well; excitement caused by the irritation of the ginger made the horse appear to be animated and full of youthful spirits.

13 Choice of Horse or Pony

Unless one has a deep purse and can afford to employ a groom, which few can these days unless using horses professionally, or unless one is a person of leisure with adequate time to look after it properly, it is not advisable to buy a thoroughbred. Apart from being more temperamental and highly-strung, and therefore only suitable for an experienced horseman as they are more difficult to handle and ride, they are also more thin-skinned and less hardy. They gall more easily and are susceptible to ailments. A thoroughbred usually must be stabled, especially in winter. This means more time and work is required to look after it. If required to hunt or do any hard or fast work, it must either be trace-clipped or clipped-out (or hunter-clipped), which necessitates rugging-up in cold weather. It also cannot be turned out in winter; even with a New Zealand rug it can only be turned out for a few hours during the day, and then only in mild weather.

For the owner-groom, there are nine varieties, at least, of native British breeds of pony from which to choose. Some of these are large and strong enough to carry a light, or even a medium weight, adult. They live semi-wild in the mountains and on the moorlands and are accustomed to fend for themselves even in the most severe winter weather. Provided they have some sort of shelter they can therefore live out all the year round if necessary.

The Shetland is the most northerly breed and is the only native breed of pony which is believed to be of prehistoric origin. Being so small they are not measured in hands but in inches. Their average height is about 36 inches, though many are considerably smaller. Because of their small size they are, of course, too small for an adult to ride, but are said to be the strongest pony in existence for their size. Relatively, they are stronger than a carthorse. They are extremely tough and hardy and in the Shetland Isles are accustomed to scratch a living from very sparse vegetation. During very severe weather they go down to the shore and eat the seaweed. The Shetland islanders use them as pack-ponies for carrying panniers of seaweed and other goods. They are very sure-footed, and live to a great age; up to forty years is not uncommon.

Shetland pony. Tough and one of the strongest ponies in the world, for its size. Not always suitable for very small children, as some are inclined to be wilful unless carefully broken and schooled. Lives to a great age, often up to forty years. PHOTO BY MILES BROTHERS

Being so small people think they should make ideal ponies for very young children to ride. But this is not altogether true as they can be very self-willed and rather stubborn, unless carefully broken-in and schooled. And being so strong they are too powerful for children to handle or control when ridden, unless on a leading-rein. They are also very broad. On the other hand their conformation makes them very suitable for driving. They have a somewhat short, thick neck and rather upright shoulder, which, though not ideal for riding, makes them eminently suited for drawing a light vehicle. In bygone days they were much sought after for work in the mines, drawing tubs of coal; today they are becoming increasingly popular for harness work. A large number have been exported for this purpose, especially to Holland and the U.S.A., and have taken many prizes in driving classes in the show-ring.

Shetlands have an affectionate disposition and on this account, and because of their small size, are about the only kind of pony which is suitable for keeping solely as a pet.

They have a heavy, rather shaggy mane. Their tails are thick and if allowed to grow too long, and not thinned out occasionally, are rather apt to over-weight them in appearance. In winter they have a long-haired outer-coat which keeps the thick woolly under-coat dry. They moult in summer, growing a coat of much finer hair. They can be any colour, including piebald and skewbald; black is perhaps the commonest.

Highland ponies are of three types: those from the island of Barra and from the many smaller Hebridean Isles. They are the original Highland ponies and are between 12·2 and 13·2 hands high. The Mainland ponies are considerably larger, being among the heaviest and strongest British ponies. The Mainland pony from Mull stands about 14·2 hands; it is honest, docile and massive. Being very strong it can easily carry even a heavy adult; in the Highlands the deerstalkers use it to carry a 20 stone deer. It is also suitable for almost any type of farm-work, for which the crofters use it. It therefore is a useful type of general purpose ride-and-drive family pony. The Scottish Riding or Garron pony, is smaller, standing about 13·2 hands. It can carry a light adult and can plod along all day, but is not very fast. It is not a good hunter, being too heavily built to jump well. These two, the Mull and Garron, are later types, owing their larger size to cross-breeding under better conditions on the mainland.

All three have sweet-natured dispositions, and are sure-footed, very strong and hardy. In recent years they have become popular for pony-trekking, especially in Scotland. Their placid, gentle temperament makes them very suitable for inexperienced beginners; the small Barra type is an ideal child's pony.

They owe their beautiful heads with large, deep-set eyes to the infusion of Arab blood. In 1535 the French King Louis XII gave James IV of Scotland some French horses to increase their size. They probably originated from Iceland and other countries within

Highland pony, showing the dun colour often found. The eel-stripe, along the back, also typical, is just visible. PHOTO BY MILES BROTHERS

A Highland pony—Garron. PHOTO BY MILES BROTHERS

the Arctic Circle, or may have come from northern Asia during the Ice Age.

Highland ponies are dish-faced, with rather short, strong necks. Dun and cream colours are preferred; duns have a distinct eel-stripe down their backs. There are dark markings below the knee. Black or brown should have no white markings. 'Fox' coloured has a silver mane and tail.

The ponies from the Fells and Dales are closely related and not unlike in appearance; they were one breed originally.

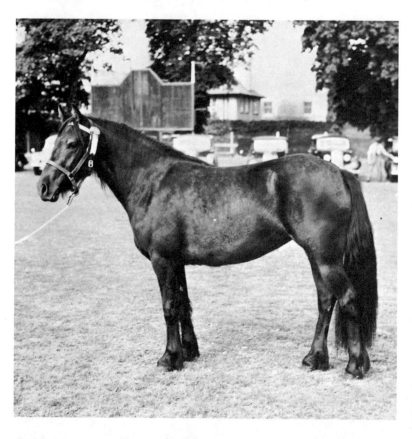

Fell pony, with characteristic long mane, long rather curly tail and feathers at fetlocks. Sweet tempered, hardy, docile and sure-footed. Can carry an adult all day. PHOTO BY MILES BROTHERS

Dales pony—akin to a Fell but rather heavier in build owing to infusion of Clydesdale blood. PHOTO BY FARMER & STOCKBREEDER

Fells come from the Lake District—Cumberland and Westmorland—west of the Pennine Chain. Standing between 13·2 and 14 hands high, they are placid with a sweet, gentle disposition, and being sturdily-built, hardy and very safe and sure-footed, make a good ride for an adult, especially a beginner. They also go well in harness. Their paces are easy and comfortable, with a long, swinging walk and trot.

They can be bay, black, dark brown, dun or grey; in fact almost any colour except chestnut. Black is probably the most usual; grey is rather unusual. A bay usually has a black mane, tail and points. Characteristic features are the 'feathers' (hair) on the heels and the long, thick, curly mane and tail. Fells have a thick winter coat and a lovely, sleek, silky summer coat.

The Dale is more heavily built, with a more upright shoulder. It somewhat resembles a small cart-horse in type, probably due to having some Clydesdale blood. It has been bred to carry weight and is stronger and larger than the Fell, standing up to 14·2 hands high. Its thickset, heavy build makes it more useful in harness for farm-work (ploughing, harrowing, etc.) than for riding. It walks freely and trots well with a rather high action; in bygone days it used to compete successfully in trotting matches. In the nineteenth century it was used as a pack-horse, carrying about 16 stone of lead in panniers, slung on each side, from the Durham and Northumberland mines to the docks. It travelled about 240 miles a week along tracks, which still exist. It lives east of the Pennines in the Dales.

It is very hardy, with a docile nature. The head is neat and pony-like with small well-shaped ears, jaw and throat. It has a short back with well-sprung ribs and good loins and hindquarters. Legs are short and sturdy, with good bone. The tail is set on rather lower than the Fell's. Like the Fell it has the characteristic feathers from the fetlocks down to the heels, and long, curling mane and tail. Black is the usual colour, but bay and brown and sometimes grey occur.

Welsh cob, the largest of the Welsh breeds. A useful harness pony.
PHOTO BY MILES BROTHERS

Welsh Mountain pony, rightly called 'one of the prettiest ponies in the world'. A child's winning show pony. PHOTO BY MILES BROTHERS

Welsh Riding pony, larger than a Welsh Mountain. From its tail carriage this one looks as though it might have some Arab blood in it. PHOTO BY MILES BROTHERS

Wales is fortunate in possessing three types of pony, the Welsh Mountain, Welsh Cob and Welsh Riding pony. The Welsh Mountain was the original breed and is one of the world's prettiest ponies; it is a most consistent winner in the show-ring. Its height is about 12·2 hands. It is strong and tough, with a docile temperament, and, being a good ride, is a first-rate child's pony. Its beautiful head resembles the Arab, with the same concave or 'dished', Arab-like profile, owing to being frequently crossed with an Arab. Its eyes are large and deep-set and its ears small and alert. Quarters are broad and powerful, with high tail-carriage. It also goes well in harness. It can be any colour except piebald or skewbald.

The Welsh Cob is completely different in height and build, though originating from the Welsh Mountain. Having a well laid-back shoulder and short back, and being a bold, natural jumper, it makes a good riding-pony and hunter for an adult.

Various countries imported the Welsh Cob for breeding trotting-ponies, while in Britain the hackney horse and pony were developed from it. Many years ago Fells were interbred with Welsh Cobs to improve their trotting action. It is a good all-round ride-and-drive pony, being equally suitable in harness and for farm-work. In bygone days farmers used them in a light gig for driving their wives to market. Being strong and docile it used to be much in demand for haulage at the Welsh coal-mine pit-heads. It stands between 14 and 15·2 hands. The head is small, with neat, alertly carried ears, set on an arched neck. Quarters are broad and powerful with a gaily-carried tail set on high. Fetlocks have a little silky hair; feet are hard. Any colour is a good colour—bay, black, brown, chestnut, cream, dun, grey or roan, but no nondescript, washy colours, or piebalds or skewbalds.

The so-called Welsh Riding pony is almost identical with the Welsh Cob from which it has evolved. Height 14·2 to 15·2 hands. It is somewhat lighter in build than the Welsh Cob, having been crossed with thoroughbreds to improve the conformation and speed.

Ponies have lived in the New Forest in Hampshire, north of Southampton, since the reign of King Canute; they roam semi-wild over some 60,000 acres. They may have been there from even earlier times. They can be seen roaming the streets in Lyndhurst, quite unperturbed by people or traffic. Unfortunately, they become too oblivious of traffic and over a hundred are killed annually on the roads. They used to vary considerably in conformation and type and were known as the wild horse, but now the variations are not so marked.

At various times thoroughbred and Arab stallions have been introduced into the herds to improve the breed. The type is now well-established since the formation of the New Forest Pony Breeding and Cattle Society. Although they roam semi-wild they are rounded up annually and branded with their owner's mark. The Agisters who look after them claim that they know every individual pony.

New Forest pony—a very useful pony for adult or child, being naturally traffic-proof from birth owing to environment. PHOTO BY MILES BROTHERS

New Forest ponies are docile, friendly and sociable; owing to their environment they are absolutely traffic-proof, making them an excellent ride for children or light adults. They also go well in harness. The head is rather large, set on a fairly short neck, with good shoulders and plenty of heart and lung room through the girth. Their quarters are their weakest feature, being rather narrow and drooping. Usual colours are bay and brown; blacks are also found,

New Forest pony—the grey colour is unusual. PHOTO BY MILES BROTHERS

and sometimes grey.

Sales of broken and unbroken New Forest ponies are held three times a year, in summer and early autumn, at Beaulieu, Hants.

Although the Exmoor pony is small in stature, it is not unusual to see them carrying farmers weighing 12 or 13 stone, and following the Devon and Somerset staghounds all day over their steep, hilly, native country. Stallions are up to 12·3 hands, mares to 12·2 hands high. They are not easy to handle, but if carefully broken in and schooled they make a good child's pony. If an Exmoor wants to it will escape from almost any enclosure.

Characteristic features are the mealy nose, mealy-rimmed eyes and similar colouring underneath the body and between the legs. Their heads, nostrils and ears are small. Fetlocks have no feathering. They are whole coloured, all bay, brown or dun, with no black, white or grey hairs. Their winter coat is usually harsh and springy, with bristles almost like nylon. Their summer coat is beautifully soft and shining.

Dartmoor ponies have lived on the moors from time immemorial. Their bleak environment makes them very hardy; in winter they have to contend with gales and scratch through snow for food.

The Dartmoor is a very pretty pony which wins many successes in the show-ring. It makes an equally good harness or child's riding

Exmoor pony—a good example. Note the mealy colouring on muzzle, flanks and hindquarters. Small, but very strong. PHOTO BY MILES BROTHERS

Dartmoor pony—an excellent child's pony when well schooled. PHOTO BY MILES BROTHERS

pony. It is honest, very active, small, and very strong for its size. It was once much in demand as a pack-pony and for use in the mines. It has a beautiful head with small ears, good shoulders and a full well-set-on tail. Its height does not usually exceed 12·2 hands. The most favoured colours are bay, black and brown, but it can be any colour except piebald or skewbald.

Ireland is an ideal country for breeding horses owing to its mild, moist climate, lush grazing and the limestone in the soil. Its native breed, the Connemara, comes from County Galway on the west coast. Traders and breeders have introduced Arab blood. It is good-looking, hardy and very tough, and is one of the best native riding-ponies for an adult. It is a useful ride-and-drive family pony.

It stands between 13 and 14 hands and has good conformation, with a neat head, good shoulders and quarters. Grey is the most usual colour, but bay, black, brown or dun are also found quite frequently.

Native ponies are now registered with the respective societies which look after the welfare of each breed.

These are:

(1) The Shetland Pony Stud Book Society, The Secretaries, 3, Golden Square, Aberdeen.

(2) The Highland Pony Society, George D. Cheyne, Esq., 32, Rutland Square, Edinburgh.

(3) The Fell Pony Society, Hon. Secretary: Miss P. Crossland, 'Packway', Windermere, Westmoreland, or, Joseph Eelph, Esq., Birkett Bank, Threkeld, Nr. Keswick.

(4) The Dales Improvement Society, E. F. Collingwood, Esq., Hollin Hill Farm, Hamsterley, Bishop Auckland, Co. Durham.

(5) The Welsh Pony and Cob Society, J. A. George, Esq., Queen's Road, Aberystwyth.

(6) The New Forest Pony Breeding and Cattle Society, Sir Berkeley Piggot, Bart., Brook Farm, Shobly, Ringwood, Hants.

(7) The Exmoor Pony Society, Lt. Col. V. C. A. Munckton, Capland Orchard, Hatch Beauchamp, Taunton, Somerset.

(8) The Dartmoor Pony Society, Miss S. Calmady-Hamlyn, M.B.E., Bearock Vean, Buckfast, Devon.

(9)   The Connemara Pony Breeders' Society, B. C. O'Sullivan, Esq., County Buildings, Prospect Hall, Galway, Eire.

A Connemara pony. Tough, yet docile. A good ride for a light adult or a child. PHOTO BY MILES BROTHERS

A registed pony of any breed will naturally cost more than one of no particular breed. There are many ponies of no special breed which will give honest, faithful service and much pleasure to their owner.

One other breed must be mentioned, though there is no breed society and it does not seem to be officially recognized. This comes from Lundy Island off the Bristol Channel. I have not seen one, or met anyone who has owned or ridden one. It apparently stands about 13·2 hands and is hardy, with quite good conformation.

Apart from these mountain and moorland ponies there are several British breeds of horses suitable for riding; these are apart from the famous Shire horses which are purely draught animals.

The Arab was first introduced into this country in the reign of William III, and can now almost be considered as a British breed, having been bred so extensively in this country since then. The stallions first imported were the Byerly Turk, the Darley Arabian and the Godolphin Arab, which were crossed with our native breeds.

In their own country the Arabs treat their horses as one of the family, good treatment of horses being part of the Moslem faith. This intimate contact with human beings over many centuries has made the Arab horse noted for its intelligence and docility, while its desert life has given it endurance and speed.

J

A lovely and typical example of an Arab horse. Note the slightly dished face and intelligent head with small ears, also the tail carriage.
PHOTO BY MILES BROTHERS

Arab horse—'Irex', reputed the most perfect Arab head.
PHOTO BY MILES BROTHERS

Good examples of an Anglo-Arab—a cross between an Arab and a thoroughbred, exhibiting some of the characteristics of each.
PHOTO BY MILES BROTHERS

Although only between 13·2 and 15 hands (little more than a pony in size) the Arab is always called a horse, and never a pony. It is one of the most graceful and beautiful breeds in the world, with small head and ears, 'dished' (concave) profile tapering to a small muzzle, large gentle eyes, and large nostrils. Its neck is graceful with a fine, silky mane. The legs are delicately formed. The tail is graceful, with fine silky hair like the mane, and is carried gaily. It has a proud, graceful carriage and lovely action.

The most usual colours are grey, white, bay and chestnut; brown occurs quite frequently; black is rare. There may be white markings on the head and/or legs.

Arabs bred in this country are registered in the Arab Horse Stud Book. The Society is The Arab Horse Society.

Owing to their spirited temperament Arabs are not really a beginner's ride, but a joy to an experienced rider.

Anglo-Arabs were originally a cross between an Arab and a thoroughbred, with no other admixture of blood. Being now so well-established, Anglo-Arabs are recognized as two distinct English and French breeds. It can be by an Arab stallion out of a thoroughbred mare, or conversely by a thoroughbred stallion out of an Arab mare. It is a good hack for the show-ring and makes a good hunter. Both parent breeds have contributed to its conformation and character.

Like the Arab, the Anglo-Arab is also registered in The Arab Horse Society's Stud Book.

The English thoroughbred can be traced back to the three Arabs already mentioned, first imported in the reign of William III, so every thoroughbred today has some Arab blood. At first Arab and English mares were used for breeding, but gradually increasingly less Arab blood was used.

The word 'thoroughbred' is a literal translation of the Arabic 'Kehilan'. Thoroughbreds today are mainly used for racing, and are most carefully bred for stamina and speed, parents that possess these qualities being chosen. Young stallion thoroughbreds are raced until they are rising four years old; if successful they are then put to stud. Some may be older before commencing stud duties. As racing increased in popularity so thoroughbreds were increasingly bred for greater speed, until, today, they are much faster than pure Arabs. Those unsuccessful in racing are of comparatively little value unless they have some specially sought-after blood-strains. They may be sold as hacks or hunters, or become show-jumpers after re-schooling; some may become polo-ponies if not too big. Unsuccessful stallions are gelded. If they do not make the grade in racing, some mares may be mated to Arab stallions to produce show hacks, Anglo-Arabs being more reliable and docile than thoroughbreds.

Having a large proportion of Arab blood, thoroughbreds have some of the best characteristics of Arab conformation, such as the small, well-shaped head and ears and the graceful, arched neck. The fairly high withers and very sloping shoulder give the thoroughbred a superb action for riding. Being bred for stamina it is deep through the girth, with well-sprung ribs, giving plenty of heart and lung room. Most thoroughbreds have a short back and high croup with good quarters. The tail is well carried, being set on high up. Legs are well-shaped, hard and clean, with strong tendons and good bone. Height may vary from under 16 hands up to 17·2 hands. Most colours are found, such as bay, black, chestnut or grey, with markings on the face and/or legs.

The Jockey Club controls all flat-racing in Britain. Thoroughbreds are registered in the General Stud Book, published by Messrs Weatherby, 15, Cavendish Square, London, W.1. There are two Societies, The Thoroughbred Owners' Association and The Thoroughbred Breeders' Association.

The Cleveland Bay is a large powerful horse between 15·3 and 16 hands, used for riding as well as for drawing stage-coaches and carriages, and for drawing vans and farm vehicles in previous times. The Royal Household still use them today for drawing the State carriages; they are also used now for breeding hacks and hunters. They originated from the fifteenth century War, or Great, horse.

The Cleveland is a fine, upstanding horse with great presence and quality, having short legs, a wide, deep, rather short body and strong, muscular loins. It has strong, powerful hindquarters, running level from the back. Legs are strong and muscular, with not less than 9 inches of bone below the knee. The legs carry no superfluous hair, and the pasterns are sloping. The tail stands well out from the body and is gaily carried. Its head is large, but well carried on a rather long, thin neck. The colour varies from bay to bay-brown, and the only markings should be a small white star, and a few grey hairs on the heels and coronet.

Cleveland Bay, the old-time coach and carriage horse, still used in the Royal Mews. A fine upstanding horse and a good ride. Originally bred from the medieval war horse. PHOTO BY SPORT & GENERAL PRESS AGENCY

Cleveland Bays now seem to be coming back into favour. The Society is The Cleveland Bay Horse Society.

In recent years some breeds of German horse, such as the Hanoverian, have been successful in show-jumping; a few have been imported into this country. They are a fine, upstanding horse with considerable presence and a good deal of quality; their build makes them well able to carry weight.

Within the last year or two quite a considerable number of Russian horses have been imported. These have done quite well in dressage and show-jumping, and seem to be growing in popularity. There are two or three distinct breeds, standing between 15·2 and 16 hands approximately.

Apart from definite breeds, there are various types whose breeding can vary, such as hacks, cobs, polo-ponies and the hackney horse and pony.

A hack is simply any horse or pony used for hacking, or general riding for pleasure. There are now special classes for show hacks, usually according to size. For most hack classes the height should not exceed 15·2 hands. Requirements are: practically perfect conformation and a very high standard of schooling. To win, a show hack must stand correctly, absolutely motionless when mounted or dismounted. It must move straight and walk out freely, the rider being able to collect or extend it at its various paces. Other essentials are: perfect manners, and ability to perform movements such as the rein-back, passage, flying change when cantering, or other dressage movements required by the judge. Hacks can be of any breed, but as perfect conformation is essential they generally have a good deal of thoroughbred, Anglo-Arab or Arab blood. They must move straight and level, close to the ground with no knee action; exactly opposite to the exaggerated knee-action of a hackney horse, or pony.

Conformation must exhibit all the points which make a good riding horse: good head; small alert ears; large, gentle, intelligent eyes; light, graceful neck, well-arched; well laid-back shoulder; good wither; depth through the girth; well-sprung ribs; strong, generous quarters; well-carried, well set-on tail; well let-down hocks; short cannon bones; clean, strong legs; good open foot. Any colour, whole or with black-points. Unexaggerated white head and/or leg markings. Bay, chestnut or grey are the most usual.

A cob is any rather thickset sturdily-built type, between 14 and 15 hands, and up to considerable weight. It makes a useful hack, often ride-and-drive, or hunter. Cobs always used to be docked, until this became illegal in Great Britain and Northern Ireland; it is still allowed in Southern Ireland.

A polo-pony was originally limited to 14·2 hands, or under in height, but can now be of any height. Any breed is used; the Argentine is noted for producing first-class polo-ponies; some have Welsh blood. Chief requirements are that it must be sure-footed, fast and handy, able to turn on the proverbial sixpence.

'Hackney' is derived from the old Norman French, *'hacquenê'*. Hackney horses stand between 15 and 16 hands and are any colour: grey is uncommon.

In the past it was popular for riding. Its natural pace is the trot, which is fast and can be maintained indefinitely. The high leg-action made it rather uncomfortable to ride. Today, the hackney is almost exclusively used for showing in harness. Its naturally high leg action has been greatly exaggerated so that the foreleg extends, moving well forward before the foot touches the ground. The knee is raised up almost touching the chest. There is an exaggerated shoulder and hock action. It is the most showy and brilliant of all harness horses. The highly arched neck with the head held well into the body is another characteristic. Legs are short and powerful with strong quarters. Haunches and hindlegs are lifted high and bent, moving well under. The tail used always to be docked, but is not now.

Hackney ponies are up to 14·2 hands and have the same high, showy action. Like hackney horses they are exclusively used for showing in harness. They are usually bay, brown or chestnut.

The Society for both hackney horses and ponies is The Hackney Horse Society.

A Hackney horse. Note the characteristic high action
PHOTO BY SPORT & GENERAL PRESS AGENCY

14 Tacking-Up

Always carry the saddle over the left arm, with its pommel pointing towards the elbow. Loop the reins over the head-band so that they do not trail along the ground, and carry the bridle either in the left hand, or over the left shoulder. This leaves the right hand free for opening doors or gates, etc.

Speak when approaching the pony. Hang up the bridle in some convenient place near by and go up to the pony. Always approach from in front in the field or in a box. If the horse or pony is in a stall, speak and put your hand on its hindquarters before entering.

Always put down the saddle—not on the ground where it may be trodden on—and short-rack the horse before tacking-up; otherwise it may turn its head and nip. Use a quick-release knot when short-racking.

Put the saddle on first. One is usually taught to do this from the near-side, this being the side from which one usually handles a pony. If uncertain of its temperament, or when handling a strange horse, always work from the near-side. The Pony Club official handbook (page 96) now advocates being able to saddle up from either side.

Saddling up from the near-side has the disadvantage that one must go round the horse to raise the flap and see that the panel is not tucked underneath, or that the girth-straps or girth are not twisted. Having lowered the girth one then has to return again to the near-side to fasten it.

By operating from the off-side one can put on the saddle, lift the flap, inspect and let down the girth before going round the horse to the near-side to fasten it. One thus only has to go round one's horse once instead of twice, saving time and unnecessary movement. I have always advocated and taught my own pupils to put the saddle on from the off-side for this reason.

When fastening the girth leave it fairly loose at first. When a saddle is put on, a horse frequently blows itself out. If it has a 'cold back' a horse may rear up if the girth is tightened immediately, especially in cold weather, and if the saddle is leather-lined. Some horses hate the feel of a cold saddle on their backs. Leaving the girth loose gives the saddle lining time to warm up before the girth is tightened.

Having put on the saddle, adjust the stirrup-leathers to the right length while the horse is still securely tied. This is much easier than doing it after putting on the bridle, when the horse can be a perfect

Measuring length of stirrup-leather before mounting. This gives an approximately correct length for the rider's leg

Adjusting stirrup-leather length when mounted. Rider's left hand is holding the reins to control his pony. Note the position of the index finger of the right hand below to guide the tongue of the buckle into the required hole, and thumb on top to press it down. Rider's foot remains in the stirrup-iron

nuisance, fidgeting and roaming about. Hold the stirrup-iron with the left hand, hold the right arm out perfectly straight with the finger-tips touching the stirrup bar, do not bend or arch the wrist. The stirrup-iron should just come underneath the right armpit when the leather is stretched taut below the right arm. Having measured the length of both leathers, run the irons up on them. Never leave the irons dangling down in the stable. If they knock against anything or get caught while leading out the horse and it became frightened, it could cause a serious accident.

Pick up the bridle and sort it out so that the reins, cheek-straps and nose-band are not twisted. Then hook it over your left forearm just below the elbow with the reins on top of the head-band and the brow-band facing the elbow.

Unbuckle the head-collar neckstrap and hold it with your left hand until your right arm is under the horse's neck. Put the head-collar down gently on the manger—do not leave it dangling or on the ground where it can be trodden on—and put your left hand on the horse's nose. Remove the right arm from under its neck and put the reins over its head, back onto its wither with the right hand. Take the top of the bridle by the head-band in the right hand and lay the bits in the palm of the left hand. While pressing the bits gently against the horse's mouth with your left hand, draw the bridle up with your right hand, in front of its face. As its mouth opens slide the bit (or bits of a double bridle) in, and simultaneously put its ears through the bridle, between the brow-band and head-band. If the horse will not open its mouth, and refuses to take the bit, gently pinch its jaw between your left-hand finger and thumb, just behind the corner incisors. This invariably makes a horse open its mouth, and there is little risk of being bitten as your fingers are between the bars of the mouth.

Then fasten the throat-lash and nose-band in that order. Put your hand underneath the horse's neck to feel that the throat-lash strap is not twisted. It should be possible to insert four fingers, held straight upright, between the strap and the horse's jowl, or your clenched fist between the strap and its cheek-bone. The throat-lash should never be tight, or it will interfere with the horse's breathing; the object of the strap is to prevent the bridle from stripping off over its head. It should be possible to insert two fingers edgeways between the nose-band and the horse's jaw, or between the nose-band and the front of the horse's nose. The nose-band should be just tight enough to stop the horse opening its mouth too wide, so that it could get its tongue over the bit, and to prevent it crossing its jaw; again, it should not be tight enough to interfere with breathing by pressure on the horse's nose.

If a double bridle is being used see that the curb bit is below the snaffle in the horse's mouth. The snaffle bit should be in the corner of the lips, but not high enough to wrinkle them.

Having fastened the throat-lash and nose-band, take the curb-chain and twist it clockwise until it lies flat in the chin-groove. Hook it onto the hook on the curb bit, about four links from the end, and then hook the last link on top as well. The curb-chain must only be tight enough to press against the horse's jaw when the curb bit is drawn back by the rein to an angle of $45°$. Then fasten the lip-strap.

If a standing martingale is being used, it should be put on before the bridle. The buckle on its neck-strap should be on the near-side. Fasten the end of the martingale strap onto the cavesson nose-band. Its other end fastens between the horse's legs onto the girth, which, therefore, should have been left unfastened after putting on the saddle.

Having put on the bridle check carefully to see that the ends of all straps are passing through their keepers and runners (the moveable leather loops which slide up and down).

Also make certain that the brow-band is not too tight or too high up, so that it is not cutting into the roots of the horse's ears. The forelock should be smoothed out over the brow-band, and the mane straightened under the head-band.

See that the bit or bits are correctly placed, neither too high up nor too low down. Check saddle fitting and girth; it will now be possible to tighten up the girths a couple of holes. Always see that your horse is comfortable. Stretch the skin under the girth so that it does not wrinkle and rub, by stretching each foreleg forward in turn; hold the leg just under the knee with the left hand and by the fetlock with the right hand.

When untacking pick up the head-collar and slip it over your left forearm with the neck-strap furthest away. Unbuckle the nose-band and throat-lash, in that order (the Pony Club rule is, when tacking-up work downwards; when untacking work upwards). Put your right arm under the horse's neck. Take the reins and top of the head-band in the left hand; slip the bridle off over the horse's head onto your

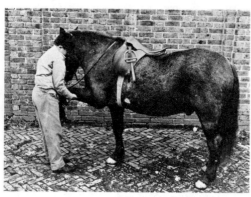

Stretching the pony's foreleg forward to prevent its skin wrinkling under the girth, causing a girth gall. Note position of the rider's two hands

right forearm, which is under its throat. This keeps the horse under control all the time while unbridling, and leaves both hands free to slip on the head-collar. It also means that the bridle is not thrown down, or the reins dangling on the ground, where it or they can be trodden on by the horse. This method is equally effective whether in the stable or out in the field. When using a double bridle, before undoing the nose-band unhook the curb-chain and unfasten the lip-strap. If a standing martingale is used slide the front end off the nose-band and put it down gently between the horse's legs. Finally, place the bridle over the left forearm ready for carrying. Always unfasten the girth from the nearside. Then go round and lay it across the saddle. If it is dirty put the muddy side uppermost. Lift the saddle up; never drag it off sideways with the girth dangling.

On taking the tack into the tack-room, always dip the bit (or bits) in water before hanging up the bridle, ready for cleaning. If saliva from the horse's mouth dries and hardens on the bit, it makes it much more difficult to clean and polish.

Always check all tack before mounting. This is particularly important if someone else has tacked-up your horse for you; they may have done it in a hurry, or they may be inexperienced, or careless. Neglect of this has been known to cause accidents.

Lift the flap to see that the panel is not tucked underneath on either side, and that the girth is not twisted, and is correctly buckled. Test if the girth is tight enough before letting down the stirrup-irons. It should be just tight enough to prevent the saddle slipping round as one mounts.

Next, look over the bridle; see that the horse's forelock is over the brow-band, and that the latter is not cutting into the base of its ears. Check the position of the bit or bits in the horse's mouth. See that the cheek-straps or throat-lash are not twisted. Note that the nose-band is in its proper place. Also check the relative tightness of both throat-lash and nose-band, as already explained. Make certain that all straps are passed through both the keepers and runners. Inspect the martingale, if worn, to see that it is not too tight, so that the horse can hold its head up to its normal position, but not higher. Check the curb-chain of a double bridle to see that it fits snugly into the chin-groove, and is not too tight. A dropped nose-band should not be too high up and its strap should pass below the bit.

If one is mounting another person, particular care should be taken to see that all these things are correct, especially for a beginner or a child, who cannot be trusted to check them for himself.

When holding a horse for someone stand in front facing its head with each hand on the rein, just below the snaffle bit. Not only has one full control in this way but the horse cannot nip one, or turn its head to nip the rider.

If a horse is very fresh and restive, or is normally difficult to mount, one should always ask someone to hold its head in this way. If one has to mount unaided, instead of gathering the reins in the left hand and resting it on the wither in the normal way, hold the cheek-straps with the left hand. Swing up into the saddle and put both feet into the irons, as quickly as possible. Quickly gather the reins in both hands, and grip firmly with the knees, ready for any

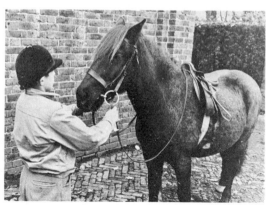

The correct way to hold a pony while waiting. Note position of hands just below the cheek rings of the jointed snaffle bit

Mounting a restive pony which is 'playing up'. Note how the assistant is holding the pony's head facing the wall, to prevent it moving forward while the rider mounts quickly

possible trouble. If there is a nearby wall turn the horse's head into the corner so that it cannot move forward.

With a difficult horse, it is sometimes a good idea to ask someone to attract its attention while one is mounting, by offering it a tit-bit. This sounds like bribery and corruption, but it does work, and is sometimes the only way of keeping the horse still for long enough to allow one to get into the saddle.

Always train a horse in the early stages of its schooling to stand still while being mounted. And having mounted always make it stand still for at least a minute; never allow it to move off immediately. Horses which are difficult to mount are usually the result of bad training, or of insufficient control by an inexperienced rider, who cannot stop it from moving off. Racehorses frequently go off almost at a full canter the moment the jockey is in the saddle.

Training a horse to stand still to be mounted takes time and patience, especially if it has already been allowed to get into bad habits of moving off and fidgeting. Ask someone to stand at its head. Then place your left foot in the stirrup-iron and raise yourself up. Stay there for a moment or two and then get down again. Repeat this over and over again, each time insisting on the horse standing still; if it does not, scold it and start again. And when it does stand still make much of it and give it a tit-bit. When the horse does stand quietly, practise mounting and sitting still, making the horse stand motionless. If it moves, scold it, dismount and try again. As soon as it stands quietly, waiting for the rider's signal to move off, reward it. Repeat this many times until the horse has formed the habit of standing still while mounting and afterwards. A horse which fidgets about while being mounted is a menace when in the company of other horses as it upsets and makes them fidget as well. It may even bump into another horse, and either unseat the rider or start a kicking match, thus causing an accident.

If a short person is riding a rather tall horse, let down the stirrup-leather so that he can put his foot into the iron, with the toe pointing downward. The leather can be adjusted to the correct length when he is in the saddle. It is undignified to hop wildly about on one leg while trying to raise the other high enough to put one's foot in the stirrup-iron, meanwhile poking the horse in the belly with one's toe. It is enough to make any horse fidget.

In such a case it is better to use a mounting-block or ask a helper to give one a leg up. To put a person up onto a horse, stand behind him slightly to the left. The rider bends his left leg up behind him. The helper holds it with his left hand in front just below the knee, and his right hand grasping it just above the ankle. At a given signal the rider bends his right knee and as he straightens it springs upward off his right leg, while at the same time the helper pushes his left leg upwards. The rider swings his right leg over the saddle as he springs up. The helper must be careful not too give too vigorous a lift or, 'vaulting ambition may o'erleap itself and land on the other side'!

If the rider is mounting without assistance, the person holding the horse's head should hold the offside stirrup-iron with his left hand, to prevent the rider's weight (particularly a heavy, rather awkward person) from dragging the saddle over towards him on the near-side.

These are courtesies which one would naturally extend to a lady rider, or a well-trained groom in a riding stable would extend to every client, in leading their horse out for them.

With children and beginners it is usually necessary to check the length of their stirrup-leathers after they have mounted. Make them take their feet out of the irons and stretch their legs down as far as they can. The underneath of the tread of the iron should come just below their ankle bone; this is the correct length for all ordinary hacking.

16 Handling in the Yard

There are numerous occasions when it may be necessary to trot a horse up in hand either for inspection for a prospective purchaser, in the show-ring or to watch its action for unsoundness.

Always lead from the near-side with your right hand on the lead-rope about eight to ten inches away from the head-collar, and the slack of the rope in the left hand. The hands should be approximately a foot apart. Do not hold the rope too near the head-collar as many horses, especially thoroughbreds and racehorses, hate their heads being held too tightly and will fuss and fidget.

If the horse is fresh and plays up, keep your right hand fairly high up with your elbow firmly into its neck, thus giving more control. If it tries to rear, lower your right hand while still keeping your elbow firmly into its neck.

To turn the horse always push it round away from you; never pull it round towards you. Pushing its head away keeps its haunches under it and therefore gives you more control. Secondly, by pulling the horse round towards you there is the risk of having your toes trodden on. Thirdly, when showing, by pushing the horse round away from you it is kept in full view of the judge; he wants to see the horse, not you.

Never look at the horse. Many, especially ponies, will stop and refuse to move if one stares them in the face. Keep level with the horse's shoulder; say 'Walk' (or 'Trot') and then move forward.

When leading a horse to be inspected for unsoundness always trot it downhill towards the person examining it, if the suspected cause of lameness is in a foreleg, and uphill if it is in a hindleg.

Always try to bring a horse in calm and cool, never hot and sweating, after work. There is an old rule, 'always walk the first half-mile out and the last mile coming home'. The only exception is in wet weather when a horse dries off more quickly if brought in warm—not hot—and is therefore less susceptible to catching a chill, than if it is cold and wet.

If the horse is hot and sweating walk it about for about 15 minutes until it has cooled off before stabling it. As soon as it is tied up in the stable rub it down thoroughly with a wisp of straw or a stable rubber

K

and pat it vigorously, especially where the saddle and girth have been, to restore the circulation. Be especially thorough in drying between its ears, between its forelegs and hindlegs, and its flanks and loins. The loins are a vulnerable part as the kidneys are in this region, and the horse is most likely to catch a chill in its loins. If it is cold its ears will feel cold. Pulling its ears gently between the fingers, or massaging them gently between both hands will help to restore circulation and warm the horse. Most horses love this 'stripping', as it is called.

If it is very sweaty or wet with rain, use the metal sweat-scraper on its neck, back and hindquarters before rubbing down. Avoid sensitive parts.

Having rubbed down put on a rug, especially over the loins to help it to dry off, and keep warm.

One way of drying a very wet horse is to put a fairly thick layer of straw along its back, covered with a large sack or rug, which is held in place with a surcingle. The straw absorbs the moisture, and the heat generated helps to dry the horse quickly.

When dry never leave the horse standing without a rug as it will be hot and can catch cold. Rug-up with a light rug and let it cool off gradually before removing the rug.

Do not leave a wet horse in from exercise standing tied up un-attended, especially in a draught. It is very liable to catch pneumonia.

Never give a drink of cold water to a horse which is hot, particularly if it is sweating. This is a certain way to give it colic. A few sips of tepid water, just to wash its mouth out, will not hurt, especially if it is led about afterwards for a few minutes.

If a horse is brought in hot and excited it may 'break-out' for hours afterwards. One must therefore keep a constant watch, as if a horse starts sweating again, having been dried off, and is left standing wet all night, it can catch cold and is liable to get pneumonia. The only remedy is to rub it down and dry it thoroughly again and then walk it round for about twenty minutes to prevent it catching cold.

A horse or pony which lives out can be turned out after work if the weather is mild. It will probably go down and roll almost im-mediately and the layer of mud will help to protect it. Also it can move about and keep itself warm. If it comes in at all warm, it is advisable to leave the saddle on for about ten to fifteen minutes before turning it out, especially if the weather is cold, or if there is a cold wind blowing, or it is raining. Having loosened the girths raise the saddle off its back and replace it. If the horse is sweating, give it a brisk rub-down and patting all over before turning it out.

A clipped or trace-clipped horse should not be turned out after work, even with a New Zealand rug on, until it is thoroughly dry and warm, especially in wet weather or with a cold wind blowing.

Sometimes after hard exercise, if a horse has been out for several hours and has not relieved itself, it may want to stale when brought in, but appear unable to do so. To persuade it to stale shake up some straw under it, and/or stand away and whistle. Many horses will immediately relieve themselves when a bed of clean straw is being put down and shaken up under them. The rustling of dry straw underneath seems to make them want to stale. It is important to make a horse stale as it is bad for it to 'go over its water'.

17 Lunging

Lunging is a valuable way of exercising a horse in snowy, frosty weather, when it is too slippery to ride or even lead it out for exercise. A ring of soiled straw or ashes can be laid down somewhere conveniently near the stables and a horse can be given forty minutes to an hour's hard work on the lunge rein, walking and trotting, and cantering if not too slippery, first on one circle and then on the other.

A very fresh horse can also be lunged for about 20 minutes, to take some of the 'steam' out of it before being ridden, especially if a nervous rider or a beginner is to be mounted.

Lunging forms a very important part in the training of a young horse, both before and after backing it. It teaches it obedience, to obey words of command such as 'stand', 'walk', 'trot', and 'canter', and helps it to learn to collect and balance itself. To prevent it becoming one-sided it should always be lunged equally on the left and right circles.

When lunging do not give tit-bits, or it will form the bad habit of wandering into the centre, expecting to be fed.

When lunging use a cavesson nose-band with a swivel ring in front for the lunge-rein, which should be of tape, about 1 inch broad and about 18 feet long. Put on a surcingle with side-reins attached from the head-collar; the side-rein (or 'dumb jockey') should be slightly shorter on the side on which it is circling, to encourage it to bend in that direction. It should never be allowed to circle round with its head facing outwards away from you in the centre. The other side-rein should be lengthened slightly. Change the relative lengths of the side-reins when altering direction.

Stand in the centre of the circle, with a fairly short lunge-rein. If the horse is circling to the left hold the rein in the left hand and the lunging whip in the right. Reverse when changing direction. The shaft of the whip should be about six feet long, with a long, thin flexible thong; when not in use it is held pointing downwards to the ground, with the thong looped up in one's hand.

Always stand still in the centre, circling round more or less on the same spot, and make the horse move round you in a circle. Do not move about as the horse moves. Stand slightly behind the horse so that you can see its tail and hindquarters as it moves round. Do not stand opposite the horse's head or shoulder. Keep well out of kicking range in case it bucks or flings up its heels in sheer high spirits.

Extend the hand holding the lunge-rein out from the shoulder slightly ahead of the horse's head, pointing in the direction you want it to go. The whip should be trailed just off the ground, behind its hindquarters. If the horse is sluggish or disobedient lightly flick its hocks or hindquarters with the whip, repeating the word of command.

Start the horse off in the direction you want, on a fairly short rein. Make it walk at first to the word of command and as it starts circling round, gradually lengthen the rein. The faster the horse is moving, the longer the rein and the bigger the circle. Keep the spare rein coiled up neatly in the hand which is holding it, so that it cannot get tangled up with your legs or the horse's: never let the rein trail slack on the ground. When you want the horse to slacken pace shorten the rein as you give the word of command.

When first teaching a young horse to lunge let someone walk round in a circle at its head. Give the word of command and let the person lead it, until the horse begins to understand that it has got to move round in a circle, and that it cannot get away.

Lunging. Trotting with arms folded to improve seat, grip and balance. Good leg position but the rider should be looking straight in front of him between his pony's ears.
TAKEN AT THE RIDING SCHOOL OF MISS PETERS, REIGATE HEATH

When a young horse is accustomed to being lunged, after it has been backed it can be lunged with a saddle on. At first take off the stirrups. Later it can be lunged with the irons run up, and then with them dangling, to accustom it to the feeling of something touching its sides. This should only be done at a walk or trot, not at a canter as the irons would hit against and frighten it. Use side-reins as before, attached to the saddle 'Ds'.

Lunging is also a very valuable training for the rider, especially a beginner, to teach him grip and balance, and to get him to sit really down in the saddle. Make him ride without bridle or reins, with his arms folded. He can have a neck-strap to hold at first to give confidence. But the sooner he can discard the neck-strap and ride with arms folded, the better. Start at a walk, then at a trot, and finally at a canter, with the neck-strap, then without. The trainer must use his discretion and be guided by his pupil's confidence and progress. But never let him become scared, or force him to do anything beyond his present capabilities. It is better to adopt the old Latin motto '*Festina lente*' ('Hasten slowly').

Touching toe on the same side at the trot. An exercise to improve the rider's seat and grip. Note leg position, heel stretched down
TAKEN AT THE RIDING SCHOOL OF MISS PETERS, REIGATE HEATH

Trunk twisting with arms sideways. An advanced exercise performed at
the trot or canter to improve seat. Note good leg position. The rider's
arms might to advantage be a little higher

Touching toe on the opposite side at the trot. A more advanced exercise
to improve seat and grip. Note rider's leg position
BOTH PICTURES TAKEN AT THE RIDING SCHOOL, REIGATE HEATH

The pupil can also perform the various mounted exercises taught
to beginners, such as touching toe on the same and opposite side
with either hand, turning round from the waist with arms stretched
sideways, arms alternately circling backwards, bending forward onto
the horse's neck from the waist, trying to stand in the stirrups,
first with hands on the horse's wither, then with one hand off, and
finally with both hands not touching the horse. These should be
practised first walking, then trotting; eventually some, like turning

from the waist with outstretched arms, and arms circling backwards, can be attempted at a slow canter, on a well-schooled, quiet horse.

After a young horse has learnt to obey and to walk, trot and canter on the lunge, when ordered, the next step is to mouth it and teach it to accept and respond to the bit. As soon as the colt is accustomed to a bit in its mouth it should be driven in long reins.

Long reins are attached to the ordinary bridle with the straight vulcanite bit, or whatever bit is being used to mouth the colt; a plain straight snaffle or a jointed egg-bit snaffle may be used instead. Personally I feel that the straight vulcanite is the best as it is the mildest bit of all and cannot harm a young horse's mouth.

Walk behind the horse, sufficiently far away to be out of reach of its heels if it plays up. At the first introduction let a helper walk at the colt's head. Make it stand still until you are ready to move. At the word 'Waa-alk', the helper leads the horse forward. At the word 'Whoa' he halts again, refusing to let the horse move. Only practise starting and stopping until the horse understands and obeys 'Walk' and 'Whoa'. Then similarly teach it to respond to the left and the right rein. Very slightly tighten the rein on the side you wish to turn; as you do so, say 'Tur-r-rn' and gently tap the horse's hind-quarters with the long lunging whip, on the opposite side to which you are turning. Practise turning right and left in this way until the horse understands and obeys.

When the horse is long-reining quietly and obediently the helper should gradually stop leading it, until eventually it will stop, walk, turn right, or left by itself in response only to the trainer walking behind.

Long-reining is a valuable way to teach the young horse to obey the reins and bit before it is backed, as there is no possibility of inadvertently pulling on its mouth, as might happen if one was in the saddle and became momentarily unbalanced if the horse played up.

It is also another good way of exercising a horse when it cannot be ridden, and can be alternated with lunging in snow, or frosty weather. It makes a change for both horse and the person in charge. After being backed it can also be long-reined with the saddle on, as well as being lunged, without or with a rider. A ridden horse cannot, of course, be long-reined.

18 Clipping

The reason for clipping a stabled horse has already been given, that a horse with a thick winter coat sweats profusely and loses condition if it does prolonged hard, fast work. Also, if one is hunting it is far harder to clean the mud off a thick coat, and it takes much longer to dry if it gets really soaked, with the increased risk of a chill.

a.

b.

c.

Types of clip
(a) Clipped out (saddle mark left)
(b) Hunter clipped (legs and saddle mark left)
(c) Trace clipped

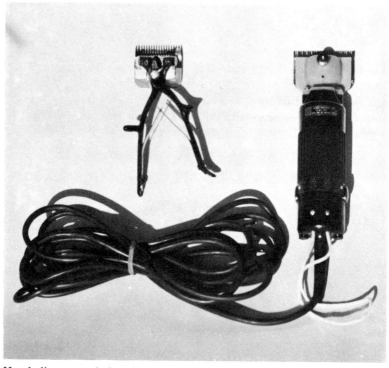

Hand clippers and electric clippers

The types of clip are: (*a*) Clipped right out; (*b*) Hunter clip; (*c*) Trace clip; and (*d*) Blanket clip.

(*a*) *Clipped right out* explains itself. There is no long hair left on the legs.

(*b*) *Hunter clip* can either be with or without a saddle patch; in the first, the saddle is left on and the horse is clipped round, leaving the long hairs in the shape of the saddle when finished. The legs are left unclipped as a protection against thorns or scratches while out.

Some favour a saddle patch on the grounds that it helps to prevent saddle galls through rubbing, especially if the saddle is leather lined, or mud gets splashed up under it.

Others say that a horse sweats under the saddle if a patch is left. They maintain that a saddle patch makes it harder to rub down and dry the horse thoroughly if it comes in wet or hot and sweating, and therefore makes it more susceptible to chills.

(c) *Trace clip* was originally only used for horses driven in harness. As the name explains, the coat is clipped out under the throat, neck and belly up to the height of the traces which supported the shafts. Legs are left unclipped.

Trace clipping is now primarily used for a horse or pony that does prolonged hard or fast work (for example, hunting) and is also turned out in a New Zealand rug.

(d) *Blanket clip*. The hair is only clipped on the neck and belly, a patch like a blanket being left on the body.

The first clip is usually some time in October; the second generally in December, and not later than the first week in January. A horse sheds its summer coat in September, when it starts looking dull and rough. The winter coat should be given time to grow through before clipping. It continues growing after the first clip, though not so thick.

To clip out a horse choose a fine, mild, dry day with no wind. Have the clippers ready, well oiled and with sharp blades. A hot, blunt blade which pulls, or a noisy machine may upset a horse. Keep the oil near so that the blades can be oiled when necessary while clipping; also have spare blades near at hand in case of a breakage. If the clippers are the old hand-type one must have a helper to turn the handle at a steady, uniform rate. Another assistant may be needed to hold the horse. Some horses will stand still, while others object strongly. It may prove necessary to use the twitch as a last resort; first let the assistant try holding up a front leg; in the latter case have plenty of straw underfoot to prevent the horse slipping, and in case it falls. For this reason if it is fidgety never tie it up tight by the head, for if it fell it could break its neck.

If possible use a roomy empty loose-box for clipping. It is a messy business and if performed in the open, hair blows about all over the yard. Approach the whole operation as calmly and quietly as possible. Do not let the horse feel that anything unusual is about to happen; horses very quickly sense anything out of the ordinary. The secret is to keep the horse as calm as possible. Some sweat easily when they become upset or excited. It is a long process needing time and much patience.

First, groom and strap the horse thoroughly to remove as much grease and dandruff as possible from its coat. It must also be absolutely dry, as the hair will pull if there is any moisture. A horse is easiest to clip after it has been exercised, dried, allowed to cool down and then thoroughly groomed. Do not try to clip a horse which is fresh. Never clip a horse when it is warm.

Start clipping on the nearside at the poll and work down the crest of the neck to the wither. Do not press heavily on the clippers or it will make unsightly ridges. Be especially careful on all tender parts of the body, or possible ticklish spots. These vary with different horses; some are very ticklish under the tummy; others by the elbow, loins, flank, near the stifle, or inside the hindlegs. Some horses are inclined to be head shy and hate their heads being touched. When 'cutting in' use the clippers on edge sideways, or at the broad end.

Leave the hair inside the ears and the long hairs on the muzzle. Be careful not to clip either the side of the mane, or root of the tail. Use a head with a broader blade (called a leg-knife) for clipping the legs as it does not cut so close. If a saddle patch is being left put on a felt numnah the size and shape of the saddle, and clip round it. Leave the lock of mane on the wither. Clipping the fetlocks and back of the tendons ruins the look of the legs for several weeks. Use a comb and scissors on these, or pull the hair if it comes out easily. When trimming the fetlocks work upwards against the hair with the comb and scissors as a barber does.

Except when clipping its head, let the horse eat from a haynet, as this distracts his attention and stops him getting bored and restless. Throw a rug over the horse's loins while clipping, as a horse will start fidgeting if it feels cold.

When clipping is finished remove all loose hairs with the body (not the dandy) brush and then rug up. A pony is very apt to catch a chill after clipping, especially in mid-winter, so extra care must be taken.

Types of clippers are: hand clippers; wheel machine clippers; electric clippers.

Hand clippers are slow, laborious and impractical. The old wheel-type machine needs an assistant to turn the handle. They can be noisy and may easily upset a highly-strung horse. They are old-fashioned and are now superseded by electric clippers, which are very light, noiseless and easy to handle, and far less liable to upset a horse.

Before using, blades should be sent away to be ground and sharpened. They should be kept carefully wrapped up in an oily rag, or grease-proof paper, free from dust.

While clipping, care must be taken that the head with the blade does not overheat. Directly it begins to show signs of getting hot, stop and allow it to cool. Similarly, directly the blade seems to be getting blunt, use a new sharp one; a blunt blade pulls the hair, and nothing upsets a horse more quickly. Stop frequently to clean the blade and blow out any dust, dandruff or fine loose hairs which have accumulated. After clipping take the head to pieces and clean it thoroughly; then oil it before putting away the clippers.

It hardly seems necessary to add that, afterwards, all loose hairs should be thoroughly swept up in the box. Otherwise, it is amazing how they will blow about and spread everywhere.

If a mane is too thick it is thinned out by pulling. To make the mane the required length, or to allow it to lie flat, it should always be pulled; never cut it with scissors or clippers. Pulling should always be done after exercise, or on a warm day, when the horse is warm, and the pores of the skin are open. Pulling in very cold weather may cause pain and make the horse fidget, as the pores of the skin are tightly shut.

Pull out the longest underneath hairs first, a few at a time, by winding them round the finger, or by using a mane comb. Pull quickly or it will hurt. Only do a little at a time each day; do not try to finish the whole mane in one session or it will make the skin sore. The top hairs, or any standing up after plaiting, should not be pulled, as doing so will make an upright fringe along the crest, which will look very ragged.

Hogging, or completely removing a mane with clippers, often improves the look of a horse or pony with a rather short, thick neck, making it appear thinner. It is also done when a ragged mane spoils a horse's appearance, or to save time and labour, by eliminating the need to look after a mane. A long, thin neck, or a ewe-neck, should not be hogged, as it only tends to accentuate the defect. Care should be taken before hogging a mane that it will suit the horse or pony. Once hogged a mane takes at least two years to grow enough to look neat, even if it then regains its former appearance, it often tends to grow ragged and bristly after being hogged. Once hogged it needs re-doing about every two or three weeks.

An assistant should stand in front and hold the horse's ears, gently forcing down its head so that it is lowered and the crest is stretched. The whole mane is then removed with clippers, preferably electric, starting at the wither and working up towards the poll. No unsightly line or ridge must be left where the coat and crest meet.

Like a mane, a tail should be thinned by pulling, and never cut with clippers or scissors, or the hairs will re-grow and become very bristly. The same method of pulling is used as for a mane. Trimming and shaping a tail by pulling is really a job for an expert; if badly done it will look as if the rats had been gnawing it, and it will take many months to re-grow and repair the damage. But a tidy, well-pulled tail adds greatly to a horse's appearance. Horses or ponies that live out during the winter should be allowed to grow their tails again for protection against the cold.

To trim, a body brush, water brush, mane comb, pair of scissors and a tail bandage will be necessary. Groom the tail thoroughly, removing all tangles and separating all the hairs. Only pull out the underneath hairs, beginning high up at the dock. Working sideways pull out the hair evenly on both sides of the tail. Do only a little at a time and work equally on both sides, as it is easy to get the tail looking lop-sided. Only pull out one or two hairs together; wind them round the fingers or around the teeth of the mane comb and give a short sharp tug. If the hair is inclined to be wiry one's fingers can become very sore, and even cut, and a little resin rubbed on them will help.

If a bang tail is wanted, cut off the end squarely. The exact length is a matter of personal taste and the horse's height and conformation. Some like it level with the hocks, while others prefer it longer, say, about four inches below the hocks. If the horse lives out, too long a a tail becomes bedraggled with mud at the end. A small pony with a very long tail looks overweighted, especially if it is also rather thick and bushy. An assistant holds the tail up, by putting his arm underneath, at the level at which the horse holds it naturally when moving. Having squared the end, pulling is continued evenly so that the tail is thinned to the end of the dock; it then becomes thicker to the end.

The end of a switch tail grows to a natural point. The tail in this case is pulled drastically for about half its length.

Never use mane clippers on the tail. As the mane comb tears the hair out and breaks it, it should only be used when the tail is thick and tangled, or when the hair is very tough and bristly.

After pulling, bandage with a stockinette tail bandage—a bandage should be used regularly to keep the tail in shape, but should not be left on for too long at a time, as it will tend to make the hair brittle; if too tight it can cause white hairs.

Before bandaging brush the tail with a damp water or body brush. Dip the brush in water and then rub it against the edge of a bucket to remove surplus moisture. Brush the tail until the hairs are damp underneath and on top, and are lying smooth. Always damp the tail and never damp the bandage. A damp bandage can shrink, causing the horse pain, and can also cause white hairs.

When starting, bring the bandage as far up under the dock, as near the root of the tail as possible. Otherwise a ring of hairs will stick out above and will look unsightly when the bandage is removed.

Bandage firmly, seeing that it is smooth, without any wrinkles. Bring each new turn of the bandage about half way down the previous turn. Continue to the end of the tail-bone and then work upwards for two or three inches, in order not to tie the bandage on the tip of the tail-bone. Tie in front with a simple bow.

When taking off a tail bandage never undo the bow and unwind but simply slide it down the horse's tail, using both hands. The bow can then be undone. Tuck the tapes in on the side on which they are sewn on and rewind the bandage as tightly as possible keeping it free from wrinkles. Hold the loose end between the legs to keep it taut while winding.

19 Care of a Hunter

Looking after a hunter falls into two categories: the care of a stabled horse, clipped-out and corn-fed; and caring for and hunting a pony or horse which lives out.

On the day before the Meet give quiet walking and trotting exercise for about $1\frac{1}{2}$ to 2 hours. At evening stables prepare as much as possible overnight for the next day. Have everything ready and laid out that will be required in the morning.

Groom and strap the horse thoroughly and plait its mane. Put on rest (stable) bandages and rug-up with the night rug. Give a deep bed of clean straw to try to avoid the horse becoming soiled with night-stains when it lies down. Give the last corn-feed fairly early, and hang up a full haynet rather late, for consumption during the night. Leave a bucket of clean water in a corner of the box.

A hunter of about 15·2 to 16·2 hands being hunted regularly should have between 10 and 14 lbs. of corn per day, depending also upon its temperament. If excitable by nature it may become unmanageable out hunting, if given too much corn.

Fill two haynets, one ready for the morning, the other for evening stables on one's return next day. Also prepare a bran mash (with salt) and leave it ready to have boiling water added next morning. If the horse is having any linseed with its morning feed, put it on to simmer overnight. Have all tack thoroughly cleaned and ready. Clean breeches and bone and polish hunting boots. It is surprising how much time all these chores consume, especially such items as boning and polishing boots.

When cleaning, all tack should be meticulously checked for signs of wear; stitchings at buckles on bridles and saddles, stirrup leathers, girth-straps, reins and so on. The rough and tumble of hunting will soon discover any weaknesses, which ordinary hacking will not. And a nasty fall can result from something breaking while one is travelling fast or perhaps jumping.

Put clothes, stock, boots, and everything else out ready overnight. Check all buttons. It can be very embarrassing, and annoying, for a vital button to 'give' at the wrong moment. So, leave nothing to chance.

All this may seem fussy and unnecessary, but one can become very careless and casual, and easily overlook some important item. In the 'good old days', grooms and valets attended to these details. But this is a 'do-it-yourself' age.

Among other items, one should carry a large safety-pin and a needle and thread (cotton breaks too easily); one should also see that one has ample loose change and other money, a flask of brandy, a pocket-knife, some string and a pocket hoof-pick. Sandwiches should be prepared and packed overnight.

Make an early start next morning. If the Meet is at 11 a.m. one should be out in the stables not later than 6.30 a.m. One's time of departure of course depends on the time of the Meet, and its distance away. Meets are earlier at the beginning of the season (i.e. from 1st November) and grow later as it advances. The first Meet may be at 8.30 or 9 a.m. while later on they are usually about 10.30 or 11 a.m. When hacking, aim at averaging between 5 and 6 m.p.h.

Put on old clothes for the early morning stable work. Inspect your horse as usual, water and tie up the haynet filled overnight. Take off the night rug and fold it neatly; put on the day rug. Then pick out feet, muck out, rearrange bedding, and 'set fair' the box ready for your return, as there will be little time to do it properly later.

Short-rack your horse, remove night-stains and quarter or groom according to the amount of time available. Check the mane plaits and replait any which may have shaken loose during the night. Put on a tail bandage, feed and leave the horse short-racked with a day rug on. Check all tack which was cleaned and put ready overnight.

While your horse is eating its breakfast go and change and have your own meal. The horse should be allowed at least an hour after eating its breakfast to digest it thoroughly before starting for the Meet.

After breakfast, pour boiling water on the bran mash, or oatmeal gruel previously mixed overnight, and cover the bucket. Remove the day rug and tack-up. Having mounted, test that the saddle is not pressing anywhere on the horse's spine. After walking for about five minutes, to allow the saddle to settle down, tighten the girths.

Tire your horse as little as possible by riding at a good walk, alternated with a steady, level trot; the old cavalry rule on route marches used to be, walk half-a-mile and trot half-a-mile alternately. A quiet canter will not greatly tire a well-schooled horse or pony.

Never arrive at the Meet with a sweating, mud-bespattered horse.

It is as well to have about fifteen minutes or so in hand, so that on arrival at the Meet one has time to dismount and check one's tack. It also rests your horse and gives it a breather. In very cold weather walk your horse about to keep it warm, either leading it on foot, or mounted.

Keep well away from other horses. Even the quietest horse is apt to get excited when it sees so many others, and may 'play up', or even kick out at another horse, or a hound that may venture too near. Always keep your horse's head turned towards a hound (or hounds). It is the unforgivable sin for your horse to kick a hound. If you know your horse is inclined to be 'a bit light behind' (liable to kick) it should have a red-ribbon tied to its tail. If another rider happens to come up from behind put your right hand behind your back as an additional warning that your horse is liable to kick. Always wait until the last when going through a gate.

When waiting while hounds are drawing a covert, keep your horse absolutely quiet, and do not talk. If the fox happens to break covert near you, put your hat on your crop and wave it.

Always ride the headlands when crossing a field; never gallop straight across. It may be sown with winter wheat or some other crop. If the going is heavy and waterlogged, ride in the water as it will be firmer. Take advantage of any good going available. After a fast gallop, if there is a check, turn your horse's head to the wind, especially if it is breathing heavily. Dismount quickly at any available opportunity to rest your horse's back and encourage it to stale if possible, by whistling to it. If your horse loses a shoe, retire immediately from the hunt and make for home. When you reach the road it is better to dismount and lead it rather than risk laming it by riding. It will also rest your horse and stretch your own legs.

When hacking home, remember that your horse, having carried you over all sorts of going for several hours, is hot and tired. So get it home the shortest way with the least possible delay. Do not hurry, but travel at a steady 'hound-jog', which soon eats up the distance.

Never keep a sweating, tired horse standing about in a biting wind while you gossip with friends: that can give your horse pneumonia. For the same reason never stop at a pub for a drink on the way home, or drop in at a friend's house for tea—however tempting—unless of course they can offer you a stable, a rug and a rub-down for your horse, while you are enjoying your tea. But even then it is best to make straight for home. It is a good idea, too, to dismount and lead your horse occasionally, especially up any steep hills.

Aim at letting your horse cool down, mentally and physically. When about a couple of miles from home, loosen the girths and ride on a long rein, to let your horse stretch its head, and neck muscles.

Even if your horse is thirsty do not let it stop and take a long drink, but there is no harm in letting it take a few sips to rinse its mouth, if one passes a clean pond or stream, or a cattle trough, provided one keeps it walking steadily afterwards.

Riding with a different length of stirrup-leather also gives your horse some relief. When your horse has cooled down, there is no harm in trotting on slowly. A hunter will usually let you know when it wants to walk, by nodding its head gently up and down.

For the last mile, dismount, slacken the girths completely loose, and lead your horse, to prevent any risk of it 'breaking-out' again on arrival at the stables. A sweating, excited horse causes the most work and is the most liable to keep on 'breaking-out' for hours afterwards. Always run up the stirrups when leading in hand, and walk on the right-hand side of the road, facing oncoming traffic.

Keep walking and trotting steadily if it is raining. A wet, warm tired horse is easier to dry than one which is wet, tired and cold.

On arrival at the stables, wash your horse's feet as far as the coronet, but no higher. Stop the water from running down into the heel by placing your thumb in it. Have a bucket of water ready in the yard. In wet weather wash feet in the box.

In the box, immediately remove the bridle and saddle, then beat a hasty retreat and let your horse go down and roll. When it has regained its feet cover its loins and quarters with a rug, turned inside out, and encourage it to stale by whistling and shaking straw under it. When it has staled put on and fasten the rug properly, unless it is very wet; in which case rub down and dry it thoroughly, or pack it with straw (Chapter 16).

If the bran mash or gruel has grown too cold, warm it up with some boiling water and give it to the horse in the bucket.

While your horse is eating or drinking the mash or gruel, fill a small haynet. As soon as it has finished, give the haynet, and wipe over your horse. Restore the circulation in the region of the saddle and girth by smartly slapping with the palm of your hand. Then give a good rub down all over, being especially careful to dry the heels. Wrap very wet and muddy legs in straw, covered by a loosely applied stable bandage. Never try to scrape or wash off wet mud; let it dry and then use the rubber curry-comb and dandy brush.

When your horse is as warm, dry and comfortable as you can make it, give it its feed and a bucket of water, while you go and change and have your meal.

A tired horse cannot digest properly; hence the small haynet immediately on arriving home to get the digestive system functioning properly. If the horse is very tired, it may even be advisable not to give the corn-feed until your final visit to the stables.

When you have changed, bathed and eaten return to the stables. Check that the horse has not 'broken-out', but otherwise do only as much cleaning as is absolutely necessary. Your horse needs rest above everything else. If it has 'broken-out' badly it will have to be brought out (rugged-up) and walked about. Dry especially the ears, throat, chest, back and loins. Feel for any thorns on its face, chest and legs, and under its belly to ascertain that most of the mud has been removed.

Pick up any droppings and remove any soiled straw, adding some fresh if necessary. Then refill the water bucket and haynet, give any last feed if due; put on the night rug and rest bandages. See that the horse is not in any draught and leave it in darkness, and peace.

There will be plenty to do in cleaning tack if you still have sufficient energy and are ultra conscientious. Otherwise wash the bits and then forget the rest until the next day.

The next day inspect your horse very thoroughly for any possible undetected cuts, bruises or sprains. See that there are no saddle or girth galls. And lead your horse out and trot it up to inspect for signs of any lameness, or strained muscles or tendons. Also, very carefully examine the feet and shoes. Having mucked out give an extra deep bed of straw to encourage the horse to lie down and rest. Do not ride your horse at all. The only exercise should be to lead it in hand for about twenty to thirty minutes, to take the stiffness out and prevent the legs from filling. The day after is the day of reckoning, as all one's gloriously muddy, dirty tack must be thoroughly cleaned, and also one's breeches, coat and boots.

If one hunts an unclipped horse or pony which lives out, one cannot expect as much hard or fast work from it, as from a fit, cornedup, stabled horse. As it is probably smothered in mud from head to tail, catch it the day before. It is impossible to dry a thick, greasy, natural coat by rubbing it, so if very wet dry it by packing with straw (Chapter 16). Pick out its feet and let it stand in a deep bed of straw. When dry get the mud off with the rubber curry-comb and dandy brush.

At evening stables, leave water and a haynet and give any short feed or corn feed. Leave the upper half of the stable door open. A horse living out does not need rugging-up.

Early next morning, inspect, water, hang up a haynet, pick out feet, and muck out. Then groom thoroughly with the dandy brush, to remove all dust; use a wisp or pat smartly all over to bring the dust to the surface of the coat. Do not plait the mane of an unclipped horse. As the tail should have been left unpulled for protection against the weather, it is also unnecessary to put on a tail bandage. Having groomed, give the corn or other short feed while you go to your own breakfast and change.

After breakfast the procedure is the same as with a clipped horse. The only difference is that one must allow considerably more time for hacking to the Meet; one can only average between 4 and 5 miles an hour, as an unclipped horse will inevitably sweat if one travels any faster. Adjust girths two or three times during the first half-hour.

On arriving at the Meet one must remember that an unclipped horse or pony has more strain on its heart and lungs, and so cannot stand up to as much fast work as the clipped, corn-fed, stabled horse. Excessive sweating will make it lose condition, but the natural grease in its coat will make it less liable to catch a chill.

On the return journey the long coat will probably not dry completely if the horse has sweated a lot. Try to bring it in reasonably cool under its long, damp coat.

On arriving at the stables take it into a loose-box and unbridle. Put on a head-collar and remove the saddle. Be careful that the horse is not standing in any draught, and throw a rug over its back and loins while examining its feet and body carefully for any thorns, cuts, scratches or bruises, and so on. Do not keep the horse standing in the stable, but give it a rub over and then turn it out into the field as soon as possible. If other horses are in the field, water and feed first before turning out; otherwise, if it is the only occupant, feed and give hay in the field, preferably in its shelter, if there is one.

Next day catch the horse, bring it in and inspect thoroughly, as in the case of the stabled horse. Give it a good grooming; it is important to remove all sweat marks completely, particularly where the saddle has been. Do not ride at all on the day after. Rest the pony.

A trace-clipped horse or pony will keep in fitter condition and will not sweat as much as one that is unclipped. It can also be dried more easily and quickly. It can live out provided that too much coat has not been removed; in very cold weather a New Zealand rug can be used on it if necessary.

20 The Horse's Foot

In many cases, the cause of lameness lies in the foot, and unless the seat of the trouble can be found and correctly treated, the horse may be out of action for an indefinite period, often through carelessness or neglect. It is essential therefore for a horsemaster to have a thorough knowledge of the structure of a horse's foot.

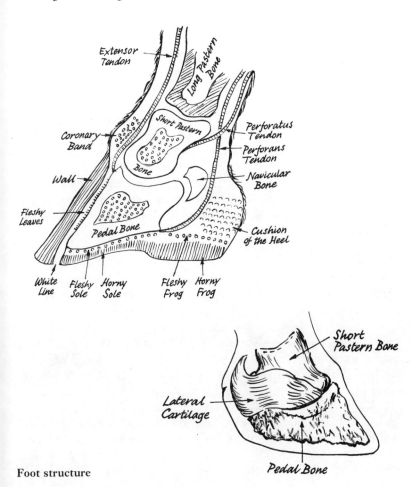

Foot structure

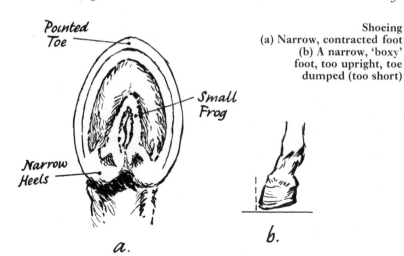

Pointed Toe

Small Frog

Narrow Heels

a.

b.

Shoeing
(a) Narrow, contracted foot
(b) A narrow, 'boxy'
foot, too upright, toe
dumped (too short)

A horse's foot is a wonderful piece of mechanism, especially designed as a shock-absorber and weight-carrier, which has to stand up to a great deal of strain, and wear and tear. When jumping, for example, at the instant of landing, all the horse's weight is momentarily on one foreleg. Again when trotting or cantering on hard ground the feet and legs have to withstand a tremendous hammering. In this connection it is interesting to consider a horse's weight: an average 16·2 hand horse weighs about 9 cwt.; a light draught horse about 10½ cwt., while a big Shire horse weighs about a ton.

From the fetlock downwards, the foot consists of the following bones (*vide* diagram, p. 157): long pastern bone, short pastern bone, pedal or coffin bone, and navicular bone. In addition, there are the tendons running up into the leg which bend, straighten and move the foot. These are: perforatus tendon, perforans tendon, and extensor tendon (running down the front of the leg and foot). The coronary band, or coronet, is where the foot is attached to the leg. The wall is the hard, horny, outer surface of the foot. The white line divides the outer insensitive wall, from the inner, sensitive fleshy leaves. These are filled with minute blood-vessels, so that the foot is literally kept bathed in blood. Hence, even a small puncture or wound in the foot will bleed excessively. Pressure of the horse's weight on these blood-vessels helps to drive the blood through them, thus promoting circulation in the extremities, farthest from the heart. There is the fleshy (inner) sole and the horny (outer) sole, the fleshy (inner) frog, and horny (outer) frog, also the bulbs or cushions of the heels.

Where the bones meet each other there is a highly-polished layer of gristle, and every joint is enclosed and bathed in 'joint-oil' to lubricate and make it work smoothly. Besides the tendons there are cartilages, attached to and extending from near the top of the coffin bone, on each side. They continue along its edge, and curving round the heel beyond is a large, springy piece of gristle, the lateral cartilage, whose outline can be seen clearly in a fine-skinned horse. It extends along the sides of the coronet; its action as a 'spring' can be felt by pressing hard on its edge, at the heels. Ligaments of considerable toughness hold the bones together while allowing them necessary movement.

The cushion of the heels, or frog pad, is a thick, tough, elastic pad, making all the back of the foot into a firm, soft cushion. It fills in the space between the wings of the coffin bone and the lateral cartilages.

The bulge round the coronet—another similar thick, but narrower, strip—is the coronary band. The fleshy sole is a similar, thinner, layer beneath the pedal bone. The surfaces of the coronary band, fleshy sole and fleshy frog are covered with many small, finger-like projections, giving them a velvety look; the horn of the hoof grows from these points.

The laminae are the five hundred to six hundred fleshy leaves covering the outer surface of the coffin bone, from top to bottom. They dovetail together very intricately with the horny leaves which are similarly arranged round the wall's inner surface.

Nerves are profusely distributed throughout the foot, so that the slightest touch on the surface can be felt, although the hoof itself is insensitive.

The horn forming the wall of the foot is hard, tough and gluey, with numerous hair-like tubes embedded in it. Its consistency may vary from being almost brick hard, to an indiarubber-like elasticity.

The wall of the foot is always growing downwards from the coronary band and outwards from the white line. Hence the necessity for having the foot trimmed periodically by the blacksmith. When unshod the toe would grow excessively long if left untrimmed; when shod the foot grows outwards over the shoe, which eventually would become almost embedded in the foot, if not previously lost. A wild horse wears its feet down and keeps them even by cantering and galloping over hard, rough ground.

It is important that a rider must be able to recognize such things as a worn shoe, risen clenches, a long foot, when to have a horse reshod, and when a remove only is necessary. The owner must also be able to know that his horse has been correctly shod and to recognize any faults in shoeing such as 'dumping', over-lowering the heels, or careless shoeing such as a 'bind', or a 'prick'. Other special knowledge is the ability to realize when a horse needs any special type of shoe, owing to bad conformation (for example, 'brushing'), corns, and so on.

If a horse does not move absolutely straight it may wear its shoe more on the inside or the outside, necessitating a shoe which is 'built-up'—thicker on one side than the other. Many horses drag their toe, particularly on a hind foot. This may be due to fatigue, faulty conformation, careless, 'sloppy' riding or possibly incipient foot trouble such as navicular disease. In bad cases the shoe may be completely worn away and even the foot worn square at the toe. In such cases a rolled toe, with a piece of extra hard tempered steel welded on at the toe to thicken the shoe, may be necessary instead of the ordinary hind-shoe with two clips, one on each side. A shoe should not be allowed to wear down until it is paper thin, but should be renewed as soon as it shows signs of real wear at the toe.

As the foot grows and the shoe wears, the nails holding it can become loosened, so that the clenches, where the nails are twisted off, hammered into the wall of the foot and then filed level, begin to rise and protrude. This can be felt by running one's finger round the side of the foot. Risen clenches are a sign that the foot is beginning to need attention; if the shoe is not worn too thin a 'remove' is the answer. The shoe is removed, the growing foot pared and filed down, and the shoe replaced. Rising clenches should not be neglected; they can be dangerous as a horse can cut itself by 'brushing' or over-reaching, if the clenches are sticking out appreciably.

The toe may grow too long, and this is a frequent cause of stumbling. The answer is a remove, or reshoeing; the toe is cut back to its correct length and shape, and the foot trimmed.

Reshoeing or a remove is necessary when the foot shows signs of growing over the shoe; this is especially noticeable at the heels at first.

Shoeing is one thing over which it is unwise to economize. The life of a shoe depends on the type of work the horse is doing, and the surface of the ground. Obviously if a horse is continuously ridden or driven on a road or very hard ground, the life of the shoes will be far less than if it is only ridden on grass. It is impossible to dogmatize. Also, some horses' feet grow more quickly than others. The weight of a horse is another factor: a heavy horse will wear out its shoes more quickly than a light pony, other things being equal. The average life of a shoe may vary accordingly from one hundred to three hundred miles and may last from a fortnight to three months.

On average a horse's feet will need trimming about every four to six weeks, regardless of whether a remove or reshoeing may be necessary.

The commonest foot ailments are sand crack, seedy toe, dropped sole, withered frog, thrush, corns, laminitis (fever in the feet), pricks or binds, matter in the foot, navicular disease, cracked heels.

Sand crack occurs at the inside quarter of the forefoot and sometimes at the toe of the hindfoot. The horn of the wall of the foot splits from the coronet downwards. The crack goes right through the thickness of the wall into the fleshy leaves (laminae) underneath. The split closes on the sensitive parts underneath, sometimes causing bleeding. It is painful and causes lameness. Sand crack usually develops through neglect, not having the foot regularly trimmed and allowing it to grow too long when a horse is turned out to grass without shoes. Fitting grass tips to the front feet prevents the development of a sand crack. Clip away the hair on the coronet, just above the top of the crack; then with a hot iron burn a horizontal line about an inch long and a quarter inch deep through the upper end of the crack, just below the coronary band. Afterwards apply a 1 in 8 Red Iodide of Mercury blister to the coronary band, above the sand crack and stimulate growth of new horn; or apply cornucrescene. Before shoeing cut away the ground surface of the foot where the sand crack would normally end, to relieve pressure.

In seedy toe, the inner and outer layer of the horn of the wall of the hoof separate, usually at the toe. This forms a hollow which becomes filled with a powdery, greasy substance. The detached outer horn should be rasped away and the part should be thoroughly cleaned, removing all the greasy powdery matter. A dressing of Stockholm tar is then applied. Then blister the coronet or apply cornucrescene to hasten the growth of new horn.

Brittle hoof mostly occurs in dry, hot weather. It makes shoeing difficult as the wall of the foot breaks away leaving insufficient room for nails. It may cause a bind, giving rise to lameness. Apply hoof or neatsfoot oil daily to the wall and round the coronet. Use cornucrescene, rubbed well into the coronary band, to stimulate new growth of horn.

Canker is a greyish fungus which attacks the sole of the foot, due to neglect in keeping a stabled horse's feet clean, or to injury. It seldom causes lameness, but must receive proper treatment. Consult a vet, and meanwhile keep the foot dry. The horse must not stand on sodden bedding. Apply an antiseptic dressing such as boric or alum powder.

False quarter is a thin layer of brittle horn which forms on the side of the wall. It looks like a groove, or series of grooves. The foot is weak, but the horse is not lame. It is an aftermath of injury to the coronary band. Sometimes the wall cracks badly, and pressure on the shoe should be eased by making a nick at the top of the crack (*vide* sand crack). Fit special shoes. Treat by blistering the coronet.

Quittor is a fistular sore in the coronet (*cf.* matter in the foot). A foot injury, such as a prick, may have become septic and pus has travelled upwards to the coronary band. Clean thoroughly with Dettol, T.C.P., or permanganate of potash (i.e., an antiseptic solution). If the wound in the foot can still be detected, open it and drain away the matter; poultice afterwards (Kaolin or Antiphlogistin). Let it heal slowly from the bottom upwards. Never let it heal over at the top before the lower part has healed, in case matter accumulates underneath.

Dropped sole may be due to bad conformation, bad shoeing, overwork and resulting fatigue, poor condition; it is rather akin to a dropped arch in the human foot. It can be helped by correct shoeing to take the weight and help support the foot. Consult the vet as to the best type of shoe for the blacksmith to fit.

A withered frog is usually the result of bad shoeing. The frog does not press firmly on the ground as it should and withers through insufficient use. The frog is nature's shock absorber and anti-skid device and should press firmly on the ground when the horse's weight is on its foot. In the past a withered frog was also caused by the blacksmith paring away the frog, to prevent it touching the ground; this evil practice is, fortunately, seldom encountered today. The remedy lies in shoeing so that as much of the frog as possible touches the ground when pressure is put on the foot. A large, healthy frog is essential.

To admit that his horse is suffering from thrush is a confession of negligence on the owner's part. Thrush is caused by dirt accumulating in the foot, particularly in the case of a stabled horse standing for long hours on muck in its box. Firstly, the box should be thoroughly mucked out and swept, and all dirty, wet straw and droppings removed. Secondly, droppings should be picked up frequently during the day so that the horse does not stand in them. Thirdly, a stabled horse's feet should be picked out at least twice a day, at morning and evening stables. Thrush can also be due to contracted heels, caused by mutilation of the frog by a bad blacksmith. Thrush attacks the cleft of the frog, producing a discharge of foul-smelling matter. It may cause lameness when severe. Thoroughly clean the cleft out with a piece of tow wrapped round a piece of stick. Use hot water with a little Dettol, or other not too strong disinfectant. Apply a dressing of dry boric powder to stop the discharge. Alternatively apply Stockholm tar, with some tow to keep it in place, or a dressing of tow soaked in some disinfectant, such as a very mild carbolic solution, about one in thirty parts of water; iodine is also excellent. The dressing is fixed in place in the cleft of the frog. Remove the shoes and have the horse reshod with tips, to put pressure on the frog. Thrush can become chronic if neglected, and a serious ailment. A good horsemaster should smell his horse's feet frequently.

Horses and ponies living out are less liable to contract thrush, except through some injury to the frog, as they are constantly cleaning their feet by moving about. Even so, their feet should be regularly examined.

Just as we can develop corns through a tight or badly fitting shoe, so a horse can also get one through an ill-fitting shoe. It is more likely to occur with cold shoeing than hot, attempting to make the foot fit the shoe, instead of the shoe fitting the foot. The shoe may be slightly too small and pinch the foot. Or it may result from leaving the shoe on too long without having a remove; the foot grows outwards and around the shoe, as well as downwards from the coronet, becoming too big for it. Corns occur at the 'seat of corn', at the angle of the heel between the wall and the bar. Low-heeled, and narrow, high-heeled feet are both liable to them. A corn shows itself as a reddish-purple discoloration. It causes pain and lameness, which gradually increase if not given attention.

The first object of treatment is to remove pressure, whatever the cause. If the corn is only small it may suffice to cut away a small part of the bruised sole and the seating of the heel of the shoe. More serious cases may need a poultice, or soaking in hot water. In the case of a festering corn, with matter gathering in the heel, the matter must first be drained by cutting away most of the affected sole and then healed from below upwards with an antiseptic dressing. The shoe should be removed and as soon as the corn shows signs of healing, fit a broad bearing shoe with the heel well seated, or a three-quarter shoe. Remove pressure as much as possible.

Nowadays a bruised sole seldom occurs, provided it is thick and hard, forming an effective protection for the sensitive parts underneath. Some horses may have a naturally rather thin sole. A heavy load or stony ground may cause it. In the old days it was fairly common owing to the old blacksmith's pernicious habit of paring away the sole until it would give to thumb pressure, or was almost paper thin. This was done because it was not understood that a hard, horny, thick sole was nature's protection. Pressure over the injury produces pain; also a red stain can be seen on the sole (not unlike a corn), owing to blood soaking through from the fleshy sole beneath. Allow the sole to grow to its natural thickness and do not pare it out. A leather sole, nailed on beneath the shoe, brings relief.

Laminitis, or 'fever in the feet' is usually caused by over-rich food, combined with' insufficient exercise. People often turn a pony out onto spring grass, when it is having little or no exercise, believing, mistakenly, that this will do it good. Apart from upsetting its digestive system, there is the risk of grass colic resulting, and laminitis almost inevitably occurs. Concussion and overwork are another cause, especially if the horse or pony has been overfed and has not been used for some time. Small ponies seem most prone to laminitis. Unshod horses can get it if they become footsore.

The laminae, or fleshy leaves, covering the coffin bone beneath the wall of the hoof, become inflamed. Laminitis usually occurs in both forefeet, rarely in a hindfoot. There is heat and the pony stands still, unwilling to pick up a foot, owing to the greatly increased pain in the other foot. When compelled to walk it potters along, putting its heels to the ground first. The blood vessels can be felt throbbing in the fetlock. In severe cases the pony is feverish and loses its appetite.

Take off the shoes and replace with thick, wide-seated bar shoes. Apply cold to the feet, and either make the pony stand in deep, wet mud, or in water, or hose for about twenty minutes several times daily, or apply cold bandages or swabs dipped in icy cold water. Change them frequently as soon as they become warm from the heat of the foot. Give a few minutes' exercise several times a day. If the pony will lie down and rest, make it comfortable in a box on a deep bed of straw. Feed only on sloppy bran mash and green food. Give a physic ball and keep the bowels freely open. Continue using wide-seated shoes for a considerable time after recovery.

A severe attack of laminitis forces the coffin bone downwards and causes a dropped sole, making it bulge just in front of the point of the frog. Once this occurs it is incurable. Past attacks of laminitis can be detected by examining the wall of the hoof; the lines showing the rate of growth are irregular and more crowded together where an attack has occurred.

A prick is the result of careless shoeing; the nail penetrates through the white line into the inner sensitive part. In the case of a bind the nail does not actually penetrate but is driven too close and presses against the sensitive inner part, causing pain. Lameness results in both cases. The shoe must be removed, and in the case of a prick do not reshoe until the injury has healed; in the case of a bind, the shoe can be replaced, as the pain ceases with removal of the pressure. A new hole for the nail must be made in the wall.

Matter in the foot may remain undetected for some time, as the original puncture in the sole may have closed completely. In such cases the matter works its way up to and out at the coronet. The original cause may have been a rusty nail or sharp piece of glass which penetrated the sole. Meanwhile the horse is acutely lame and there is considerable heat in the foot.

The matter should be let out through an opening made in the horn, which should be large enough to let it discharge freely. The matter is usually greyish in colour and the amount varies—it may be considerable or only trifling. Syringe the wound several times a day with some antiseptic solution and keep it open until all discharge has ceased. Never let it heal up on top, but let it heal slowly upwards from the bottom of the wound. Exclude the entry of dirt with a tow pad and put a boot on the foot. Standing the foot in warm water softens the horn and relieves the pain.

If the sole or frog is injured and a boot is unavailable a dressing can be kept in place by slipping a piece of tin under the edges of the shoe pressing it flat.

Navicular disease is a disease of the navicular bone and nearly always occurs in a forefoot. The navicular bone and its surrounding structure become inflamed. It takes some time to develop and is, unfortunately, incurable according to all text-books. It causes lameness which may be intermittent in the early stages; and may wear off after a little exercise. When resting, the horse points the affected foot, placing it slightly in front of the other forefoot, with the heel only just touching the ground. When exercising it seems to prefer walking on the crown of the road, rather than at the side. The heels are contracted and the frog shrinks, as a rule.

Directly navicular disease is suspected call in the vet. It is most advisable to have the foot X-rayed to confirm the diagnosis. In the early stages navicular can be detected on the X-ray plate by markings on the navicular bone. In an advanced stage the bone and the ligaments will be found to be locked solidly together.

In the earlier stages injections of Cortisone in the heel can be tried by the vet, but it must be used with caution as it can have some odd effects. In treating a case in its early stages try cold water bandages on the pastern and heel for about twenty minutes daily. After thoroughly drying rub Bone Radiol well into the heel, to try to penetrate through to the navicular bone. Turn the pony out and completely rest it, only bringing it in for daily treatment. It may be necessary to continue treatment for some considerable time and to rest the pony completely for several months. When it appears to be going sound it should only be very lightly hacked for several more months; and trotting on hard surfaces and cantering or jumping should be avoided.

Cracked heels usually result from carelessness—the heels are not thoroughly dried after washing the horse's feet. They may occur in frosty weather when a horse or pony is living out in a very wet field. Small cracks develop transversely across the heels, which become hot and sore. There is considerable pain which causes lameness.

If discovered at once before the cracks have opened up, apply glycerine or vaseline; clean, unused motor grease is also effective.

Whatever is used should be rubbed in thoroughly. If the cracks have opened and are infected so that there is a slight discharge, apply 'White Lotion', or dust on boric powder. Bring the pony up from grass and keep it stabled until the cracks have completely healed. It should be led out twice a day, for about twenty minutes, to exercise it, and naturally must not be ridden.

If neglected, cracked heels can develop into greasy heels, which is a nasty discharge. This can become serious, and the vet should be called. In mild cases, thoroughly wash and dry the affected heel (or heels) and apply a mild astringent, or bandage on wads of tow soaked in White Lotion. If greasy heel continues for some time the skin may become very much thickened. Serious cases do not yield readily to treatment, and are best left to the vet.

Keeping a horse's feet in good condition depends very much on having a good blacksmith. Unfortunately, blacksmiths today seem to be a dying race. Many of them are well past middle age, and when these retire eventually the shoeing problem will become acute. There are not many young ones to take their place, and few of them seem to have apprentices as they did in the old days. Although a good blacksmith can earn good money and many have a lucrative business combining shoeing with light agricultural engineering and welding, it is said that young lads leaving school will not take up the craft, chiefly because it means hard manual work and an ability to handle all types of horses. Farriery is a craft and takes several years to learn. Blacksmiths have their representative trade organization which fixes the prices for shoeing. This official body is doing all it can to attract youngsters into the profession and shoeing competitions are held at some County Agricultural Shows, but a lot more needs to be done to attract recruits. Before the army was mechanized it used to train good farriers, and a number of these started their own businesses when they left the army. So, if one can find a good local blacksmith one should treasure him like gold. Shall we all ultimately have to learn to shoe our own horses and ponies? Or will science produce some kind of easily applied plastic shoe, which will stay on and not wear out too quickly? Even so, we should still have to be able to trim and rasp our horses' feet.

For hot shoeing a blacksmith uses an anvil with a square body and a sharp rounded beak. Many travelling blacksmiths, serving a large area, now make the shoes at their forge and then cold shoe. A few

M

carry round a portable electric or calor-gas forge and an anvil and so can still hot-shoe when they visit their customers. Hot shoeing is preferable to cold shoeing as the blacksmith can make the shoe and alter it to fit the horse's foot while actually shoeing, and so obtain a more accurate fit.

The anvil must be so solid and heavy that a strong blow on the beak cannot move it. Its body is used for 'welding' and 'drawing' the metal into a bar. The beak is used for turning the drawn-out bar into the shape of a shoe. A blacksmith knows from experience exactly what length of metal is required for any sized shoe. There are two holes in the anvil body, the large for taking the shanks of the 'tool' and the half-round 'cutter'; the smaller is for a 'nail-cutter'.

Fire tongs have long handles and very long jaws, when new. In use the metal burns away and the jaws vary in length. The long handle allows the blacksmith to handle the iron without approaching too close to the fire. The blacksmith's shovel is called a slice.

Shoe tongs have shorter handles; their jaws are also shorter and vary in width. Inside tongs have jaws which close tightly for handling narrow bars; outside tongs have wider jaws for handling thick iron bars. These tongs are used for shaping the hot shoes at the anvil.

The turning, or hand, hammer weighs about 4 lbs. and is used at the anvil. It has one flat and one convex face; the sides are used for drawing clips and are therefore rather angular.

The sledge hammer weighs about 9 lbs., and with it the hot metal is welded, drawn to the required length and thickness and then hammered through the 'swedge' or 'tool'. It is also used for driving the stamp through the web and for cutting the heels.

The swedge, crease, concave tool, or simply the tool is the mould through which the hot metal is pulled while being hammered to give it the required concave shape.

The fuller is a blunt chisel fastened to a handle like a hammer. It is hammered into the metal while it is being drawn along, to make a groove. If too sharp, a fuller can easily cut a hot shoe in two, if hit too hard.

The stamp is a punch for making the nail holes; its point is the same shape as the head of the nail. When in position it is struck lightly and then heavily until it pierces the web. The point of the stamp must be held at an angle at the toe of the shoe to make a wider hole than at the heels. The angle is varied so that the holes are graded in size. Coarse holes are made near the inner edge to enable the nails to enter a good thickness of horn at the toe; the holes are finer, opening nearer the outer edge of the web as the wall becomes thinner towards the heels.

The pritchel is a long steel punch with its head shaped like the head of a horseshoe nail. Its point should exactly correspond to the neck of the nail. Being driven into hot metal makes it lose its shape quickly, so that the blacksmith frequently has to repoint and retemper it.

After making the nail holes with the stamp, they are completed with the pritchel. Punching out the unfinished hole is first completed; the shoe is then turned over and 'back pritchelled' to eliminate the burr or rough edge which might strip the nail while it is being driven home. In theory the nail hole should be so accurately stamped and pritchelled that it exactly fits the nail head, but in fact there are slight errors. When back-pritchelling, the nail hole is made slightly larger than the neck of the nail, so that the blacksmith can 'pitch' the nail in or out when hammering it in. If accurately done it helps to keep the nail firm, but if overdone the neck of the hole becomes so enlarged that the nail may become loose. Although the hole should be the exact shape of the nail head, it should also be slightly smaller so that when the nail projects slightly from the shoe it can be driven right home, making it more secure.

Nowadays shoes can be bought ready-made for the blacksmith to select the required size and shape it to the horse's foot. But many smiths still turn their own shoes from a new bar of iron, cut off to the required length. They can also be made from 'old stuff', i.e. worn-out shoes, but few smiths bother to use these. This method was used in the Army, and the shoes produced were of good, tough quality, owing to the amount of hammering needed. One and a half worn shoes are required to make one new shoe. A worn shoe is bent double at the toe and half of another shoe is wedged between its branches, giving three thicknesses of metal. The doubled end is raised to welding heat and quickly placed on the anvil; the three pieces become welded together into one by two or three rapid blows. It also makes a convenient shape for the tongs to grasp. The other end is then also brought to welding heat. The resulting lump of metal is called a 'mould'. Heating the metal is called 'taking a heat', and the smith judges its intensity by looking at the metal as it lies in the fire. At the correct heat it is removed from the fire, swung once to shake off loose flakes and cinders, and then hammered into a rod sufficiently long to form half of the new shoe. When it is the correct length, the smith 'turns' the shape of the half shoe; the concave shape is produced and the heels are cut out at the correct slope. Having turned the shoe over the fullering is pressed out and the nail holes are stamped, starting from the toe. The position of the nail holes is first lightly marked; the stamp is then driven through, or nearly so, with one or two hard blows. An expert can do all this without having to reheat the shoe. The other half of the shoe is then similarly made, the clips are drawn and the holes are pritchelled. To draw the clip the smith holds the edge of the web over the edge of the anvil and strikes the desired position with the edge of the hammer.

A well-fitting shoe should be absolutely level and press evenly along the entire wall, the bars, the white line, and the naturally flat outer rim of the sole. It should exactly follow the shape of the entire hoof; each heel should be levelled off so that horn and iron are exactly aligned.

The hind shoe of a riding horse is set back slightly from the toe so that an over-reach when moving fast, or when jumping, cannot cause any injury.

While forging it, the shoe is shaped as accurately as possible, by comparing it with the old shoe. It is then brought hot to the foot, and held in contact long enough to scorch the horn brown where it touches. While doing this the smith mentally notes any further slight alterations in shape that may be needed, and also the position of the clips. He then takes the shoe and accordingly hammers it into shape. This process may be repeated several times until he is satisfied that the shoe fits perfectly. Hot shoeing ensures a perfect fit, because the brown appearance of the burnt horn shows where the web of the shoe touches the hoof. These burnt parts are then rasped down until the entire shoe makes perfect contact; this is shown by a complete, even brown rim. Small pieces of horn are then removed to allow the clips to fit flush with the wall. The shoe is then cooled and filed up, and is ready to be nailed on.

The smith takes the foot squarely and firmly between his knees. Having laid the shoe accurately in position one nail is driven in at the toe. After readjusting the position if necessary, the opposite toe nail is hammered in, securing the shoe so that it cannot shift. The remaining nails are then driven in on each side, from toe to heel. As few nails as possible are used to hold the shoe to avoid making more holes than are absolutely essential, in the wall.

The nails at the toe are driven in first because they hold the shoe firmly in the required position, and because the horn is thickest at the toe, which makes it easier to drive the first nail. The horn decreases in thickness towards the heel so that more care is needed. The nail enters near the white line and is pitched (sloped) at an angle which will bring it out high enough up the wall to give it a firm hold. The smith must take care not to prick or bind (q.v.) when driving in the nails. Those driven too close to the sensitive inner part are called 'coarse', while those very near the edge of the wall are called 'fine'. If they penetrate far up the wall they are said to be 'high', while those coming out near the ground are called 'shallow'.

The blacksmith judges whether a nail is being correctly driven by sound and feel. The sound of each blow alters as the point penetrates the soft horn near the white line towards the harder outside wall. From experience he can hear any deviation from the normal. He also repeatedly touches the spot with his finger-tip, where he expects the point to appear; this gives him a good idea of its direction. Nails should penetrate at medium height, those at the toe being a little higher than at the heel. If there are more nails on one side than the other, the first to be omitted is the inside heel nail, as this is the most difficult to drive safely and is the least necessary.

The projecting point of each nail is twisted off with the claw of the hammer and bent flat against the wall, to avoid injuring the smith's hand or leg.

The closed jaws of the pincers are pressed firmly up against the broken ends of the nails, which are then hammered well home. A small part of the shank is thus turned up, which is called the clench. The clenches are then hammered firmly into the wall. Sometimes the smith makes a tiny groove with the edge of the rasp, to receive the clench. The embedded clenches are then rasped down flush with the wall. The edge of the rasp is run round between the shoe and the hoof, to bevel the rim of the hoof so that it does not split. The clips are hammered lightly to correspond with the slope of the wall, either before or after clenching up.

A blacksmith's charges vary according to the size of the pony or horse, from under 12·2 hands and then from 12·2 hands upwards, increasing for every hand up to a 17·2 hand horse. The current average seems to be about 30/– for a 12·2, 32/– for a 13·2, and 35/– for a 14·2 pony and *pro rata*.

The weight of shoes generally used is about 4 to 5 lbs. per set for hunters, 8 to 14 lbs. per set for light draught horses, up to 20 lbs. for heavy draught and shire horses. For racing, special aluminium racing plates are used, weighing only from $\frac{1}{2}$ lb. to 1 lb. per set. These are fitted before the race (the horse is 'plated up') and removed immediately afterwards. Very light concave fullered shoes, weighing approx. 6 oz. each are used for training. Shoes for ponies up to 14·2 hands and light hunters and riding horses up to 15·2 hands weigh proportionately according to their size.

As light a shoe as possible should always be fitted, provided it wears sufficiently long to avoid too frequent shoeing. Constant nailing breaks the wall of the foot.

Various types of shoes are used for different purposes. Carriage horses are usually shod with Rodway shoes with a double fullering, that on the inner side having no nail holes; or ordinary plain shoes with calkins on the hind feet. Plain shoes are used for all types of draught horses; if machine-made they are fullered, with large calkins, and sometimes toe pieces, which are a piece of iron welded edgewise on across the ground surface of the toe. The object is to help the horse to get an extra grip when starting to pull a heavy load.

Concave, fullered shoes, either flat or with small calkins and wedge heels are normally used for hunters and hacks. Sometimes the hind shoes have 'square' toes to lessen the possibility of over-reaching.

In special cases tips, not more than half the length of the ordinary shoe, are used, to bring the frog onto the ground. They are used when the frog is either small or has shrivelled for some reason, through accident, disease or past bad shoeing.

If a horse stumbles or drags its toe a rolled or dubbed toe is used; the toe of the hoof is rasped short and the shoe is turned up. If used on a hindfoot side clips are used instead of the normal centre clip. Alternatively, the metal of the shoe is made as thin as possible at the toe to prevent it coming in contact with the ground too soon.

Feather-edged shoes are used when a horse brushes through going too close behind. The inner branch of the shoe is made very narrow and fits close in under the wall. No nails are used on the inner branch of a feather-edged shoe.

A three-quarter shoe is used to relieve pressure on the seat of corn, by removing between one and two inches from the heel.

When a horse is turned out to grass for any length of time and its shoes are removed, grass tips are fitted on the forefeet to stop the hoof cracking.

A special type of shoe is the 'Gragagrip', which has a thin, flexible steel bridge with a rubber pad at the ground surface. The steel plate cracks the first time it receives any weight, which gives it as much flexibility as possible. The frog has no continuous pressure on it and can descend and press on the steel bridge every time the foot touches the ground. The foot does not touch the rubber and dirt cannot accumulate under the plate. The greater part of the foot is left open. There are four thicknesses, $\frac{1}{4}''$, $\frac{3}{8}''$, $\frac{1}{2}''$, $\frac{5}{8}''$, for all shoe sizes, fore or hind. The blacksmith rivets the steel bridge to the shoe before it is nailed on. The walls and the frog must be level and the bridge must lie straight across the heels. For a normal foot the rubber must only be of shoe thickness and touches each side of the shoe. If the frog is prominent use Gragagrips which are thinner than the shoes, or thicken the heels of the shoes. With a withered or shrunken frog use Gragagrips which are thicker than the shoes, or thin the heels of the shoes. Continuous shoeing with Gragagrips helps to develop a strong, healthy frog.

There are several methods of preventing slipping on icy roads or snow. Roughing generally means all anti-slipping devices. Strictly speaking it means removing the shoes and turning down the heels to form calkins, if these are not already present. These calkins are sharpened to a chisel edge: the one at the outer heel lies across the heel, that on the inner heel points forward.

Frost nails are sharp-headed nails which replace the ordinary nails at the heels. Sometimes they are also used at the toes.

Frost or screw cogs are screwed into specially-made holes in each heel, and may also be in each toe. To prevent the horse being injured at night they are removed with keys (or 'taps'), being replaced with blunt cogs ('blanks'); these stop the edges from burring over, and preserve the screw threads in the holes. Heads are of various shapes. They are better than ordinary frost nails.

Mordax studs are easily fitted and remain permanently in the shoes until they wear out. While the shoes are hot they are drilled

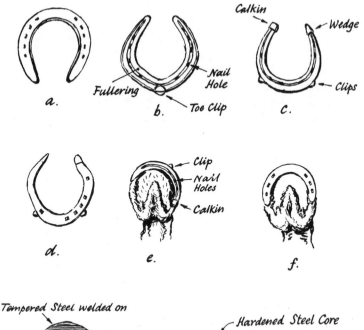

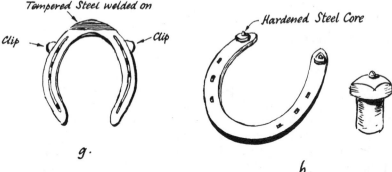

Types of Shoes
(a) Plain, unfullered shoe (stamped)
(b) Hunter fore shoe (fullered)
(c) Hunter hind shoe (fullered)
(d) Feather-edged shoe
(e) Three-quarter shoe
(f) Grass tip
(g) Hind shoe with 'rolled' toe to prevent dragging
(h) Mordax studs (to prevent slipping)

or punched with tapered holes. After cooling the shoes the studs are driven in up to their shoulders. When the horse is reshod they are punched out. The centre of the stud has a core of especially hard metal, and the makers guarantee them for at least 530 miles for hacking and hunting under normal conditions; for light harness horses they are guaranteed for at least 250 miles.

One should be fitted in the heel of each hindfoot and forefoot. They should not be fitted in the toes of forefeet for riding.

When examining the foot of a newly-shod horse, note the following points. When the foot is on the ground:

(1) Clenches: even, flat and broad, neither too high nor too low. They should not be driven into old nail-holes.
(2) The wall should not be rasped.
(3) The foot should not be dumped; i.e., the foot has not been shortened to fit the shoe.
(4) The shoe fits the foot accurately.
(5) Clips should be low and broad.

On lifting the foot up and examining underneath:

(1) Nails driven home.
(2) The frog and sole should not be cut away or pared. Any ragged pieces of the frog can be removed.
(3) Heels not opened up. They should be level in height.
(4) A perfect fit between foot and shoe, with no intervening space. A perfectly even bearing.
(5) Shoe properly finished off.
(6) Heels should not be too short. The shoe fits the foot perfectly all round its circumference.
(7) The shoe allows the frog to press firmly on the ground and does not interfere with it in any way.

After examining the feet have the horse trotted up for signs of any lameness, i.e., a possible prick or a bind.

Faults in shoeing are not now so often found, but one should know, and be able to recognize them.

To avoid over-lowering the wall is a matter of skill and experience. It can happen most easily with a flat spreading foot, or when a smith is shoeing an unknown horse for the first time.

An uneven bearing surface is due to lowering one side more than the other, the cause of which is carelessness or inexperience.

Dumping is a serious fault, consisting of filing away the front of the wall at the toe, until the foot fits the shoe. If for any reason the toe must be shortened the ground surface should be rasped away, and not the wall. Rasping the wall produces a narrow bearing surface of the foot; also rasping away the hard outside horn leaves the soft, moist layers beneath exposed; they then become brittle. Driving nails into the brittle horn splits and breaks it off, so that the shoe works loose and is lost. In the case of a flat foot it may very occasionally be necessary to dump so that the nails can be driven in high enough up the wall to hold the shoe firmly.

At one time it was thought to be correct to pare the sole until it could be pressed down by one's thumb. It was thought that the natural thick protecting sole made the foot less elastic. As in the case of the dumped toe, the soft horn revealed by paring quickly became dry and brittle. Clay and cow dung mixed was plastered in at night to keep the foot 'cool'. The sole became so brittle that the horse could not be reshod until it had rested long enough for the sole to regrow and thicken. Paring the sole is never practised now.

Paring the frog is also no longer practised. Old smiths thought that the frog was delicate and would be injured if it touched the ground. Their idea of prevention was to remove the frog. This produced a shrivelled frog, very prone to thrush. Its usefulness as a shock-absorber was destroyed and it was easily bruised by an uneven road-surface.

Opening the heels meant cutting away the bars of the foot in order to make the heels apparently wider. Besides weakening the heels, they eventually contract. Again, this practice is, fortunately, almost non-existent nowadays.

Over-lowering the heels occurs fairly frequently owing to a misconception concerning frog-pressure. The horn at the heels is also easier to rasp away than at the toe. Over-lowering weakens the heels, throws more weight on tendons and ligaments, and may result in lameness.

All these are faults in preparing a foot to be shod.

When fitting, excessive burning of the horn, when hot shoeing, is done sometimes under the erroneous impression that it gives the shoe a firmer seating. It, in fact, does the reverse as the charred horn becomes very brittle, and crumbles away under the shoe. This produces an uneven fit, probably causing a loose shoe. A few smiths over-burn to make rasping easier.

Over-lowering the sole occurs through carelessness. It may sometimes happen the first time a horse with an unusually thin, flat sole is being shod.

Dumping may arise when making the shoe and, also when fitting, trying to make the foot fit the shoe, which is too small. Dumping was practised owing to the mistaken idea that the foot should look smaller and neater than it actually was; so the circumference of the shoe was made less than that of the hoof, the wall being rasped away until the foot fitted the shoe.

Too long a shoe is a fault which may occur, especially in cold shoeing. If the shoe projects beyond the heels on the forefoot it can be torn off by the toe of the hindfoot. The correct length is up to the end of the heel; the shoe is then bevelled off in line with the heel.

Too short a shoe is another fault more likely to occur in cold shoeing. It makes the heels more liable to be bruised, as the shoe has insufficient bearing on the bars.

The shoe must not be wider than the foot. If it projects beyond it, the result may be to make the horse strike the opposite leg (brushing). Again this is more likely to occur through inaccurate fitting when cold shoeing, and the smith does not have the horse present when he makes the shoes.

Pricks and binds are the two most likely faults to occur when nailing on the shoe. Horses with small feet and thin walls run the most risk of these occurring. 'High' and 'shallow' driving of the nails are both faults if the horse has a well-shaped foot with strong, thick walls. But either may be necessary if the horn is brittle or much broken away, or to prevent possible injury to a weak foot.

The most usual fault is rasping the surface of the wall, in the belief that it makes it look smarter. The wall should not be rasped above the clenches. The clenches should only be rasped sufficiently to make them flush against the wall. Rasping below the clenches should only be where the foot and shoe meet and not a means of camouflaging a badly-fitted shoe. The less the wall is rasped, the better the workmanship.

21 Lameness

Besides the foot, lameness may occur through heat and swelling in the horse's legs. The way to detect heat is to place the hand firmly on the part where heat is suspected, hold it there for a few moments and then place it on the same part on the other leg. If there is any heat it will be felt by contrast. A horse's leg normally should feel cool.

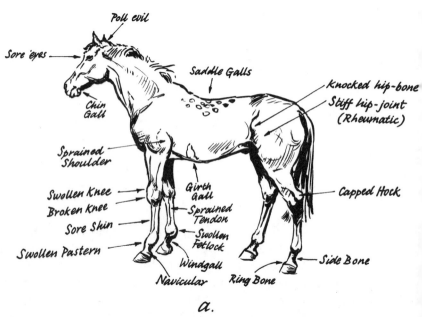

First aid: Ailments
(a) Location of injuries

Swelling can usually be felt by running one's hand slowly down the horse's leg, where it is suspected, and then comparing it with the same part of the opposite leg. The leg should feel firm and free from any extraneous lumps or bumps. It very much depends upon the type of swelling for which one is feeling. In some cases the

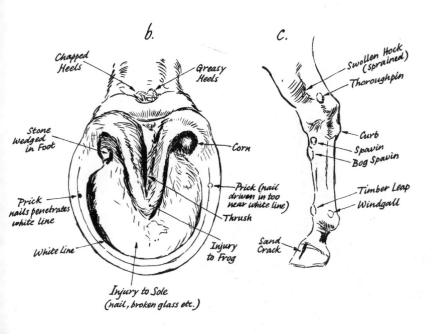

b.

Chapped Heels

Greasy Heels

Stone Wedged in Foot

Corn

Prick nails penetrates white line

Prick (nail driven in too near white line)

Thrush

White Line

Injury to Frog

Injury to Sole (nail, broken glass etc.)

c.

Swollen Hock (sprained)

Thoroughpin

Curb

Spavin

Bog Spavin

Timber Leap

Windgall

Sand Crack

(b) Foot
(c) Hind-leg

swelling may feel soft and spongy and leave a slight indentation when pressed fairly hard with the thumb. A swelling, if due to a strain, such as a strained tendon, is usually accompanied by heat. If the part felt is painful the horse will usually tell you by moving its leg uneasily and being shy about letting you touch it.

Swelling nearly always means the presence of fluid, especially when present at the joints. If there is no injury or other cause of lameness in the foot, work upwards from the coronet to the shoulder in the foreleg and from the coronet to the hip joint in the hindleg.

Possible causes in the foreleg are ring-bones, side-bones, wind-galls, swollen fetlock, filled legs (Monday morning leg), splints, sore shins, sprained tendons or ligaments, big (swollen) knee, broken-knee, capped elbow and sprained shoulder.

In the hindlegs besides ring-bone, side-bone, windgall and swollen fetlock, examine for bone spavin, bog spavin, curb, thorough-

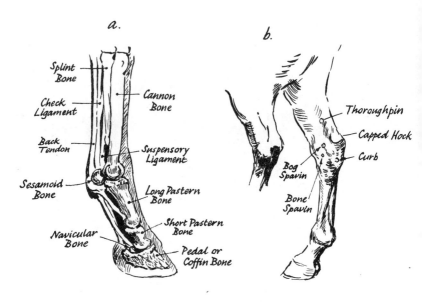

a.

Splint Bone
Check Ligament
Back Tendon
Sesamoid Bone
Navicular Bone

Cannon Bone
Suspensory Ligament
Long Pastern Bone
Short Pastern Bone
Pedal or Coffin Bone

b.

Thoroughpin
Capped Hock
Curb
Bog Spavin
Bone Spavin

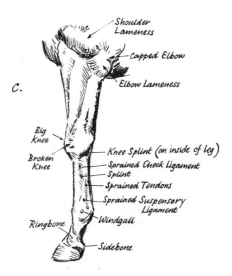

c.

Shoulder Lameness
Capped Elbow
Elbow Lameness
Big Knee
Broken Knee
Knee Splint (on inside of leg)
Sprained Check Ligament
Splint
Sprained Tendons
Sprained Suspensory Ligament
Ringbone
Windgall
Sidebone

Seats of lameness
(a) Foreleg
(b) Off hindleg
(c) Near foreleg

pin, capped hock, displaced stifle joint and injury to the hip joint.

Ring-bones can occur anywhere between the coronet and fetlock, and are bony enlargements of the pastern. They form slowly and are more serious when a joint is involved. They can cause severe, continuous lameness and may permanently stop the horse doing any fast work. Ring-bones can occur on all four legs, and are sometimes caused by irritation from the rope when a horse is hobbled, especially by the hindlegs. They are less severe in the forelegs. They are sometimes hereditary, or may result from a blow or concussion.

Rest is essential, without shoes, either in a box with deep straw or turned out on soft ground. Daily hosing, or cold bandages may help, also blistering. Later, special shoes may be necessary. Consult a vet.

Side-bones are ossified cartilages at the sides of the foot in the region of the heel, which loses its flexibility. It may be hereditary but is generally caused by concussion or strain. Shires and other heavy horses are more prone to develop side-bones. The wall bulges and the shoe wears very unevenly. If detected in the early stages, development may be arrested by hot fomentations and massage with embrocation. Special shoes will be needed. Consult a vet.

Sesamoiditis means that the sesamoid bones behind the fetlock become inflamed. Injury to the bones or the tendons or ligaments causes inflammation. The joint swells and is tender, and appears to be displaced forwards. The horse is lame and takes short steps, with a rather 'pottering' action. If treated in the early stages cold water and rest will help to reduce the inflammation. Use a loose, thick layer of gamgee or cotton wool securely bandaged on with some firm material such as calico, to give support without pressure. Remove and rebandage daily. Blistering may help later.

Windgalls are enlarged joint oil-sacs above and at the sides of the fetlocks; they can also occur at the knees and hocks. Fluid exudes from the joint oil-sacs which have become inflamed by concussion. They are visible as small, round, soft swellings which are easily compressed by the thumb. At one time they were thought to contain air, hence their name. When first formed they are often painful and cause lameness. Later, when formed, they are not serious and cause little trouble. They may become painful if the horse brushes them. Hand-rubbing may help. Also treat with Kaolin paste, and after three days, apply lead lotion.

Swollen fetlock is due to a sprain. The whole joint swells and is painful, with severe lameness. It may be the result of a twist, caused, for instance, by putting a foot into a hole while cantering. Treat with Kaolin paste for three days, then hose frequently and apply cotton-wool pads soaked in lead lotion. Rest until all swelling disappears.

Sore shins occasionally result from extra strenuous exercise, such as racing or a very hard day's hunting. Lameness results from heat and pain in the lower part of the cannon bones, with possibly some swelling which feels 'doughy' to the touch. Rest until completely recovered. To relieve the pain apply hot water, followed by cold bandages. Some sort of working blister, such as 'Workalin' may be used.

So-called 'sprains' may happen to tendons or ligaments, or both. Usually they are not really sprained, which means that the tendon or ligament has been stretched; this seldom occurs. The causes are inflammation, a break in some of the fibres, or injury to the sheath which encloses the tendon. There is heat and swelling, and pain causes lameness. The cause may be overwork, too much trotting on a hard road, or hard work on ground which is either very hard, or too soft and heavy.

If a horse has naturally weak tendons it should be worked in bandages, either gamgee (or cotton wool) and bandage, or a plain stockinette bandage fastened with a double strap and a buckle.

Rest until heat and swelling subside. Meanwhile hose, or stand in cold running water (not of course in winter), bandage tightly over a thick, even cotton-wool pad. Or apply a cold compress. One method is to use a loose linen bandage, kept constantly moist by a piece of string running beneath the bandage, the other end of the string is in a pail of water, supported above the leg, so that the water permeates down the string. Massage with embrocation.

Weak tendons can be helped by working blisters such as Workalin or a leg paint, of which a number of kinds can be bought.

The check and suspensory ligaments, both at the back of the cannon bone, are among the most likely to suffer injury.

Small bony swellings, called splints, form on the splint bone, cannon bone, or on both, usually on the inside of the foreleg. While forming they can cause lameness, but become painless when formed, unless the knee joint is involved, or there is pressure on the suspensory ligament. They cause little trouble when a horse is older than six years. The cause may be hereditary, concussion or a direct injury. The splint's position is shown by its extreme tenderness, even if it can neither be seen nor felt. In the early stages give the same treatment as for a sprain: complete rest, alternate hot and cold fomentations, hosing, massage with green oils or embrocation; any of these can be helpful.

A swollen (big) knee indicates the presence of fluid, similar to water on the knee in a human being. The cause may be a fall, without actually breaking the skin, or a hard knock, probably sustained when jumping. Sometimes a horse may hit itself against something in the stable. There is considerable heat and pain, the horse cannot bear to put any weight on that leg and consequently goes extremely lame. It also cannot bend its knee, because of the pain. Complete rest is essential. The most important thing is to get rid of the fluid as quickly as possible and to prevent the knee becoming permanently stiff. Keep the patient in a large loose-box with a deep bed of straw, and keep as quiet as possible. It may take some time to get rid of the fluid. Hose twice or thrice daily for at least thirty minutes at a time. Use hot and cold fomentations, in between periods of hosing, followed by gentle application of embrocation or green oils. A Kaolin or an 'Antiphlogistine' poultice left on all night and applied as hot as possible may help to draw the fluid. Blistering may help to draw it out if it proves obstinate and other remedies have failed.

Broken knees are invariably the result of a fall; the cause may be faulty conformation, poor condition, overwork and fatigue, careless riding such as cantering on the road, or bad riding, slopping along on a loose rein and not keeping the horse properly collected and up to its bit. Stumbling may be due to a stone in the foot or possibly incipient navicular. Too long a toe may cause it. If the fall is due to bad conformation or poor condition, and not purely accidental, then the horse is unsafe to ride, especially at anything faster than a walk. As a precaution never go out without knee-caps. Broken knees are a blemish which knock pounds off a horse's value. Even if the cause is an accident and the horse is perfectly sound people view broken knees with justifiable suspicion. Their unspoken query is, if it goes down once, is it likely to fall again?

If an oily fluid oozes from the cut it means that the wound has penetrated into the joint oil-sac. This is serious and the vet should be called immediately. There is also the risk that the bone may be fractured or chipped. In the case of a large open wound, it is safer to have an anti-tetanus injection. Absolute cleanliness is essential. Hosing is one of the best ways of washing dirt out of the wound. Do not aim a strong jet directly at it but let the water trickle down. This also helps to stop bleeding and reduces any swelling. Keeping the leg bent helps to make removal of dirt easier.

Hose daily and then apply an antiseptic solution. After bathing, apply a healing ointment (for example, Boot's Pink Healing Ointment is excellent). The wound should granulate and be a healthy pink; it should heal inwards gradually from the outside edges. Do not bandage. Sulphanilamide powder dusted on helps to dry up the wound and is very healing. I have used Boot's Pink Healing Ointment, dusted over with Sulphanilamide, very successfully on open wounds.

Elbow lameness is indicated by the horse standing with its leg bent. The cause may be rheumatism, a sprain or a fracture, and treatment must depend on the correct diagnosis. If uncertain consult the vet.

Capped elbow results from lying on a hard surface (for example, insufficient straw bedding in the box), or pressure of a hind shoe. There is swelling, with possibly a bare patch and hardening of the skin. The skin may be broken. Apply alternate hot and cold fomentations twice daily to reduce the swelling. If the skin is broken bathe with antiseptic and dust on Sulphanilamide. Use a sausage boot, fitted round the pastern, to prevent any further occurrence.

Shoulder lameness is indicated by an outward movement of the leg when trotting, stiffness, or dragging the toe. Stand in front of the horse, hold its leg with both hands, just above and below the knee, raise the leg and pull it towards you. If there is any shoulder lameness the horse will wince and try to pull its leg back away from you. Cause may be liver or stomach disorders, as well as rheumatism, sprain or an injury. If due to rheumatism, treatment under an infrared ray lamp will help, together with massaging with embrocation. Rheumatism may be due to damp bedding or stabling. If the cause is a sprain, hose twice daily for at least thirty minutes at a time; give prolonged complete rest. If in any doubt regarding the cause, consult a vet.

In the hindlegs, as far as the hock, the seats of lameness are the same as in the forelegs, starting from the foot and working upwards.

Around the hock area possible causes of trouble are, bog spavin, bone spavin, curb, capped hock, thoroughpin and lymphangitis (Monday morning leg or big leg). The stifle and hip joints are also possible centres of trouble.

Bog spavin is an enlargement on the inner and upper part of the hock joint. The joint's oil sac distends, usually as the result of strain, but it may be hereditary. Usually, only one hock is affected, so that one can detect the enlargement by comparing it with the other hock. The joint becomes stiff and the foot may be dragged, wearing the toe of the shoe. Test by bending the joint, bringing the foot as close up as possible to the stifle. If the horse is then trotted away directly the foot is lowered, there will be marked lameness. A bog spavin swelling is soft and does not invariably cause lameness. Use a special truss to give pressure, massage with embrocation, or blister; rest.

In the case of bone spavin, the small bones at the lower, inner part of the hock grow together, forming a solid mass and causing lameness. The enlargement can be felt with one's hand. It can also be detected by comparing the two hocks, while standing in front, outside each foreleg in turn and looking at the inside of the hock. Lameness usually only occurs while the spavin is forming; once the bones have firmly united lameness may not persist, but the toe is generally dragged. Usually the horse is able to work. The cause is strain and overwork. Treatment, in the early stages, consists of rest, hosing or other cold applications, massaging with embrocation, or blistering.

Curb is a sprained ligament at the back, about 4 or 5 inches below the point of the hock, usually caused by jumping or galloping on muddy, heavy ground. Neglect can result in a permanent enlargement and chronic lameness. When it first occurs it is swollen and painful. If treated immediately it is fairly easily cured by rest, hosing or other cold applications to reduce the inflammation, or blistering. Give laxative food, such as hot bran mash with a little Epsom Salts, for the evening feed. Relieve strain on the leg by shoeing with calkins or high heels.

A sprained or 'sprung' hock may only affect the ligaments, or it may also involve the bones or tendons. There is tenderness and heat, causing great pain and perhaps high fever. The cause may be fast work, jumping or drawing too heavy a load in the case of draught horses. Call in the vet immediately. Usual treatment is prolonged rest, with hosing or other cold-water applications.

As already stated, the usual cause of a capped hock is lying on hard ground, with insufficient bedding in the case of a stabled horse. As in the case of a capped elbow (*q.v.*) there is swelling; the hair may be worn off, and the skin may become calloused, or broken. Reduce the swelling with hot and cold fomentations applied twice daily; if the skin is broken bathe with an antiseptic solution and apply Pink Healing Ointment, and/or dust on Sulphanilamide powder. If the skin has become hardened try to soften by bathing with warm water and then applying some sort of skin cream. If the horse has been lying out on very hard ground bring it in and give it a deep straw bed. At night put on a hock cap—a padded leather cover which straps round the hock joint.

A thoroughpin or 'through-pin' derived its name from the fact that it is a fluid swelling on either side of the hock, which can be pressed with the finger from one side to the other. It occurs above the point of the hock, at the back. It can be hereditary or may result from a strain. It may only cause slight lameness and unless severe is not serious. Rest and massage will probably disperse the fluid; also apply pressure, using a thoroughpin truss or a rubber bandage. Fit shoes with high heels. In a serious case the vet may draw off the fluid.

Lymphangitis (Monday morning leg or big leg) must not be confused with the swollen hindlegs which occur in some cases of glanders farcy, or epizootic lymphangitis, which is a serious, highly contagious disease. Monday morning leg, big leg, or weed, occurs usually in one, or both hindlegs, but occasionally in the forelegs.

Riding-school or other hard-worked riding or draught horses get it after standing idle for a day's rest. Hence 'Monday morning leg', when carriage horses were rested and stood in the stable all day on Sunday. Either or both legs suddenly swell enormously, probably with knotted cords down the insides of the thighs; a little sticky fluid may ooze from the skin if the condition is severe. Tenderness and severe pain cause acute lameness. The horse may also be constipated and feverish.

To relieve the pain hose, or apply hot fomentations. Give $\frac{1}{2}$ to 1 pint doses of linseed oil to cure the constipation and put on a special diet of warm bran mashes, which are also slightly laxative,

green food and roots (for example, carrots, turnips or swedes); avoid
foods containing much protein. Follow the hosing or hot fomentations by massaging gently with embrocation. Two or three days'
treatment will bring an improvement but lameness will persist for
several days longer. When the lameness is less acute give walking
exercises for short periods twice or thrice daily. Do not return to
normal work and food too suddenly when the horse has recovered.
To prevent a recurrence, reduce the amount of food when the horse
is not working, especially cutting down the amount of corn. Do not
allow a stabled horse to remain standing all day in its box but give it
some light exercise. Best of all turn it out to grass for at least part
of the day so that it exercises itself.

The stifle may be affected in several ways: it may become slipped
or dislocated at the patella or knee cap (as in the case of a human
being). Young colts are especially prone to this when galloping about
and turning suddenly. The patella is easily put back into place,
sometimes without help, by the natural action of the muscles. If help
is necessary, pass a rope between the forelegs around the pastern
and pull forward until the foot is flat on the ground, while pushing
the horse back; then press the bone forward and downward and hold
it in place while moving the horse forward once more. Once replaced
the bone should remain in position. Call in the vet or obtain other
skilled help. The stifle can also be sprained, but this can receive the
usual treatment: rest, hosing or other cold water applications, hot
and cold fomentations, massage with embrocation or green oils. The
joint may be bruised, and, if it is, rest is the only treatment required.
Injury may be caused by a fall, sudden twist when moving quickly,
or, in the case of a harness horse, starting with a heavy load; also
accidents in the stable, becoming cast in its box, slipping, trying to
turn in a stall or other narrow space, or hitting the stifle joint against
something, such as a doorway. The horse goes lame and drags its
leg stiffly, with its toe scraping the ground. Heat and swelling are
present; with a displaced (slipped) stifle the bone is visible as an
enlargement on the outside of the stifle.

Lameness in the hip joint may be due to rheumatism as well as to
an injury, caused by knocking the hip against a projection, through
carelessness while being led out of the stable; the cause may also be a
sprain. Correct diagnosis really depends on knowing the circumstances when the injury occurred. The horse finds it difficult to

move its leg; as it moves, the leg swings outwards and the toe is dragged. The leg also appears to be shorter than the other. Heat and tenderness cause severe pain. Prolonged rest is necessary; relieve the pain with hosing or cold applications. If the muscles are very badly torn, a cure may be impossible and the horse may have to be put down.

If the cause is rheumatism, apply heat, give infra-red ray treatment or massage with green oils or embrocation. Keep the part moving and prevent it becoming stiff by gentle exercise for short periods two or three times daily.

Detecting the cause of lameness is sometimes quite a problem, the first difficulty being to discover on which leg a horse is going lame. The best way is to have it trotted toward and away from you, preferably up and down a slight incline. If lame in a foreleg it will be more obvious going downhill, and if in a hindleg, when going uphill. The reason for this is that more weight naturally falls on a foreleg when going downhill, while the weight is more on the hind-legs when moving up an incline. The horse tends to 'favour' the injured leg by taking as much weight as possible off it and placing it on the sound one. When trotting it nods its head as the sound foot reaches the ground.

If lame in a hindleg the hock of the sound leg rises higher and dips lower than that of the lame one when the horse is trotted away from you. This dipping of the hock is due to the extra weight being placed on the sound leg. The horse again nods its head as the uninjured leg reaches the ground.

Lameness is harder to detect if it occurs in both forelegs or both hindlegs. The horse will then take shorter strides than normal and potter along. It is most difficult to tell which leg is affected when the horse is only slightly lame.

If very lame in one foreleg the diagonal hindleg also seems to be affected when trotting away from one.

Resting a hindleg is quite usual, but if lame in a foreleg the horse may point or rest it in front of the other leg, when standing quietly in the stable. Constantly lifting the foot indicates pain.

Having found the affected leg one should start with the under-neath (ground surface) of the foot and then work systematically upwards, testing at all possible seats of lameness, already mentioned, in turn for heat or swelling. But the foot should always first be thoroughly examined and the shoe removed, as in a large majority of cases the trouble is there. If there is foot trouble the hoof itself can feel hot, and there may be heat round the coronet and just above it on the pastern. The chances of possible trouble seem to grow progressively less the higher one ascends the leg. That is, for example, the chances of the trouble being in the shoulder are less likely than say in the fetlock, or between the fetlock and knee or hock joints. But even so one should not rule out the shoulder, stifle or hip joints as possible seats of lameness, and they should also be carefully examined.

One form of lameness in a hindleg not previously mentioned is stringhalt. When trotting the horse tends to raise its hindleg to an exaggerated height and put it out stiffly, backwards, instead of with the normal action. The hamstring or tendon at the back of the gaskin or second thigh is affected. Unfortunately, it seems to be incurable and gradually becomes progressively worse until eventually the horse should be destroyed. A horse with stringhalt should not be ridden; in its early stages it might be used for light work in harness at a walking pace, or a slow trot. Both hindlegs may be affected and lifted abnormally high. The action is quite unmistakable, whether in only one hindleg, or in both. Consult a vet directly you notice any sign of it.

Shivering is a most serious unsoundness which quite easily passes undetected at an examination for soundness. A long road or rail journey may produce symptoms. The disease is probably caused by pathological changes in the spinal cord. All classes of horses can be affected, especially draught and harness breeds. It is uncommon in ponies.

The symptoms are characteristic. On lifting a hindleg or when backing the leg is suddenly raised, semi-flexed and abducted, shaking or shivering while suspended. The superficial thigh muscles and quarter quiver and the tail is raised and tremulous. The animal may show symptoms while being shod, or when moved over smartly in its stall or box. As with other nervous diseases, excitement may cause symptoms as when led out of the box into the open, or into a straw bed or onto a wooden floor. Some thin-skinned horses may snatch up a hindleg owing to the straw irritating the heel. A shiverer usually does not lie down when indoors, and then loses condition. It may go down when out at pasture, and may improve.

Tests

(1) When in its box or stall notice if the horse 'cocks' his tail or leg. Make it move over to one side and then the other.

(2) Back it sharply and turn to both sides, noticing how it lifts its legs.

(3) Lift up each hindleg, one after the other, holding them up for a few seconds. Note any unusual difficulty in raising them and whether it shivers or not.

(4) Offer a drink of cold water, noticing if it cocks its tail or leg when drinking.

(5) Prick the coronet with a pin, or lightly hammer the top of the hoof.

There is no treatment. As O'Connor states, hunters which occasionally shiver may hunt and jump for several seasons but eventually lose power behind and, though able to gallop and willing to jump, cannot clear an obstacle with the hindfeet or rise sufficiently to jump a moderate fence. Spasms tend to increase both in frequency and severity—until the horse becomes unusable.

22 Health

It is fortunately comparatively easy to recognize signs of good health or the opposite, if one has some understanding and experience of horses.

The healthy appetite (a healthy horse is normally a good eater), smooth, shiny coat, bright eye, and alert head-carriage with ears pricked forward and constantly on the move are all signs of good condition. Without being fat, a healthy horse in hard condition is well covered and muscled up, with well filled-out flanks and hind-quarters. It moves freely and with a springy step and looks interestedly about it. Turned out in a field, it will canter or gallop round the field with head and tail held high, giving a few bucks, or springing sideways. When ridden, it may toss its head and try to give a few playful bucks.

A horse that is off-colour in any way quickly shows signs of it and easily feels very sorry for itself. Loss of appetite, a dull, staring coat, with the hair standing out instead of lying sleekly down, a dull eye, with head drooping listlessly and ears flopping, or laid back. In some cases, according to the cause of ill-health, the horse will lose condition, and grow thin, while its flanks and hindquarters fall in and look hollow. A sick horse moves slowly and lifelessly, with head and tail drooping, or the latter tucked in between its legs. When standing in the field or stable it appears 'tucked up' and probably rests a hind-leg for hours on end. It does not try to move about. When ridden it moves lethargically, and needs kicking on; it has no apparent interest in life or anything around it. Even raising a trot seems an effort, and it may stumble. All these are warning danger signals of impending trouble, and the wise horsemaster will recognize and constantly be on the watch for them.

When one considers what a complex piece of mechanism a horse is, it is surprising really that he does not suffer from more ailments or injuries than he does. Although large, a horse is not nearly as tough as his size would suggest, and so it behoves the owner to be able to know and recognize the symptoms. A horse can become ill so quickly and unexpectedly; for instance, an attack of colic can come on, apparently out of the blue, within about half-an-hour, in what was to all appearances, a perfectly healthy horse.

Diseases caused by bacterial infections, of course, take some time to develop, but even so the horse begins to show signs of being off colour before the illness actually appears—for example, gradual loss of appetite, apathy instead of alertness.

The state of the droppings are one indication of health, or otherwise. Normally they are passed about six to eight times a day. They should be neither too hard nor too soft, but firm, and should crumble slightly when they hit the ground. They should be almost odourless and rather shiny and smooth in appearance, being coated with a slight coating of slime. Their colour largely depends upon the nature of the food being eaten, but normally is between a lightish yellow-brown (when the main diet is hay, and/or corn and bran) to a darkish greeny-brown as when the horse or pony is out at grass. The droppings of a horse at grass may sometimes be loose, especially in spring when the grass is rather rich. If any food is passing undigested through the intestines, it will appear in the droppings, and be a danger-signal that all may not be absolutely well with the digestive system. The trouble may lie in the teeth, causing inability to masticate thoroughly before swallowing. Whole oats, especially when given to an old horse, may appear, undigested, in the droppings—hence crushed oats are better. Droppings should also be examined frequently for the presence of worms; if suspected, a sample should be sent to the vet for a worm-count. Some kinds of worms can actually be seen quite easily in the droppings.

Although so many possible things can go wrong, it is comparatively easy to keep a horse fit and in good condition, year in and year out, provided one pays attention to such things as general cleanliness of horse, food and stables, correct feeding, proper exercise, and regular grooming.

Other signs of illness are: heavy breathing, with heaving flanks, as if the horse had just been galloping; feverishness, shown by excessive thirst; if feverish the base of the horse's ears may feel abnormally warm. The normal temperature for a horse is between 100·5° and 101°. Sweating is another danger signal and usually a sign of pain. Fast pulse: the pulse is taken under the horse's jaw at the large artery situated there; the normal rate is 35 to 40 per minute. Normal rate of respiration is between 10 and 15 per minute. Pulse and respiration should both be counted when the horse is standing absolutely quiet in the stable, as any excitement or movement tends to increase them. Quickened breathing accompanied by general restlessness indicates considerable pain.

In good health the membranes lining the eyes, nostrils and mouth should be pink and moist. They become red and dry with fever, have a yellowish tinge in liver complaints, pale if anaemic, and with purple spots if blood impurities are present.

The urine is normally rather thick and yellowish, but has a bright colour if the patient is feverish.

The position of the legs also gives several indications that all is not well: resting or pointing a forefoot in front of the other to relieve it of weight shows foot trouble. If both forefeet are placed forward it indicates trouble in both. Holding the forelegs wide apart usually suggests trouble in the chest. Constantly scraping the toe and pawing the ground may be due to navicular disease. Drawing one or both hindfeet well forward, with obvious reluctance to back is a sign of trouble in either or both feet. Inability to get up from the ground may be due to spinal injury, sprained back muscles or lockjaw (tetanus). General restlessness, constant lying down and rising again usually indicate stomach pains (colic); the breathing is quick and laboured when the pain is severe. Constant rubbing of one leg against the other, or stamping, are often due to irritation caused by mites. Cart horses with heavily feathered heels often get these 'itchy heels'. If the horse constantly scratches, bites or rubs itself against something, suspect lice. Ungroomed ponies with thick winter coats are especially liable to them.

A fit horse's skin should feel elastic and supple and should move freely. When unwell it feels tight and 'hide-bound'.

Normally a healthy horse is a good eater, eating up everything set before it. Some go to extremes and are gross, greedy feeders. A few may be faddy eaters, or shy feeders who will only eat when alone or when everything is quiet. If fed in a field some horses will allow themselves to be bullied and driven away from their food by others. If a horse starts leaving its food it may be getting too much at one feed; try cutting down the amount until the horse finishes it all or giving more frequent smaller feeds. Or it may indicate the need for a change of diet. Like us, the horse may get tired of the same food day after day. Some few horses are genuinely bad eaters; they are the horsemaster's despair as they remain looking thin and half-starved, and their condition never seems to improve, however much food one tries to make them eat.

Narrow, deep wounds, such as those caused by something penetrating the foot, are the most likely to give trouble, and the hardest to heal. Matter may accumulate at the bottom and then they have to be drained. On no account must they be allowed to heal over at the top, with pus forming underneath, but must be kept open and allowed to heal slowly from below upwards. An open, surface wound, even though of large area, is much easier to heal, provided it is kept clean, for it will granulate over and gradually heal inwards from its circumference.

Apart from accidental wounds such as scratches, and tears from barbed wire, a horse may cut itself quite badly through brushing, high and low over-reaches. Treads may also occur, either self-inflicted (rare) or by another horse treading on its foot. The skin may be torn, with a flap hanging loose, or there may be quite a deep cut on the outside of the pastern, midway between the coronet and fetlock. Galls can be caused by badly fitting tack, or tack being carelessly fastened too tightly, or too loosely. A curb-chain if fastened too tightly can cause a rub under the chin, in the chin or curb-groove. A badly-fitting head-collar or nose-band may rub the cheek-bone; or a bridle may gall the base of the ears if the brow-band is too tight. Saddle galls can result from a badly-fitting saddle, one that is girthed up too loosely, or by a bad rider, who rolls about in his saddle. They can occur anywhere from the withers, along the sides of the ribs to where the cantle rests. Or if the saddle is too low and presses down on the spine, despite the space provided by the gullet, the tops of the vertebrae may become rubbed, as they are very near the surface, with only a thin layer of skin. Girth galls can be caused by a girth being fastened either too loosely, or too tightly, or by using a dirty, stiff leather girth. Incidentally the leather lining of a saddle can gall a horse if allowed to become greasy, dirty and hard.

Galls can vary in severity from rubbing off a patch of hair to an actual abrasion of the skin. Saddle pressure on the wither can cause a deep wound, called a fistula, which is difficult to cure and takes a long time to heal.

A horse which has been galled should not be used until it has healed. If for any reason a horse with a saddle gall must be used, fit a numnah under the saddle, with a piece cut out of it over the position of the gall, to relieve any pressure on it.

A girth gall can be similarly treated by passing the girth through a length of motor-cycle inner-tubing.

These, however, are only emergency makeshifts. The real answer is not to use the horse at all.

Galls, if the skin is broken, should be treated as wounds and all wounds must be kept perfectly clean, and in summer protected from flies. When healed, harden off with a saturated solution of salt and water, a solution of alum, or surgical spirit. Do not use surgical spirit if the skin is broken.

A horse fresh up from grass, in soft condition, will gall more easily than one in hard condition. Before starting to use a horse which has not been ridden for some time harden off the back and sides where there is pressure from the saddle and girth with either salt and water, alum solution or surgical spirit.

Bit injuries to the mouth can be caused by using too narrow a bit, or from having a snaffle bit too high up so that it tears the skin at the corners of the lips. Getting its tongue over the bit can tear the root of the tongue. A curb bit with too high a port can injure the roof of the mouth by pressing upwards against it.

Apart from giving a horse a hard mouth through hardening of the skin covering the bars of the mouth, deadening all feeling eventually, heavy hands, pulling at the mouth, or rough handling by a bad or careless rider can injure the lips or the corners, and/or other parts of the mouth.

Wash the mouth with a weak permanganate of potash solution and do not use the horse until its mouth has completely healed. Then use only the mildest of bits such as a straight rubber or vulcanite snaffle.

If a horse keeps its mouth constantly open while being ridden, air enters and dries it so that it is liable to be lacerated or torn by the bit or bits.

Hosing (in summer) is one of the best means of cleaning a wound; letting cold water trickle over it will wash away any grit or other dirt. When thoroughly clean, wash with some antiseptic solution such as Dettol, T.C.P., or permanganate of potash. Then dust with boric powder or sulphanilamide, either with or without first applying some healing ointment, such as Germolene, Boracic ointment, Boot's Pink Healing ointment or Ayreton's Antiseptic ointment. Repeat the treatment twice daily until completely healed.

If there is a flap of torn skin, either replace it and bandage lightly with a covering piece of lint, soaked in disinfectant solution, to try to heal by first intention, or carefully cut away the torn skin with surgically clean scissors, which have either been passed through a flame or dipped in boiling water or strong disinfectant. As much as possible avoid touching the wound with one's hands. Before touching a wound one should always wash one's hands with carbolic soap or in fairly strong disinfectant.

If the wound is at all serious, or has been caused by some dirty object like rusty barbed wire, call the vet to give an anti-tetanus injection. Even a small cut could cause tetanus. This is especially important if the wound was received outdoors, or if the horse is living out. Some soils harbour tetanus germs more than others and the bacteria can lie dormant in the soil for a long time. There is especial danger when a field has been heavily grazed by horses over a considerable period.

Always cut away the hair surrounding a wound. It is not often advisable or possible to apply a bandage. If not too large in area, sometimes it is better to apply a light lint dressing covered by a piece of gauze or waterproof, and kept in place with strips of adhesive plaster, just to prevent dirt and flies from entering. If the wound is on a leg, not too high up, it may be possible to bandage, although a horse usually seems to succeed in getting it off; one finds yards of filthy bandage wrapped round the horse's feet or trailing about the box floor in the morning. A bandage should never be applied tightly, but loosely, in order to allow for swelling; a tight bandage will stop the circulation and produce swelling. A cut or open wound is usually accompanied by a certain amount of bruising of the surrounding area, which almost inevitably causes some swelling. Therefore I favour the school of thought which says, do not bandage, cover the wound, keep it clean by daily attention and allow nature to play her healing part.

One difficulty, if the wound is on a foreleg, or anywhere accessible, is that the horse will invariably try to lick it, or pull off any dressing. As far as possible, nature is the best healer, provided the wound is kept clean and healthy. Wild animals through fights and other causes sustain some terrible wounds. It is surprising how these heal naturally without the aid of artificial disinfectants and healing powders or ointments. A wild animal's saliva is a wonderful natural healing antiseptic. The animal licks the wound and goes on doing so, thereby cleaning it, and if it is in a normally healthy state it usually heals fairly quickly.

The amount of bleeding from a wound depends on its size, depth and position. A foot wound bleeds profusely because a horse's foot is literally bathed in blood. If not excessive, a certain amount of bleeding is a good thing as it helps to remove dirt and grit—and quite a lot of blood apparently can be lost without dangerous consequences. Venous bleeding oozes and wells up slowly, unless the wound actually cuts a vein; it stops naturally in time due to clotting of the blood. Blood from a vein is a darker purplish red colour, due to comparative lack of oxygen in it.

Bleeding from an artery is another matter and should be arrested as quickly as possible. If a large artery is severed, bleeding from it could cause death in from about fifteen to twenty minutes. Therefore apply some sort of tourniquet and summon the vet as quickly as possible. In an emergency pressing hard with the thumb on the artery below the wound (on the side nearest the heart) will help to check excessive bleeding until help can be found. If the wound is in a position where it can be applied, a flat stone in a handkerchief, twisted tightly round with a stick or pencil, so that the stone is pressed hard against the artery, forms quite an effective tourniquet; this method has often been used in the hunting field. If the ends of the severed artery are visible it may be possible to clip the ends, or tie each with a piece of hair from the horse's mane or tail. Arterial blood is bright red, owing to the oxygen in it from the lungs, and escapes in spurts, corresponding to the heart beats. It does not coagulate to form a clot like venous blood.

If the horse is down on the ground and it is necessary to keep it down, to prevent excessive bleeding, the best thing to do is to sit on its head.

24 Forms of Treatment

Fomenting with hot water is used for relieving pain, for strains and reducing heat and swelling. Alternate applications of very hot and very cold water will help to reduce swellings. Have a kettle of boiling water, two cloths and two buckets, one full of icy cold water. Fill the empty bucket with boiling water, dip a cloth in it and wring it out nearly dry. Apply it as hot as the hand can bear to the affected part and leave it wrapped round until it starts to cool. Then apply the second cloth, dipped into the cold water and wrung out. Leave it on until the heat from the affected part begins to warm the cloth. Continue alternately with the hot and cold for at least twenty minutes. This is a valuable treatment for sprains, torn ligaments, etc. Afterwards, bandage lightly with a rest bandage.

Letting water trickle from a hose is most useful for reducing heat and swelling and for any sprains or strains. If it is possible to keep the horse tied up and cold water trickling onto the affected part for about an hour, so much the better. Do not use in winter. Hosing is one of the best ways of cleaning a cut and helping to stop slow venous bleeding, as it helps to clot the blood. Hosing is also helpful in a case of laminitis.

Tubbing is used when it is necessary to bathe the foot, if the horse can be persuaded to stand its foot in the tub without knocking it over. Some horses will, others will not. A broad, shallow tub is better than a rather narrow, deep one.

Poulticing can be used to extract matter, or some object embedded in the skin, such as a thorn. It is also useful in the case of an abscess, to help bring it to a head, so that it can be lanced by the vet, if this is necessary.

Kaolin and Antiphlogistin are both excellent poultices. They should be applied as hot as possible, covered with a woollen bandage tied fairly loosely, to keep in the heat, and should be left on all night. A bread poultice should not be used as it is an ideal breeding ground for bacteria and goes sour very quickly for this reason. Linseed Meal can be used.

To poultice the foot, or leg, make a bag or stocking out of a clean sack. Fit tapes to its opening. If the foot is to be poulticed fill the bottom of the sack with the poultice and then persuade the horse to put its foot into it, drawing the sack up as high as possible round its leg, so that its foot is embedded in the poultice. Tie the top of the sack, not too tightly, round the horse's leg above its knee so that it cannot slip down.

Bran makes quite a good poultice, but like bread is apt to turn sour and should therefore not be left on too long. Twelve hours is the maximum length of time for a bran or linseed poultice.

Blistering is used in certain cases, such as windgalls, already described (Chapter 21). It is used as a counter-irritant and for drawing fluid to the surface when there is inflammation. There are many proprietary brands of blister on the market, 1 in 8 Red Mercuric Iodide is one commonly used. Mercuric chloride and turpentine blisters are not recommended as they are very painful, cause sloughing, and their effect does not last. The hair should first be clipped away from the part to be blistered. A cantharides blister can be used for recently formed bony enlargements such as ring-bones. After blistering a horse must be rested until the blistered part has healed.

If a horse must be kept working, some form of 'working blister' such as Workalin can be used. This does not incapacitate the horse, though it may remove the hair.

Firing is used to strengthen weak tendons. It thickens the skin. A horse, especially a young racehorse, is sometimes fired before any trouble has occurred to strengthen tendons and as a preventative. This is sometimes found in young racehorses and hunters imported from Ireland. A red-hot electric needle is now used for firing. A vet will give his opinion as to whether firing is advisable in any particular case.

When a foot is denerved the main nerves connecting it to the leg are severed so that it has no feeling in it. It is an operation which should only be performed if all else has failed, or when a horse is suffering considerable pain. The horse may be sound and be safe to hack quietly, but it would be dangerous, and cruel, to use it for hunting or show-jumping. In a case of navicular disease the foot is occasionally denerved as a last resort to prevent pain.

25 Ailments

While prevention is better than cure, the stable manager must be familiar with the common contagious, infectious and non-infectious ailments, and with the necessary steps to take to prevent them spreading. He should also know what active treatment to give pending the vet's arrival, and what after care is necessary during convalescence.

Scrupulous cleanliness of the stables and everything in them is the best prevention of disease, coupled with sufficient food of the right kind and adequate daily exercise. A healthy horse in hard condition is far less susceptible to illness. Boxes must be properly mucked out daily and swept, together with any passages. Keep mucking-out tools and wheelbarrow clean. Drains should be disinfected fairly often. A weekly sprinkling of disinfectant on the floor helps to allay dust and keeps the stables sweet and clean. All grooming kit should be washed periodically with disinfectant. Thorough grooming and/or strapping, is essential. Keep night and day rugs and stable blankets well aired. Before storing winter blankets or heavy night rugs for the summer, wash and dry thoroughly; let them air in the sun. All feeding bowls should be kept absolutely spotless; also water buckets. Remove any stale food from the manger.

Should a disease be introduced into the stables by a horse from outside, isolate it immediately as far as possible from all others. Wash down the walls and floor of any box in which it has stood with strong disinfectant (Jeyes Ibcol, or Carbolic). Then if the stable walls are limewashed, do them again. Burn all bedding. Wash all grooming kit, feed bowls, or anything else which has been in contact with the horse, in strong disinfectant. After washing put any blankets or cloths such as stable rubbers out to dry in the fresh air and sunshine. Do not go from an infected to a healthy animal. When leaving the infected stable wash your gum boots in strong disinfectant to avoid the risk of carrying infection out into the yard. Wash hands and arms up to the elbow in strong disinfectant.

Keep all grooming kit, feed bowls and blankets used for the infected horse in its box, i.e. right away from everything else. If these rules of hygiene are observed risk of infection will be greatly reduced.

The risk of infection is one which every stable manager runs when taking a strange horse at livery. The wise man will give any new arrival a period of quarantine (at least three weeks) before allowing it to associate with any of his own mounts. There is less risk if turned out to grass, but any new horse should be carefully watched daily during the quarantine period.

Treatment of illness until the vet arrives largely depends on the nature of the ailment. But isolate the patient immediately, and keep it warm and quiet. Take its temperature, pulse and respiration, noting them for the vet. Whether the animal should lie down or not again depends on the nature of the illness. If it is colic, for instance, the horse must not be allowed to lie down or roll about, for fear of a twisted gut; put on a head-collar and lead it about until the vet arrives.

Convalescence after care consists of prolonged rest, continued with sufficient gentle walking exercise, leading the horse, to help its digestion and bowels. The animal may require building up so give a condition powder such as Vi-Minerol, and so on, and such diet as the vet prescribes. Generally, the patient should have an ample supply of green meat. In summer, turning out to grass for a few hours daily in the sunshine, provided the temperature is not too high and there is shade available, is beneficial.

Most contagious diseases must immediately be reported to the Authorities, or the police. The vet will almost certainly do this, but do not leave it to chance, as you are responsible and may be heavily fined for not reporting it.

Fever symptoms are high temperature, rapid breathing and pulse. The horse is usually constipated and any urine passed is high-coloured. There may be spasms of shivering. Fever itself is not a disease, but one of the symptoms of some contagious disease. Keep the patient as comfortable as possible, with deep bedding; put on rest bandages. It is most important to get the bowels working properly, especially if constipated. Give an enema, about blood heat, twice or thrice daily. Only give half the normal grain ration, or no grain at all, but plenty of green food. Keep a full bucket of clean water near the horse to drink at will; change the water frequently.

Anthrax was one of the scourges, especially in the East, before the cavalry was mechanized. It is a bacterial disease, fatal to horses, and can attack men. The germ usually comes through the food or water.

Loss of appetite and high fever are followed by rapidly increasing swellings on various parts of the body. Membranes lining the eye and nose appear purple and spotted. There is a blood discharge from the nose, and sometimes, the bowels. Death soon follows. Fast increasing swelling occurs in the throat and feels rather doughy and soft; a finger pressed into it leaves a dent. The chest and belly may both swell, chest swelling being accompanied by colic pains. There is finally a rusty or bloody discharge from the nostrils. The horse dies in from twenty-four to forty-eight hours. If any animal is found dead suddenly, suspect anthrax at once. Immediately notify the Authorities or police. The body should preferably be burned, or buried more than six feet deep in quicklime. The burial ground must be well away from buildings, any cultivation, or running water and clearly sign-posted: 'Foul Ground—Anthrax.' Cremation is far better than burial. The whole stable and yard must be well disinfected.

Glanders-farcy is another very contagious disease, occasionally caught by man. It used to be another scourge of the cavalry regiments, especially in India.

It may lie dormant in the system for a long time before developing. It can be spread to other horses by discharges from the patient and very strict precautions must be taken. Anyone in contact with the sufferer must not go near another horse; nor must anything belonging to it. Notify the Authorities immediately.

The symptoms are a slight, sticky discharge from the nose, usually one nostril, with a hard lump under the jaw on the same side as the discharge. The lump does not move freely but feels as though stuck on to the jaw. Farcy-buds, or small sores, having the same sticky discharge, may appear in the nostril and on other parts of the body, with no signs of healing. When they occur on the legs the disease is called 'farcy', but it is identical with glanders. Glanders-farcy ulcers are small, angry-looking sores with ragged edges; after bursting they have a glutinous, not very copious, discharge. The ulcers are in line, one under the other, on the nose, the inner sides of the legs, and sometimes on the face and neck. The neighbouring lympha-tic vessels stand out like knotted cords under the skin. The disease is incurable and after diagnosis the victim should be destroyed. Segre-gate any horses which may have been in contact. Stables and all grooming kit, and so on, must be rigorously disinfected. Take the temperature daily of all segregated horses; slight, irregular fever is the first symptom of the disease. Also inspect daily the nose, under the jaw and the inner sides of the legs. Mallein is used for diagnosing any suspected cases. A healthy horse does not react to an injection, but if affected the temperature rises and a swelling appears where the injection was given. Burn all carcases.

Epizootic lymphangitis is another very contagious disease. Horses can catch it from mules and donkeys. It does not affect humans. Its cause is bacterial and the germ may be dormant in the system for some time. A chain of small abscesses develops along the lymphatic vessels, and on any other part of the body, though most often on the legs; these swell and the disease appears very similar to glanders-farcy. Unlike glanders, however, the sores heal readily. It also differs from glanders in that the matter is thick and white, or creamy; the swollen lymphatics and the abscesses which result, always start from a wound; there is usually no pain or fever. The patient or suspect does not react to the mallein test. Infection occurs by direct contact, matter being carried from an infected wound to a healthy one, either through flies, or by carelessness when dressing an infected wound, using the same materials on a healthy wound. It is a serious disease, notifiable to the Authorities. All suspects should be strictly isolated and horses affected must be destroyed at once. Fortunately the disease seems to have been stamped out in the British Isles, but it still exists in many countries abroad.

Mange is a notifiable contagious disease which spreads very easily and is difficult to cure. It is caused by small insects living in, or on, the skin. In dry mange the insects are underneath the skin. In the moist type they are on the skin surface. Both types first start on the head, withers and back, and sometimes, but more rarely, on the quarters. Dry mange has small pimples about the size of a pin's head; the hair falls from these, leaving a bald patch about the size of a pea. In moist mange, a moist patch rapidly increases in size, and becomes bald. There is severe irritation with both kinds. The horse smacks its lips or nibbles with them, and leans or rubs against one's hand if one gently scratches an affected part. It leans heavily on the brush when groomed, and if free, the horse will rub itself so violently against anything rough, that the skin will bleed.

Isolate all cases and suspects. Disinfect the stables thoroughly together with all rugs (rugs are one of the main causes of contagion), stable rubbers and grooming kits, which have been used on the victims. Horses with mange should be clipped, singed and washed with hard soap and warm water. Then apply a mixture of 1 pint sulphur to 8 pints sperm oil, all over the body. Never apply linseed oil. Rub in the mixture first with the hands and then with an old body brush, for two days. On the third day again wash thoroughly with hard soap and warm water; be very careful to see that all the sulphur and sperm oil mixture is removed, or it will cause blistering. Having removed the dressing make the horse sweat, and groom thoroughly for ten days. Then repeat the dressing, washing and grooming. If itchiness or any other signs of mange still remain, apply a third dressing, followed by thorough washing and grooming. Another excellent remedy is twelve pints lime, thirty pints sulphur to one hundred pints of water. Apply the dressing a little warmer than normal body temperature. If a number of horses have to be treated this is the most economical method as a trough or sheep dip can be used and the horses passed through it daily. Give a plentiful diet and daily exercise.

Influenza, though it need not be notified, is contagious. Bad sanitation is one main cause, and it occurs when large numbers of horses are suddenly collected together. The eye membrane becomes swollen and highly coloured, giving the name pink eye to the disease. There is fever and great lassitude. The air passages and chest can be affected, with discharge from nose and eyes, similar to catarrh. Pneumonia, lung inflammation, may follow. The legs may swell rapidly and occasionally there is diarrhoea. As the disease easily spreads all usual disinfecting precautions should be taken. The horse is very weak and quickly becomes thin. There is often no appetite, or it is capricious. Do everything possible to persuade the horse to eat, to maintain its strength. Careful nursing is most important; keep well rugged-up and warm, out of draughts, and put on warm woollen rest bandages. A long convalescence is necessary to restore strength and condition.

Strangles is a serious contagious disease which should be reported. It is often closely connected with one form of pneumonia. The horse's appetite disappears and it becomes thin. It is also feverish and an abscess develops between the branches of the lower jaw, with a discharge of catarrh from the nose. Having burst, the abscess usually heals quickly. At first the swelling is hard and diffused, but after a few days becomes localized between the jaws and grows soft. Give plenty of food to maintain the horse's strength. Keep the bowels open and soft. The discharge from the abscess when it bursts, or has been opened, must be burnt immediately. Everything in contact with the horse must be thoroughly disinfected.

Ringworm is caused by a fungus growing at the root of the hairs and produces bald patches, about the size of a florin, covered with greyish scales. It is contagious, but not necessarily serious and need not be reported. The hair surrounding the bald patch must be clipped away. Apply tincture of iodine or iodine ointment on and around the patch.

Contagious stomatitis produces blisters inside the mouth, on the lips, gums and tongue. Sometimes they develop on the outside of the lips, and the nostrils. Isolate all patients and use separate water taps and buckets. Disinfect the entire stables and all water buckets, feed-bowls, and so on. Apply a 1 per cent solution of potassium permanganate.

Infectious diseases are chiefly passed on by germs in the air, and not through actual contact. Isolate the patient immediately and disinfect its box and everything it has used. Spray the stables with some good germicidal spray, twice daily. Keep them scrupulously clean, and disinfect the floors and walls by spraying them after mucking out.

Coughs seem to go all through a stable suddenly, especially in spring and autumn. Horses living in are much more susceptible to colds and coughs than those living out the whole time. Draughts and sudden changes in temperature in the stables seem to be the main cause. Draughts can be deadly, especially if a horse comes in very warm, and possibly sweating, after exercise. Coughs and colds also precede influenza epidemics.

A cold is catarrh which inflames the nostril membranes, causing discharge. Coughs result from an inflamed throat membrane (sore throat). Coughs and colds are frequently both present together. At first the discharge from the nose is watery, but it thickens after a few days, having first a greyish, and then a yellow colour. It is odourless and runs freely from both nostrils. A hot, dry throat membrane causes a short, painful cough; the presence of much phlegm produces a longer and hoarser cough. Swallowing food or touching the horse's throat will make it cough. When the throat is very swollen and painful the horse cannot swallow and the food returns down the nostrils. Fever may accompany a severe cold and every care should be taken to prevent pneumonia (lung inflammation). Colds and coughs may be incipient strangles or pneumonia. Keep the horse warm, well rugged up, and out of draughts; put on woollen rest bandages. Give a deep bed of straw. Steam the head by filling a pillow case with straw; pour a few drops of eucalyptus or Friar's Balsam on the straw, and then pour on boiling water. Hang the bag on the horse's head like the old-fashioned cabby's nosebag. A nosebag, if obtainable, makes an excellent receptacle. Steaming promotes a free discharge, which should frequently be wiped away with cotton wool soaked in some disinfectant solution. Give a cough electuary, and rub the throat with liniment. If the throat is very painful only give such soft food as can easily be swallowed, such as rather sloppy, warm bran mash. This will also help to keep the bowels open; they should be kept free and rather soft. The horse must not be allowed to become constipated. Rug-up extra warmly and lead out daily for about ten to fifteen minutes walking exercise: do not exercise if it is raining. If one has a covered school in which to exercise, so much the better. Coughs may also be due to dusty hay, or to broken wind. A chronic cough may be caused by worms.

As already mentioned, a feverish cold, accompanied by a cough, may be the first stage of pneumonia, or may very easily lead to it. Pneumonia must be regarded as contagious so far as other horses are concerned. The horse loses its appetite and rapidly becomes thin. There is fever, with a fast pulse and quickened respiration. The eye membranes become inflamed, and a reddish nasal discharge frequently occurs, accompanied by a cough. The horse stands with its forelegs apart, and a dull sound is produced by tapping the ribs covering the lungs, due to fluid congestion. Good nursing is essential. Keep the patient warm and out of draughts. Rug up and put on woollen rest bandages. Give a deep bed of straw. Apply hot blankets to the chest and give small (half pint) doses of linseed oil, to give relief. Try every variety of food to tempt the horse to eat. Leave small quantities of several different kinds of food in the stable at night. Leave water within easy reach and replace with fresh directly it becomes fouled. If constipated give warm enemas, and plenty of green food. If the horse is weak give a stimulant, for example, a carbonate of ammonia ball. A long convalescence is necessary after recovery so that the lungs may regain their former elasticity.

Pustulous eczema (impetigo) is highly contagious and infectious. Isolate and thoroughly disinfect the box and everything used by the infected horse. The skin irritates and discharges, causing matted hair. Dirt, neglect and digestive trouble, probably due to incorrect feeding or dirty food, are usual causes. Give a laxative or an enema. Change the diet; reduce the corn ration, replacing it with plenty of green food, carrots and bran mash. Clip hair from the parts affected. Wash thoroughly with warm water and carbolic soap. A poultice may be applied where possible to draw out the matter. Afterwards apply an antiseptic ointment. Put ½ oz. potassium nitrate and potassium bicarbonate in the drinking water. Call in the vet.

There is a less common dry form in which the hair falls out, leaving grey scales, and the skin wrinkles and thickens. It may be confused with mange, but only a vet can decide, as microscopic examination is necessary. Wash with disinfectant, apply sulphanilamide, and consult the vet. Mange is parasitic; eczema is not.

26 Other Ailments

It has already been stressed that an anti-tetanus injection should always be given in the case of cuts and abrasions which are any more than small and superficial. And even the smallest scratch should be washed with disinfectant and kept scrupulously clean until healed.

The tetanus or lockjaw germ infests the ground, so that the most dangerous injuries are those to the feet, and broken knees, where the injured part comes into contact with the soil.

Symptoms are stiffness and muscular spasms in the jaw (hence the name 'lock-jaw'), neck and back; it may also affect other muscles. The tail becomes drawn to one side and quivers. The jaw becomes fixed, and the third eyelid or haw becomes visible when the head is raised. As the horse tries to eat, unsuccessfully, its mouth may become covered with food. Isolate the sufferer and keep as quiet as possible away from all noise, as it becomes very easily startled. Make up a bed which is noiseless to walk on and does not rustle. Give plenty of boiled, sloppy food which can be sucked down. Leave ample food and water within easy reach and leave the horse for twelve hours at a time. The best treatment is absolute quiet. Find any wounds and thoroughly clean with antiseptics. If the horse lives over ten days it generally recovers, but needs very careful nursing.

A horse's wind can be broken by too much fast work when it is not in hard 'hunting fit' condition, or if worked fast when suffering from a cold and/or cough. Once the wind has been damaged it can never be completely cured, though it may be relieved. After any effort there may be difficulty in breathing out and expelling the air from the lungs. This is most noticeable if watching the flanks. Instead of the flank rising and falling steadily and gradually, broken wind causes a double effort to expel the air. There may also be a noise; normal breathing is quite silent. Broken wind causes the belly muscles to be 'caught up'. There is a chronic, short, husky cough. Incorrect feeding can cause broken wind by over-distending the stomach with too much bulky food, making it press on the lungs. Fast work too soon after a meal can also cause broken wind.

Decrease the amount of bulk food and compensate by giving more concentrates (or 'short' feeds). Hay and all other food should be slightly damped. Keep the atmosphere as free from dust as possible. Steaming the nostrils with a medicated vapour (Friar's Balsam, eucalyptus) may bring some relief. The diet should include carrots.

Broken wind is caused by actual damage to, or tearing of, the lung tissue, which when it heals forms thickened scar tissue. One expression used for a broken-winded horse is, 'thick in the wind', which more or less accurately describes the condition. Once a horse's wind has been broken it can only be used for slow work, such as light hacking, mostly at walking pace and not more than a slow trot.

Many horses get broken-winded through selfish, thoughtless and careless riders who over-gallop them and only think of their own pleasure. Riding-school horses are especially liable to this treatment by clients who want their 'money's worth', unless very strictly controlled. That is one reason why I have never allowed my own ponies out unaccompanied. You simply cannot trust other people to ride your horse as you would ride it yourself.

Roaring is the characteristic whistling or roaring noise which a horse makes in deep breathing, such as during a gallop, when its larynx muscles have been affected after some chest complaint; there may also be a hereditary pre-disposition. One side of the larynx has become paralysed, making the windpipe opening abnormally small. One can try treating it as for a sore throat, but the only effective treatment, especially in bad cases, is to have the horse 'Hobdayed' or 'tubed'. Hobdaying is an operation named after the famous veterinary surgeon, Professor Sir Frederick Hobday, C.M.G., F.R.C.V.S. (1870–1939), Principal and Dean of the Royal Veterinary College, London. The operation consists of inserting a tube into the windpipe to facilitate respiration. The horse breathes directly into the lungs through the tube, instead of its nostrils. The opening of the tube is covered with very fine gauze to prevent the entrance of dust or larger foreign bodies, it has to be unscrewed, taken out and thoroughly cleaned daily. If successful, the horse can live a normal, active life; some even compete in important events, such as Badminton.

Two forms of colic exist: spasmodic and flatulent (windy) colic. Both are potentially serious, so no time should be lost in calling in the vet. Meanwhile, keep the horse walking about and do not allow it to lie down and roll.

In spasmodic colic pain occurs at intervals and is not continuous. In between spasms the horse seems perfectly well until another one occurs suddenly. Pain is obviously intense as the sufferer is usually violent, pawing, stamping, kicking at its belly and lying or throwing itself down and rolling. It must not be allowed to roll as it may twist the gut, which is fatal, as a rule. When walking it crouches in its loins and stretches out its hindlegs as if trying to stale. It also keeps looking round and snatching at its sides; sweat occurs in patches, or all over the body in very severe cases. Breathing is rapid and distressed (laboured), but there is no rise in temperature. The mouth goes dry and the eye membrane becomes bright red. Within five minutes many, or all, of these symptoms will occur; after the attack the pain stops as suddenly and the horse seems to have recovered, for a few minutes, until the next attack. The pains occur longer and more often, with fewer intervals between. The stomach may appear distended and the skin stretched tight like a drum. There is severe constipation. Most of the causes originate from bad management; watering after feeding, instead of before; giving the horse cold water to drink when it is hot, and especially if sweating; overfeeding; giving food which is dusty or in a receptacle not kept scrupulously clean; working when exhausted; giving a heavy meal to an exhausted horse, when its digestion is unable to cope with it; turning out suddenly in late spring onto very lush new grass; mouldy hay; newly cut hay; lawn mowings not absolutely freshly cut, which have started to ferment; swallowing some foreign body which gets stuck in the intestine, causing an obstruction and the formation of gas from undigested food. To relieve pain give two wineglassfuls of brandy, gin or whisky to three parts of water. Apply hot blankets to the belly. Give a chloral hydrate ball for immediate relief of pain. To make the bowels act, give a large enema every thirty minutes. Other remedies for relieving pain which may be tried are: 2 teaspoonfuls of ginger; 4 oz. brandy or whisky; 1 to 2 oz. of turpentine mixed with 1 pint of oil, or beaten up with eggs and milk.

Flatulent (windy) colic is due to the bowels becoming distended with gas from fermented food. The belly swells, making the horse look unnaturally rotund. The horse does not become so violent or throw itself about so much, but seems rather sleepy, uneasy and fidgety; it scrapes at the ground and wanders slowly round, as though wanting to lie down, but afraid to do so. There is continuous, instead of intermittent, pain, and the pulse is fast. There is no temperature. Usually accompanied by severe constipation. Treat mild cases of flatulent colic with a mild laxative, for example ½ to 1 pint of linseed oil. The vet usually gives an injection to quieten the horse and make it sleepy; often this effects a cure, but if not he may give another some eight to twelve hours later.

It is advisable to sit up all night with the horse, especially when suffering from spasmodic colic, in case the attack becomes more severe and it starts throwing itself down. Keep a head-collar on it so that it can be led about if this occurs. During convalescence, keep the horse on warm, sloppy bran mashes with about 2 teaspoonfuls of linseed oil added per feed; give this for two or three days and then give some green meat, for example brussels sprouts, and so forth, cut up fine, to keep the bowels open and active. To prevent constipation, exercise daily for twenty to thirty minutes, leading in hand. Do not ride for at least a week until fully recovered and back on normal diet. Some vets prescribe a little hay, immediately following an attack, while others forbid it.

Constipation sometimes occurs by itself, but is usually a symptom or accompaniment of some illness, for example, a cold, pneumonia, colic (*q.v.*); it may also result from indigestion. Insufficient exercise can cause it. Give more steady (not fast) exercise. Change the diet and, especially in winter, give more green food; apples in reasonable quantity are also good, but too many can cause colic. Sloppy bran mash, given warm with linseed oil added, and a pinch of salt, is a mild laxative. If these do not overcome it give a fairly large, warm enema.

After administering an enema hold the tail down for about a minute to give the solution a chance to work effectively, otherwise it may be expelled before it has properly entered the bowel.

Lampas only occurs in foals or colts when their teeth are changing. The gum behind the incisor teeth of the upper jaw becomes inflamed, just as an infant gets inflamed gums when teething. Adult horses do not get it. It is due to food working up between the teeth; remove this and only give soft foods. The horse's palate immediately behind the incisors is often below their level, and this condition is frequently mistaken for lampas. Like babies, young horses are often rather fractious and irritable while changing their teeth and need sympathetic and tactful, yet firm, handling.

Worms are a real source of danger and are most likely to occur when a number of horses are kept continuously in a field without adequately resting it. Worms are passed in the droppings a can be picked up in the grass by another previously unaffected hors while grazing. There are three kinds, the round worm, red worm and whip worm. If suspected, treatment should be given immediately their presence is confirmed. Send a sample of droppings to the vet for a worm count. If neglected a horse can become very ill, and may die. The horse rapidly grows thin and loses condition, even though its appetite considerably increases. The skin becomes tight (hidebound), the ribs show and the coat is dull and staring. There is considerable thirst. Worms attack the bowels, literally eating them away. Colic may be another symptom. Worms may be treated by giving the affected horse thiabendazole, with its proprietary derivative equizole, which is in the form of a pony cube and may be mixed in with the feed.

The round worm is stiff, white and about the thickness of a pencil. It is very long (6 to 14 inches). Starve the horse and keep without water for twenty-four hours. Then drench with 2 tablespoons oil of turpentine, and 1 pint linseed oil. In severe cases the vet may have to use a stomach pump. The modern treatment is piperazine, given with phenothiazine, which is not dangerous. It is more effective against immature worms. Piperazine adipate is almost 100 per cent effective against both mature and immature worms.

The red worm is the most dangerous of all parasites which attack a horse, for it is a bloodsucker which eats into the intestines. It is reddish in colour, and approximately 2 inches long. It can usually be detected in the droppings. Neglect causes death. Give phenothiosone powder in water as a drench; or mixed with food. Piperazine adipate is also recommended. Careful nursing is essential. Give plenty of best quality food. Starve and keep without water for twenty-four hours before dosing. An infected horse may take anything up to six months to recover. When recovered have a worm count taken to ensure freedom.

The paddock must be ploughed and thoroughly cleansed with quicklime. Leave it ploughed up during the winter so that the frost and rain can break up the soil; resow the following spring. Cattle are unaffected by the worms which attack horses. They should therefore be allowed to graze a worm-infested paddock. In doing so, not only will they eat all the coarse grass which horses leave, but in grazing will devour countless thousands of worms and their eggs spread by the horses' droppings.

The whip or thread worm is about $1\frac{3}{4}$ inches long and very thin. It attacks the rectum, causing intense irritation, which results in continuous tail rubbing. To relieve irritation apply mercuric or carbolic ointment. Give an enema, using a handful of salts to a gallon of tepid water, and administer piperazine adipate (10 grammes).

No droppings from worm-infected horses must ever be put on the manure heap. Either burn, or bury them in a pit containing quicklime. In fact, regard worms as a contagious disease.

The gad-fly, or bot-fly lays its eggs in the grass and these stick to the horse's legs, and even the underside of its belly—depending on the length of the grass—as tiny yellow specks, smaller than a pin's head. Sometimes a horse's legs are literally smothered in them. The horse licks its legs, thereby transferring the eggs to its stomach, where they hatch out as stomach bots. They may or may not be expelled in the droppings, but if a horse is suspected of being infested by these worms, starve it for twenty-four hours and then drench with 2 tablespoons turpentine in 1 pint linseed oil. The eggs stick tenaciously to the legs and picking them off is a long and tedious job. The best way is to scrape them off with a blunt knife (taking care not to cut the horse). Or they can be singed off, which is rather a tricky business. They will also wipe off with a damp paraffin rag, or with warm water and soap.

Mallenders is a skin trouble akin to eczema which attacks the foreleg at the back of the knee joint. Sallenders is a similar infection which occurs at the front of the hock. The oil glands which keep the skin soft at the knee and hock joints, where bending the joints might cause friction, become inflamed and irritated by dust, or mud. Its origin is often hereditary. The skin cracks or becomes raw, and bending the joints tends to keep the cracks open. Pain may cause temporary lameness. Wash and dry thoroughly. Dissolve a small quantity of salts in warm water, and use a hard soap. When absolutely dry apply an astringent, antiseptic lotion. After, rub in zinc or iodine ointment, Vaseline, Ayreton's Antiseptic ointment, or Boot's Pink Healing ointment. Continue treatment for several days after the part has apparently healed.

Mud fever is most frequently due to carelessness or neglect. It is a serious ailment which can put a horse out of work for a long time, and even cause death if neglected. It most often occurs when the mud is imperfectly washed off a horse's legs and belly after returning from work, especially when warm water is used in cold weather and the skin is not thoroughly dried afterwards. Never wash mud off in winter; let it dry and then remove thoroughly with a rubber curry comb and dandy brush. It is somewhat similar to greasy heels. The mud irritates the skin which becomes inflamed and discharges. Mud and matter cake together forming a firm, scabby surface. Wash with hard soap and warm water with a little salts dissolved in it. When thoroughly dry, apply an astringent lotion. Severe cases are often difficult to cure. Consult a vet.

Horses are more susceptible to sunstroke than is generally realized, even in the British Isles. It is not for nothing that Spanish and Portuguese horses wear those rather comic hats. Never turn a horse out in hot sunshine without a shelter, even a tree. Sunstroke affects the atlas (behind the ears) and the spine. Put the patient in a cool, dark place and keep very quiet. Bathe head and spine with cold water. Feed on soft food, and when recovered give a laxative. Rest for several days and then only give light work.

Staggers is akin to sunstroke and may result from strenuous work in hot sunny weather. There may be pressure by some part of the tack or harness on the large neck blood vessels, causing brain congestion. The horse suddenly falls and cannot rise again. It may reel as it walks; frequently the hindquarters become completely paralysed. Some remain quiet when they fall while others become very violent and have to be held down. Treat as for sunstroke.

Sometimes staggers may be due to an affection of the brain, for example, pressure or an abscess on the brain. If staggers occurs frequently suspect this to be the cause and consult a vet. In this case the horse may drop suddenly in its box, or while being led out, for no apparent reason. Also, while not actually falling, its behaviour may be peculiar at times. Obviously such a horse is unsafe to ride or drive.

Poll evil may produce similar symptoms to staggers. The cause is a blow on the head, between the ears (i.e. on the poll), which produces an abscess. The horse refuses to let its head or ears be touched and becomes uncertain and abnormal in behaviour. It is curable. Consult a vet. Never hit a horse anywhere on or near the head.

Sore eyes usually occur in summer and are caused by flies. The eyes become very sore and discharge. They may water copiously and the membranes become very red and inflamed. Matter may collect in the corners during the night. Stable by day and graze at night, or provide a shelter so that the horse can escape from flies during the heat of the day. Leave the forelock long to protect the eyes, or let the horse wear an eyeshade. (Incidentally, it is sheer cruelty to turn a docked horse out in summer; having no long tail to swish it is completely at the mercy of the flies.) Bathe with weak, tepid potassium permanganate or boracic. Cold weak tea is also very soothing. Use a separate piece of cotton-wool for each eye. After bathing apply Golden Eye ointment at least twice daily.

Ponies living out are liable to become infested with lice in winter, when they have their thick coats, especially if they are not caught and groomed daily. Two kinds infest horses, biting and sucking lice, and both thrive on dirty conditions and neglect. Buildings and trees can transfer them to horses which are not infested. Cleanliness of the horse and its surroundings, whether stabled or living out, is the best preventative. Sucking lice usually infest the roots of long hair, such as manes and tails. Biting lice mostly live in the coat. The horse loses condition and its coat becomes dull and falls out. There is also irritation of the skin. The insects are visible when the hair is parted. If possible, clip the horse, burning the hair where it falls, then singe to destroy the lice and apply paraffin emulsion. Alternatively, dust 'Gammaexane' powder thoroughly into the coat, working it down into the roots with one's fingers. Apply twice, with a week in between each application; the first time should kill the insects and the second any eggs which may be hatching. Disinfect thoroughly everything which has been in contact with the horse, including the building, especially woodwork and all grooming kit and rugs. Do not use the same grooming kit on another horse. The lice that infest horses cannot live on humans; similarly the fleas and lice that live on domestic animals and humans cannot live on horses.

Nits also infest horses, again through dirt, neglect and irregular grooming. Treat as for lice and again thoroughly disinfect everything.

Nettlerash is a minor complaint which, nevertheless, nearly drives a horse frantic, owing to the irritation. Anyone who has suffered from it themselves, will sympathize. Flat, hard lumps of various sizes suddenly appear, irregularly scattered over the body; they are like those caused by stinging nettles, and vanish in a few hours. Bites and stings may cause it. Or it may be caused by the blood being out of order temporarily, perhaps through too much protein in the diet for the amount of work being done. The causes may be summed up as bad management, such as incorrect feeding, insufficient exercise, or the horse standing about unattended to and becoming chilled after returning hot from exercise. Prevention is better than cure. Improve the general management, check and, if necessary, alter the diet. Give a tepid bran mash. Let the horse cool gradually after work and do not give it a drink while it is warm; avoid giving very cold water, especially in the depth of winter. Nettlerash may be an accompanying symptom of febrile diseases, especially surra.

Surra is a fever caused by a parasite in the blood which affects most animals, but especially horses, mules and camels. It is a tropical disease not found in the British Isles and generally occurs in the rainy season. Symptoms are an intermittent fever which comes and goes or becomes less every few days. Eye and nose membranes become yellowish in colour, and develop dark red spots on them. Nettlerash appears on the body, and later its lower surface and the legs swell. The sufferer rapidly wastes away and loses strength, death usually occurring in about six weeks from the time it became ill. It used to cause heavy losses especially among camels, but now one intravenous injection of a new drug, naganol, is usually enough to effect a cure. It also cures horses, but for a complete cure five injections are required, two intravenous and three intra-thecal.

Warble flies normally attack cattle, but sometimes horses and ponies, in the summer. The fly lays its eggs on the lower part of the legs, and the horse, bull or cow, then licks them off and they hatch in its throat. The larvae burrow their way under the skin to the shoulders and back, where they can be located as a hard lump. Rub some antiseptic ointment well into the skin, or wash with fairly strong Dettol, to kill the grubs, which can then be squeezed out. If warble flies are very prevalent, for instance, when a horse is in the same field as cattle, putting a dressing of Stockholm Tar on the legs may prevent the flies from striking there.

Horse-flies are another summer menace which abound in some districts and nearly drive the poor horses mad. They are large grey flies which suck the blood, settling on any part of the horse, often on the belly or inside of the hindlegs, or on the neck, where the horse cannot reach them. Their bite hurts, as the writer has good cause to know, and the irritation lasts for quite a time afterwards. They even attack when one is out riding and if one can kill one by slapping and squashing it, one's hand is quite red with the blood already sucked from the horses. Horses living out can lose condition through the amount of blood sucked from them, and also because they get practically no rest. The sole really effective remedy is to turn them out to graze only at night; a field-shelter helps.

Flies are a constant torment to horses (and riders) in summer. They seem attracted to horses and swarm round them in clouds, giving them no peace. They also give them sore eyes (*q.v.*).

Citronella oil, mycel cream and 'Extra-Tail' are all supposed to repel flies. Extra-Tail is sprayed on; some horses will not allow one to use a spray on them—the hissing seems to alarm them. If so, put some on the hand and then rub it in, especially on the face and legs. Citronella and mycel are also rubbed in by hand. Apply before turning the horse out. 'Extra-Tail' is claimed to be effective for several hours against all flies including horse-flies.

Another preventative is 1 pint ordinary paraffin oil, $1\frac{1}{4}$ lb. soft soap and 2 gallons water, preferably rain-water. Dissolve the soap in 1 gallon of water, then mix in the paraffin to form an emulsion. When emulsified add the second gallon of water. The mixture may be further diluted. Sponge it on all over the horse, taking care that it does not enter its eyes. It has the advantage of being a comparatively cheap remedy when several horses have to be treated.

27 Stable Vices

A horsemaster is bound to meet some form of stable vice over the years, and crib-biting is perhaps one of the commonest, and probably originally starts through boredom, when a horse is confined to the stable for long hours with nothing to do. The crib-biter seizes a post or any other wooden object between its teeth, arches its neck and gulps down air with a grunt. A bad case will even stop to do this in the middle of feeding, and will attach itself to any object whether outside or in the stable. One bad case I met even tried to bite the flat surface of an iron manger, when there was nothing else in its box. When turned out it bit the fence posts.

This is why I have advocated (Chapter 1) keeping the box as devoid of fittings as possible, and suggested that any manger or other wooden object should be covered with a sheet of zinc.

A confirmed crib-biter looks poor and thin, however much food it has, because it is always gulping down air. This also interferes with its digestion, making it more susceptible to colic. The stomach looks distended and feels and sounds tight if gently tapped.

The vice is incurable. The only answer is to have the horse out and occupy it as much as possible. When not being ridden turn it out. Do not let it remain standing idle in the stable for longer than necessary every day. Divide its hay feeds into small portions and see that it always has a haynet to nibble at to keep it amused.

Keep a crib-biter away from other horses, otherwise they will imitate and soon all will be doing it. Unfortunately, horses are very imitative and will quickly copy a stable vice.

One method of prevention is to make it wear a flute bit when stabled. This is a hollow bit with holes in it, which stops air being drawn in when the horse tries to gulp it down. Another method is to attach a stick to its head-collar, so that when it tries to arch its neck preparatory to gulping down air, the stick pokes into its neck and stops it. Also, try muzzling, except at feeding-time. Or, smear anything which could be bitten with something unpleasant tasting like soap, or bitter aloes mixed with treacle. Do not give a salt lick; it may encourage it or even have been the initial cause.

Wind-sucking is a similar vice, except that the horse does not seize anything between its teeth, but simply arches its neck and gulps down air. What has been said about crib-biting also applies to wind-*i* sucking. Try using a gullet plate and cribbing strap, obtainable from a saddler. Also try using the flute bit.

Sometimes the habit of licking the walls, through boredom, can start crib-biting or wind-sucking. Or the food may be inadequate or lacking either in sufficient bulk or minerals. Internal parasites may have been the original cause.

Weaving is a habit frequently indulged in by wild animals, especially elephants, kept in captivity. The animal waves it head and neck and rocks itself from side to side, while lifting and lowering each forefoot in turn, or even crossing them. This continues for hours, the animal giving itself no rest. It is a nervous habit caused by boredom and enforced idleness. A horse will swing its head, neck and forefeet from side to side, generally over the lower half of the door. Sometimes it also rocks, lifting its forefeet in turn or crossing them. Neighbouring horses will quickly imitate a weaver. Try to prevent the head moving sideways by using short pillar reins (though this does not attack the cause). Again keep the horse idle in the stable as little as possible and give as much work and exercise as possible. Turn it out when not being ridden. A 'bad eater' in the stable frequently picks up and is better and more alert at its work when living out. When stabled keep occupied and amused with a haynet, or even a salt-lick. It seldom seems to make a weaver start gnawing at walls or crib-biting. A permanent cure is almost impossible. A confirmed weaver which has been kept out at grass for years will immediately restart directly it is stabled. It does not seem to make a horse lose condition appreciably, unlike wind-sucking or crib-biting.

Bed-eating is a pernicious habit, to which some horses that are gross feeders are particularly prone. Giving oat straw encourages, and may start the habit as horses like it. Insufficient bulk food (i.e. hay) may be another cause. It is a habit to discourage, but not an easy one to break, as habitual bed-eaters are not too fastidious and will eat the soiled as well as the clean straw, which is not good for them. Sprinkling the bed lightly with a weak disinfectant solution may discourage it. Eating the walls of the stable may simply be a depraved appetite. If the walls are whitewashed it may indicate a deficiency in the mineral diet. It may even be due to plain hunger if horses are insufficiently fed, to worms or parasites, or just plain boredom. Paint the wall with 1 part tar to 5 parts naphtha.

Dung-eating is another depraved appetite in which some horses indulge. They will eat their own droppings. Worms or parasites, or mineral deficiency may cause this filthy habit. Check on the diet, both as to amount, ingredients and balance. Indigestion may also cause it. In both cases, wall- and dung-eating, if more food and/or a change of diet does not effect a cure, consult a vet.

In the case of dung-eating stop the horse eating off the ground. Pass a strap behind the poll to hang down just below the throat-lash; loop it onto another strap over the nostrils, like a nose-band. When the horse tries to lower its head the two straps press respectively on its neck muscles and nostrils, which stops it extending its neck.

Kicking may start in several ways—itchy heels (usually only cart-horses), rats in the stable at night, boredom, or fear. In the case of itchy heels the horse keeps stamping its foot, or feet, to relieve the irritation. A horse will also kick if rats are moving about in the stable at night, partly due to uneasiness and fear. Sometimes a dim light left on all night in the stable helps to stop this. A horse may start pawing or kicking at a partition through sheer boredom, especially if it is alone in the stable. A bored horse apparently likes the noise; the more monotonous the sound the more it amuses them. Having nothing better to occupy them they start kicking at the box door or stall partition. Other horses, unfortunately, soon learn to imitate. Try padding the door and partitions with straw-filled sacks to deaden the sound and minimize the risk of injury. Or hang a bunch of gorse or any other prickly plant where the horse kicks, so that it pricks itself. The effect must be watched carefully as it may kick all the more through panic.

A horse will also start kicking through jealousy, or to attract attention if it hears another horse being led out of the stable, or at meal times, if it thinks another horse is being fed and it is not. Other horses again will quickly imitate until there is pandemonium in the stables, especially at meal times.

Fear is a very deep-rooted cause of kicking which may date back to rough, bad handling as an unbroken youngster, or be due to bad breaking. This is kicking of a different sort; the horse does not just kick or paw at the box, or stall partition merely for the sake of making a noise, but, whether in a field or loose box, will lay its ears back, tuck its tail in between its legs and turn its hindquarters towards anyone who approaches it, sometimes edging backwards towards the person, and then suddenly letting fly with its heels. The whole attitude says plainly, 'Keep away from me, or else . . . !' This kicking through nervousness or fear is dangerous. Punishment is worse than useless as it aggravates the fear. The only way of overcoming it is by winning the horse's confidence, making it realize eventually that it has nothing to fear when approached, and therefore that there is no need for self-defence. This may be a long, tedious process, requiring much time and patience, and often, a good deal of courage. Always offer the horse a tit-bit when approaching it, whether in the field or stable. Never show any signs of fear, or hesitancy. Always approach from the front, and speak first, move slowly and quietly and handle gently but firmly, with many caresses. Tie the horse up and spend hours in the stable either moving about, doing odd jobs near it, or just sitting by its head; take a book in and read. Occasionally speak to the horse; get up and offer it a tit-bit. While doing so, speak soothingly, make much of it and pat its neck or gently rub under its jaw—most horses love this. In this way try to overcome its suspicions. Persevere daily with this treatment, for many weeks if necessary.

When grooming take extra care to avoid any ticklish spots. Hold the tail when grooming its hindquarters or hindlegs; or hold its hock or hamstring (the top of the gaskin or second thigh) firmly so that any warning movement is instantly felt (usually a slight tightening of the muscles), and adequate precautions can be taken. If you feel any movement speak soothingly and temporarily stop grooming that particular part. In the case of a really vicious kicker put plenty of straw down, and having tightly short-racked the horse, ask an assistant to hold up a front leg while you are grooming; a horse cannot kick while only standing on three legs; or strap a front leg up if help is unavailable. From time to time let the horse stand on four legs to rest it; and/or change the front leg being held up.

Mares usually are more prone to kick than geldings; they can be especially uncertain when in season, particularly in early spring and summer.

Stallions do not kick so much with their hindlegs but rear up and strike out forwards with their front legs, again particularly during the mating season, and if there are any mares nearby.

If your horse kicks out despite your precautions, scold sharply and slap it smartly on the hindquarters to make it realize its attentions are not appreciated. Short-rack while grooming and give some hay to occupy its attention.

A kicking block is another preventative; it is a shackle, with a few links of heavy chain and a smooth wooden ball attached. If the horse kicks, the chain and ball hit its legs. Or, sandbags or other heavy weights can be tied to its legs, or they can be hung behind the horse so that they swing back and hit it when struck. Watch the effects of these precautions carefully as they may add to the fear, thereby making the horse still more liable to kick.

Always remember that the closer one stands, the safer one is because the kick has less force. A swishing tail and laid-back ears, together with showing the whites of the eyes, are warnings of imminent trouble. When trying to win a horse's confidence do not make the common mistake of trying to rub its nose or face as the majority of horses hate it.

Biting can begin as a playful nip, and unless checked at the outset can easily develop into a dangerous vice. It is a mistake to give a horse indiscriminate tit-bits at odd times, or whenever one sees it. The horse expects something every time it sees its owner, and if it does not receive anything it becomes annoyed and starts nipping. For the same reason the owner should never let his horse put its nose into his pockets, looking for food. By all means give a tit-bit when catching, after a ride, when turning out just before releasing your horse, or as a reward, occasionally, when it has done something exceptionally well, say a dressage movement, or after jumping a clear round.

If a horse tries to turn round and nip while being groomed, either put your elbow out suddenly, so that it knocks its nose against it, at the same time scolding it and saying 'No!', sharply. Or give it a smart slap on its nose with your hand, again saying 'No!' in a scolding tone of voice, or slap it hard on the neck with the back of your hand, again scolding it sharply. Never hit it on the head, as this will make it head-shy. Punishment for trying to nip (or for anything else) must always be meted out immediately—even thirty seconds to a minute after is too late; the horse will not understand why it has been hit and will become frightened and resentful. If punished immediately the horse realizes why and bears no ill-will. It quickly learns to know that it is doing wrong.

To prevent a horse nipping it should always be short-racked, before grooming, especially if it is a stranger with which one is unfamiliar.

Never tease a horse as this also will only teach it to bite. When grooming, be as gentle as possible at any ticklish spots; also be careful when girthing up not to pull the girth tight too suddenly, or, not to pull it too tight.

A really vicious biter shows the whites of its eyes, lays back its ears and really goes for one with teeth bared. Apart from short-racking when grooming, one can use either a muzzle or a side-stick, which is a suitably thick and long stick which is securely fastened to the head-collar nose-band, with the other end attached to the pad of a surcingle. This restricts the movement of the horse's head and prevents it turning round. One can also use a thick wood, or hard rubber snaffle bit which causes a certain amount of pain to the horse's mouth when it bites.

If one has sufficient time and patience it is possible to cure a vicious biter by spending enough time in its box trying to gain its confidence as with a dangerous kicker, since the origin of the vice may have been teasing or other bad handling.

28 More Vices

Although riding itself does not come within the scope of this book, every good stable-manager should know how to handle a horse. This is a part of horsemastership, and for this reason such vices as bolting, bucking, napping, rearing and rolling are being dealt with here.

Bolting can be traced to several possible causes: wolf-teeth, rough, heavy hands which jag the horse's mouth, too severe a bit, a worn bit with a jagged edge (especially likely with an old jointed snaffle) or anything else which causes pain in the mouth may drive a horse nearly frantic, eventually making it bolt in its efforts to escape; similarly a badly-fitting bridle or saddle may be causing pain which is driving the poor brute to distraction; sometimes, especially with a young horse unfamiliar with strange sights or sounds, something may make it take fright and bolt in sheer panic in an effort to escape. When a horse bolts it is usually in a state of blind, unreasoning fear and is therefore beyond control, because it is beyond any appeals to reason through the ordinary aids. It logically follows after shying, though a horse may suddenly bolt without first shying or swinging round.

A very nervous, highly-strung horse which is inclined to bolt suddenly is a danger to itself, its rider, and to other people, and few experiences are more frightening than being on a runaway horse, or behind one in a trap.

As it is temporarily insane and beyond reasoning, one's only hope of pulling it up is through pain in its mouth. It's a case of 'It's either you or me, and it's not going to be me.' This is the only occasion when all consideration for its mouth must be thrown to the winds.

Do not panic as well as the horse but sit down in the saddle and concentrate on keeping there. Assume the galloping position, knees gripping tightly with hands low on its neck and forward. It is the rider's superior wits versus the horse's brute strength. The first thing to do is to try and check its speed and to regain control through the bit. Pulling on the reins is useless: the horse has the bit between its teeth and has set its jaw, so the harder one pulls the harder it pulls in return. And in a tug-of-war the horse must win every time. If on the road try to turn its head into a hedge. Failing that look for an open gate into a field. Galloping uncontrolled along a slippery road with present-day traffic is far too dangerous. Make the reins very short; give with your hands, then suddenly pull back as hard as possible with both reins, and continue doing this. Try to make the horse 'give' with its jaw and respond to the bit.

If this fails drop your left hand low while raising the right. Then pull up your left hand hard and quickly and drop your right, going diagonally across the horse's mouth. Immediately repeat using the opposite hands. A third method is to saw at the horse's mouth alternately with each rein. Provided one keeps cool these remedies can quickly be used in turn.

If there is an open gate ride into the field and make the horse keep going round it, in diminishing circles. When it eventually tires and tries to slow down keep it galloping on round the field until it is really dead-beat and lathers. And find the heaviest going possible—riding it to a standstill has permanently cured a horse that bolts.

Beginners often think a horse is bolting when it is simply enjoying a good gallop through sheer *joie de vivre*. In such a case find a long safe stretch and gallop some of the nonsense out of your horse, and enjoy the fun.

Two or three playful, high-spirited bucks when first coming out of the stable are merely signs of a healthy, happy horse. But they can develop if unchecked into a habit and become real bucking, with the avowed intention of unseating the rider. If a horse once succeeds in catching its rider unawares and bucking him off, it will try it on again.

In real, serious bucking, the horse drops its head between its fore-legs, arches its back almost double and kicks up and back with both hindlegs. To understand what real bucking is watch a Wild West rodeo bucking broncho.

Playful bucking must be discouraged with a sharp reprimand lest it becomes a habit and develops into genuine bucking. Keep the horse's head up and sit up, gripping extra tightly with the knees. Lean back, throwing your weight backwards onto the horse's loins—its weakest part—which prevents it throwing up its heels. Hold the reins very tight and short, and keep the hands low. Never let them go up in the air.

A bucking pony is a tiring, and extremely uncomfortable ride. A horse may give a harmless, playful buck or two before settling down to work, when first taken out to be lunged.

Stallions rear up more frequently than mares or geldings. Any horse that rears often is dangerous. Get rid of it. The habit may have originated through bad handling when a colt. The person breaking it in may have been impatient in the very first stage of teaching it to be led in a head-collar. If an attempt is made to drag it forward, it naturally tries to pull backwards and rears. Or a horse may rear

Stallions are more prone to rear than mares or geldings. A persistent rearer when ridden is too dangerous to keep. PHOTO BY SPORT & GENERAL PRESS AGENCY

up suddenly in fright. It may at some time have had a blow on the head, and fear of being hit again may make it rear in an effort to back away.

Wolf-teeth, sharp teeth which should be filed, a painful or too severe bit, or a badly-fitting bridle (usually too small) may cause rearing; also, a badly-fitting saddle.

Before finally condemning a horse or pony that consistently rears try to look for every possible cause.

As the horse goes up throw your arms round its neck and your weight forward as much as possible. Grip the saddle as tightly as possible with your knees while curving the calves of your legs and ankles round the horse's sides and belly. Drop the reins altogether if necessary but never pull them backwards towards you; you may pull the pony over backwards on top of you.

Or, hold the cheek-straps of the bridle and lean forwards as far as possible. Holding the bit near the snaffle cheek-rings try to pull the horse's head down. If you can pull it sideways, the idea is to make it overbalance and so lower its forelegs.

There is no real cure for a horse that habitually rears. Experts claim that deliberately pulling it over backwards can effect a cure. But it is extremely dangerous as the rider may not jump clear and be rolled on, while the horse may do itself a serious internal or spinal injury, or may have its back broken.

Too tight a curb-chain or too severe a curb bit may cause rearing. A really tight martingale may help to prevent it.

Napping is a most annoying habit which originates in allowing it to have too much of its own way. It occurs particularly with ponies ridden by children or beginners, who are not strong or knowledgeable enough to make it obey them. Instead of obeying the pony tries an evasion, opposing the rider's will and often ending by imposing its own will on the rider.

A nappy horse will try every kind of evasion to get its own way; it will suddenly stop still and refuse to move forward, or it will go round in circles, sidle sideways, buck or even attempt to rear up, rather than move forward. Or it may refuse to go in the direction its rider wishes and will try every means to go the opposite way.

Some, such as racehorses or riding school hacks, accustomed always to going out in a string, will refuse to go out alone.

The answer is a strong, forceful rider who will stand no nonsense,

Ponies especially delight in trying to roll when tacked-up. PHOTO BY
SPORTS & GENERAL PRESS AGENCY

and complete re-schooling. Even a well-schooled horse can quickly
be ruined if ridden too frequently by inexperienced riders. Never give
way to a nappy horse even if it takes an hour to win; and never
dismount. A horse regards dismounting as a victory and a confession
of fear or weakness by the rider.

In re-educating, it may be necessary to go back to long-reining
and lunging to teach the horse obedience and forward movement.
Lunging, with a good rider in the saddle, is valuable retraining.

Some, ponies especially, delight in trying to roll when saddled.
They give a beginner little warning, and can be dangerous if caught
unawares as the rider may get trapped underneath and rolled on. An
experienced rider knows the warning signs, pawing the ground with a
foreleg and a slight bending at the knees, while the pony lowers its
head. If a pony is known to be prone to roll, drive it forward with
whip and leg at the first sign of pawing the ground, or make it
circle quickly—in fact anything to distract its attention. Then make

it trot on and keep it trotting fairly quickly. If too late to prevent it going down quickly remove both feet from the irons and jump off, but keep a tight hold on the reins. With the reins over its head try to bring the horse or pony to its feet before it rolls on the saddle and perhaps breaks the tree. Be careful that the bridle does not strip off over its head in trying to get it onto its feet. Some ponies try to roll whenever they come across a pond or a stream. I knew of one that invariably gave its young mistress a ducking in summer!

Rolling is more likely in autumn or spring when a horse is moulting. The loose hairs may irritate, or its skin may itch. It may also roll if one dismounts and loosens the girth, so, remove the saddle if stopping for a rest. Knot the reins so that they cannot be broken by becoming entangled in the horse's legs.

Apart from the danger of breaking the tree, it is unpleasant to have to ride home with a saddle and bridle plastered with mud, which also entails a lot of extra tack-cleaning.

29 Breeding

Caring for a mare in foal, and of a mare and foal, both come within the sphere of good stable management. The private owner of a mare may wish to use her for breeding for some reason: through unforeseen circumstances it may be impossible to ride for some time, and the owner may not merely wish to turn his mare out and let her remain idle during this period; or the mare may have suffered an injury which has left some permanent blemish or unsoundness, which makes riding her no longer possible, yet the mare is in no pain; for example, she may be permanently lame, yet perfectly fit otherwise. Being a much-loved favourite, the owner naturally does not want her destroyed, so the obvious solution is to use her as a brood-mare.

Breeding a foal can also be quite profitable, if it turns out a good one. Besides there is the fun of handling, breaking, schooling and making the young colt, if one has the time, and the joy of having achieved something when one rides a horse one has bred and schooled oneself.

Before sending her to be mated, have the mare thoroughly examined by a vet to ensure as far as possible that she is sound and suitable for breeding and that there will be no snags. The best age at which to mate is between five and six years; four is rather young, while anything over twelve may be a little old and involve some risk in having a first foal. If a mare has already had other foals successfully, she may safely have one even at twenty. Some brood-mares have even had their last foals at over twenty-one.

It is also advisable before mating to insure the mare against foaling risk. There are reputable insurance companies which specialize in all forms of horse insurance, including foaling risks; the insurance can cover the foal as well, after birth. Although it will not restore a much-loved favourite to life, it will give some financial compensation if anything goes wrong, and avoid what otherwise would be a serious financial loss as well.

The next step is to decide on a suitable stallion. It is important to choose one with a sweet temperament, and known to be absolutely free from any vices, and from any hereditary unsoundness or defects

R

which could be transmitted to the foal. Some stallions impress their character, conformation and even colour very strongly on their progeny. Choose one with a good temperament and conformation; if it has been successful in the show-ring, or as a show-jumper, this may also be inherited by its offspring.

Do not mate with a stallion which is much bigger than the mare. Too big a stallion may produce a foal which is too large for the dam to carry safely. This may cause grave foaling risks, and is sheer cruelty, as it causes much pain in giving birth. Although it is done, the writer does not like to hear of pony mares being mated with thoroughbred stallions, nor of Shire stallions being mated with considerably smaller thoroughbred mares.

Some stallions at stud are advertised at so much for the stud fee, plus one guinea for the groom, with a no foal, no fee guarantee, or no foal, free return visit offer; this is by far the most satisfactory arrangement. The fee includes the mare's keep at the stud until she is known to be safely in foal; it does not include transport.

Have the mare served in May or early June so that the foal would normally be born in April or early May. This gives it the best chance as it has all the summer and (one hopes) good weather before it, to give it a good start. But as we all know, it is the prerogative of the fair sex to be unpunctual and to keep one waiting, and it is possible that the lady may keep one on tenterhooks for as long as a month before the foal arrives. And then it frequently arrives at the most inopportune time, often between 2 and 3 a.m.

I know of at least two cases: in one, 'Mum' kept us waiting for four weeks over the official birthday; in the other she kept us guessing for at least two to three weeks, and right up to the end nobody seemed quite sure. Some mares' figures are not at all obvious, even in advanced pregnancy.

A mare's oestrous periods normally begin in February and last until July. She comes into season every three weeks, each period lasting up to five days. During one of these she may be effectively served.

When in season mares need handling with some tact and care as they are very 'touchy', and are liable to kick, or even go for one. In fact this touchiness and irritability when being handled is one sign that she is coming into season. She may be difficult to catch, even though normally she comes to call. She will be restless and awkward about being groomed. If ridden she may neigh frequently, especially if she sees another horse, much to her rider's embarrassment. And woe betide one if she sees an entire in a field while one is out riding. If one has not the means to provide a proper foaling box, it is probably best to let the foal be born quite naturally out in the field, provided the vet has previously done everything possible to ensure that there are not likely to be any complications.

Do not allow any geldings or, especially, other mares in the same field, as they will interfere with the mother and/or foal, through jealousy. Mother and foal must have a field to themselves, well away from any others, where they can enjoy peace and quiet.

Unless one is going in seriously for breeding, for racing or showing, the special breeding of the sire is not so important. Though naturally it is very nice to have a well-bred foal. But stud fees for top class stallions are apt to be expensive. In racing of course, both dam and sire are carefully chosen for speed and stamina, and so on. One way of getting a well-bred foal at a moderate stud fee is by using a premium stallion, which can be done under certain conditions. A premium stallion is allotted a certain area, and travels that county during the breeding season. The mare is served on one's own premises.

As stallions only serve a certain number of mares in a season, a good stallion of proved high-fertility rate is much in demand, and may be fully booked for a year ahead. So one must plan well in advance. This also applies to stallions standing at reputable studs. Advertisements of stallions at stud appear each week in *Horse and Hound* during the mating season.

After mating, when the mare is returned as being safely in foal, the stable manager's task of pre-natal care begins. The urine test is the most reliable to prove whether a mare is barren or in foal. But it can only be used early in pregnancy. A vet can usually tell by a thorough examination, but even this sometimes proves incorrect. I once bought a mare which I became certain, soon after, was in foal, but three vets said she was not. All three were proved wrong when, on going down early one morning to see my mare as usual, I found a new arrival during the night standing by its proud and anxious mother. Luckily, having had my suspicions, I had only exercised her lightly. I attribute the entirely natural, trouble-free birth to the fact that she had been gently ridden and exercised up to a week before the foal was born.

Sometimes in advanced pregnancy, the foal can be felt moving in the mother, and a vet with a stethoscope may hear its heart beating. A mare can normally be worked to within a month or two before the expected date of foaling. After this she can be gently ridden if the work is gradually decreased in duration and amount.

Regular exercise is essential for health, but the mare must not have any strain or undue exertion; she should not be used in harness, nor ridden on soft, heavy going. Gentle riding at a walk, or even a slow trot, on grass, will do no harm; nor will road-work if kept to a walk, and any jarring is avoided. During the last fortnight to a week, she should only be led in hand, and not ridden.

The normal gestation period is eleven months, as compared to nine months for a human baby and two years for an elephant; a whale is said to have the longest gestation period of all mammals.

During the last six to eight weeks before parturition, the udder begins to swell: this is one of the most reliable signs. It is most apparent in the morning and exercise reduces the swelling. Wax begins to form on the teats. This usually disappears and milk begins to ooze within twelve hours of foaling.

Feeding is most important and must be of the best quality and generous in quantity. The mare should be allowed to graze for a gradually increasing length of time daily; turning her out suddenly for too long may upset her digestion.

Should one have a large loose box the mare should be brought into it at night during the last month. There should be a deep straw bedding. If the box is too small it restricts free movement and there is the risk of the mare getting cast. It should be at least 12 feet square. It should be well lit and well ventilated, without any draughts, and must be kept spotlessly clean. Before being used it must be thoroughly washed out and disinfected, including walls, floor and ceiling. If obtainable use long wheat straw and keep it as free from chaff as possible. Keep the box also free from dust.

Interfere as little as possible with the mare; it should be possible to see, without disturbing her.

As the end of the last month approaches give an occasional bran mash to help keep the bowels working normally and prevent constipation.

Try to arrange for the vet to be available on call when the day arrives in case there are any unforeseen complications. When foaling begins the owner should have someone knowledgeable with him, whom the mare knows and trusts, in case help is needed. Naturally the vet is the best person if he can be present when labour begins. About fifteen minutes after labour begins both forefeet appear first, with the head straight and slightly behind them. If more than about twenty minutes have elapsed the presentation of the foetus may be abnormal, and need help. An experienced helper can assist by inserting his hand gently and feeling any abnormality; he may then be able to adjust the head, or a leg carefully into the best position. His hand should first have been washed in some mild disinfectant and then dipped in olive oil to lubricate it. It may also be necessary to assist the appearance of the foetus by drawing it out; this also helps to reduce labour pains, even in a normal birth.

Immediately it is born see that the foal can breathe and is free from the foetal membranes. If it does not start breathing slap its sides and press its belly and end ribs gently at regular intervals to start the lungs working.

Normally, a foal will be on its feet and feeding about thirty minutes after being born.

When a foal is born unassisted and naturally outside, the umbilical cord breaks during birth, or the mother afterwards bites it through. If the foal is born in a loose-box it may be necessary to cut it; tie it first with tape about one or two inches from the belly and then cut with scissors or a knife, previously made surgically clean; sometimes it is tied twice and severed in between. Then apply iodine or mild disinfectant to the navel to prevent any risk of infection. Remove and burn all soiled bedding and replace it with clean straw. The after-birth should be burnt, or buried if in a field.

Provided the mother is well, leave her alone with her foal until she has licked it. If she shows no signs of doing so rubbing salt into the foal's coat may encourage her. If she still refuses this maternal duty thoroughly dry the foal with some soft hay, or soft cloth. When dry give the mother a bran and linseed mash. Then leave them alone. Firmly discourage all visitors. Peace and quiet are what they need.

Above all, avoid all fuss and 'flap'. Remember that hundreds of foals are born annually in a wild state without any human aid. Any anxiety seems to communicate itself in some extraordinary way to the mare, and will only upset her. If one is a 'fusser' by nature, leave it to the vet and his assistant and go out until it is all safely over.

If the foal was not born outside keep it and its mother in the box for several days. If the weather is good they can then be turned out daily for up to a couple of hours.

The more the foal is handled, right from birth, the better, as it will make breaking much easier later on.

By the time it is a month old the foal will have begun to nibble grass. If fed with its mother it will learn to eat other kinds of food by imitating her.

Start working the mare again lightly and let the foal run beside her; but do not over-exercise it. Occasionally take the mare out alone. The first time this happens there may be difficulty; there will be anguished shrieks and yells from the baby, who wants to come as well, and the mother may try not to leave it. But making her leave the foal for an hour or so is good training for the future inevitable weaning.

Do not let the foal suckle when the mare is tired or hot.

The next stage is to teach the foal to wear a small head-collar, or foal-slip, and then accustom it to being led. At first let the foal follow while an assistant leads the mare. It must then gradually be taught to be led by itself. It should be given several short 'lessons' (about fifteen minutes) several times every day, until it learns to follow obediently.

By the sixth month the mare's supply of milk will have been decreasing gradually, and it will be noticed that she may repel the foal when it tries to suckle. This tendency grows stronger as time passes and is nature's way of indicating that the foal should be weaned. The weaning process will take about a week, and mare and foal should be completely separated.

Dry the mare off by feeding her on best quality old hay, and do not allow her too much to drink; one method of helping the process is to apply black treacle to the teats. It may be necessary to draw off a little milk at first by hand, but stripping will only encourage the production of more.

If possible give the foal a companion—best of all, another foal. Catch and handle it daily, continuing its lessons in leading and obedience, and let it graze for an hour or two.

Food must be of best quality, and plentiful; give it crushed oats and linseed (boiled overnight, and the resulting jelly next morning added to the feed), plus cod liver oil in small doses.

During the first winter the essentials are shelter, good food ¿ adequate exercise. Unless it gets a good start during its first year will lose ground which it will not easily recover later.

During the daily lessons in being led, teach the foal to obey simple orders such as 'Whoa', 'Stand', 'Walk on' and 'Back'. Also gradually introduce it to the idea of being groomed by stroking it all over; also pick up its feet, which will prepare it for the idea of being shod later on. Teach it stable manners and gradually accustom it to the idea of being tied up and eventually to being short-racked for grooming. It must also learn to obey when told to 'move over', or 'stand'. 'Steady' is one of the most useful orders, both in and out of the stable.

If the foal violently resents being stroked at first, try doing so with a soft pad attached to the end of a long pole; stroke its hind-quarters gently with this several times daily until it accepts it.

A well-handled, well-disciplined foal, accustomed to obeying the voice and to being groomed, will hardly need 'breaking' in the usually accepted sense; the process will have been so gradual and gentle that it will merely be a matter of education, introducing it progressively step by step to new ideas. It will have acquired complete confidence. I dislike the implication of the word 'breaking'; we do not want to 'break' the foal, but rather to educate and develop its mind and character. I much prefer the idea of 'making' a horse. Breaking implies destroying something. Surely we do not want to destroy, but rather to make or create something of use and beauty out of the raw material at our disposal? One strict rule should be observed, that one person and only one, should have the handling of the foal; nobody else should be allowed to touch or feed it.

Foals are inclined to be 'cheeky', and because they are so attractive (like most young things), they are often allowed to get away with murder. Kind yet strict discipline is essential. Never give it tit-bits, or allow anyone else to do so; if it attempts to nip, slap it smartly on the nose and reprimand it sharply with your voice. Do this immediately. It understands and respects strictly fair and just, deserved, punishment, but punishment for something it does not understand, or if undeserved, will be resented and may cause fear, bad temper and sullen obstinacy.

The feet must now be trimmed regularly, and it is essential to have a good blacksmith who is gentle, quiet and good tempered, yet firm.

This training will occupy the next two years of the colt's (or filly's) life. 'Making', i.e. formal education with eventual mouthing, bitting and saddling should not be undertaken until it is at least three years old; four years is even better, as before this its muscles and balance are not fully under control, while its bones are still soft. It should certainly not be backed or ridden before it is four years old, and then only by a lightweight rider and for short periods at a time, without any really strenuous work. It is true that racehorses begin their racing career at between two and three years, but unfortunately they are all too often regarded merely as money-making machines. And how many horses break down in the process? And what happens to those that do, or to those that fail to make the grade, even if they do not actually break down? What an outcry there would be if a child of ten was given the rigorous training of a mature athlete and was made to attempt to beat, say, the 100 yards record.

At about three years old the start of the colt's formal education can begin by lunging it. This will train its muscles gradually and help it to learn to balance itself. Always lunge equally on both left and right circles. It is a curious fact that most horses seem to find it easier naturally to turn to the left than to the right. Lunge at first at the walk and simultaneously make it obey the vocal commands, 'Halt' ('Whoa' or 'Stop'), 'Stand', and 'Walk on'. Then similarly teach it to lunge at the trot, obeying the command to walk, when given. Eventually teach it to lunge at the canter, always obeying vocal commands for transitions from one pace to another. This work can well occupy the next year to eighteen months.

It can also gradually be introduced to long-reining, to accustom it to the idea of being made to go on from behind, and also to obey signals to turn right or left. At the Spanish Riding School in Vienna, a lot of time is spent training the young Lippizaners in long-reins. This is preparatory work towards the idea eventually of obeying signals given by the bit through the reins, whether the horse is being ridden or driven.

Mouthing can begin at about three years old, just to accustom the colt to having something in its mouth. Use a wooden or vulcanite mouthing bit with 'keys'; smear it with treacle and let it be worn in the box, for about thirty minutes at first; gradually increase the time to an hour; eventually let it wear the mouthing bit for the whole morning. At first smear treacle on the bit; trying to lick it off will encourage the youngster to play with its bit and take an interest in it, and will also help to keep its mouth moist by encouraging the free flow of saliva. It also teaches it to accept the bit willingly. Nothing is more annoying than the daily struggle when a horse refuses to take the bit when being bridled. And usually this was due to a struggle and the mouthing bit being forced into its mouth at first.

Sometimes a horse can be cured of the bad habit of refusing to take the bit, by smearing it with treacle a few times, before bridling. Bribery and corruption? Possibly, but the end justifies the means. Every time there is a fight, fresh resistance is built up and bridling is associated with an unpleasant experience in the horse's mind, so that it will try every means of evasion to avoid taking the bit.

When the young horse has become thoroughly obedient on the lunge and when being long-reined it is time to think of introducing it to the idea of carrying a weight on its back. First put a sack secured with a surcingle. Gradually fill the sack with straw until it will carry a filled sack while being lunged. This may be resented by a few bucks at first. Beware of the youngster that appears to be too docile. Either it lacks any spirit of character, or resentment may inwardly be boiling up; and one day the explosion will come, suddenly. In which case, do not fight force with force. The horse being the stronger must win, and once it discovers its superior strength and that it can be the master, you will have a rebel against authority on your hands. Go back to the beginning and start the lesson all over again, possibly for several weeks.

The next stage after the weighted sack is to put a saddle, without stirrups, on its back. Let it be long-reined and lunged with this until it accepts the idea and is obedient to all vocal commands. Then put on the stirrup-irons and let them dangle to accustom the youngster to this new idea of having something touching its sides. Again long-rein and lunge until obedient.

The next step will be backing. Proceed gradually. At the first lesson just stand by the horse and lean on the saddle, while an assistant holds its head and distracts its attention, possibly with a carrot or some pony cubes. Repeat this several times, gradually leaning more and more heavily on the saddle, until the horse takes no notice.

When the horse accepts this and stands quietly, put your foot in the stirrup, put your weight on it for a few seconds and then lower yourself again. Repeat a number of times, gradually increasing the time during which your foot remains in the stirrup. Do this for several lessons if necessary until the horse takes no notice. Always have an assistant at its head. These lessons should always be given after about twenty minutes' lunging so that the horse has let off steam first.

Next, raise yourself up in the stirrup and lie across the saddle for a few seconds; then lower yourself. Again continue until the horse accepts it, and each time remain lying across the saddle for a little longer. You may have to do this for about a week, if necessary, or even longer.

Finally, vault as quietly as possible into the saddle and sit still for a few seconds. Keep repeating this, each time remaining mounted a little longer. The lesson has been learnt when you can stay there for several minutes without any fuss on the horse's part.

At the next lesson mount and sit perfectly still while your assistant leads the horse forward at a gentle walk. When the horse walks on quietly without offering any resistance, let your assistant lunge you on both circles at a walk.

Do not attempt anything faster than a walk for several weeks, until you have taught your horse to obey guidance in direction through its mouth, and until it has learnt to understand and obey the leg aids.

At this point, except for being lunged, no assistant is necessary. It is now entirely a conversation between you and your horse, without the intervention of any third party. You are trying through its mouth and your leg aids to teach your horse to understand and obey a sign language.

Give all lessons in the corner of a quiet field away from all possible distractions. Or in a covered school if available. Give several short lessons daily; start with twenty minutes and gradually increase their duration, but not more than forty to forty-five minutes at the most. Like all youngsters, your horse has no great power of concentration at first. Its mind will wander and its attention is easily distracted. If the lesson is too long it will only become bored and fed-up. After a lesson, ride it quietly round the field for about ten minutes on a long rein to let it stretch out its neck and rest its neck muscles.

When the horse has learned to obey the rein and leg aids hack it quietly about and let it see and hear as many new sights and sounds as possible. Always lunge for about twenty minutes before riding.

Check any tendency to 'hot-up'. Accustom it to going in the company of other horses; at first let it go out with a staid, bridle-wise old horse that will act as 'schoolmaster'; and never more than a walking pace.

The best way to teach a horse the aids to trot is by riding it on the lunge, teaching it the leg aids first. If it tends to hot-up, slow down to a halt or walk and start again.

If you have a dog, so much the better. Let the horse get thoroughly accustomed to it. Train the dog not to go near your horse's heels, but otherwise if it barks and gambols about, so much the better. Your horse will meet many irresponsible dogs out later on, so the sooner it learns to ignore them, the better.

Making and elementary schooling will take about two years. By the time it is five the horse should understand the aids to walk, trot and canter; it should be accustomed to and able to pass all ordinary traffic, and be familiar with dogs and all ordinary sights and sounds.

Its more advanced education can now proceed by teaching it to rein back, and to turn on the forehand and haunches, leading up to more advanced dressage. At five it should also be ready to start jumping and can be shown hounds.

Again a wise old horse as schoolmaster is most helpful. At first let it have free jumping over low obstacles in a jumping lane. Most horses enjoy this, especially if there is a reward at the end of the lane. When first teaching it to jump when ridden, make it trot over cavelletti to learn balance and collection and to pick up its feet. Then let it follow a schoolmaster over low jumps, which should be solid, and not easily knocked down, to teach the young horse to respect them. Never overface a beginner; let it gain confidence and learn to balance itself over low jumps: 2 ft to 2 ft 6 ins is quite high enough. Gradually introduce a variety of obstacles, the more varied the better, always following its schoolmaster at first. After a time, when out hacking, put it over a narrow ditch, or other small obstacle.

When first introducing it to hounds, take it to the Meet accompanied by its schoolmaster. When hounds move off, move off quietly, as well—in the opposite direction, and go for a quiet hack.

Use a straight vulcanite snaffle for the first bit and early schooling until the horse's mouth is 'made' and it accepts the bit and bridles to it.

Only the trainer should ride the young horse until it is thoroughly schooled and really understands and obeys the aids. No two people ride exactly alike and slightly different application of the aids may cause confusion in the horse's mind.

Some people may like to keep a stallion instead of, or as well as, their own mare. They may use it for servicing their own mare (or mares) thus saving a substantial amount in stud fees; or they may stand the stallion at stud and let mares visit it, if they have the facilities and space, thus making it quite profitable; or they may show the stallion in hopes that it may win one of the premium awards. The stallion should be registered, either as a thoroughbred, Arab, Anglo-Arab, or one of the breeds of native British ponies.

Many people think that stallions by their nature must be unmanageable, and dangerous to handle, and only to be ridden and looked after by the most experienced horseman and stud-hand. If properly handled and schooled the majority need be no more difficult to ride and handle than a mare or gelding, and are perfectly docile in the stable. They can be ridden even when visiting a mare to perform their stud duties, and afterwards. Indeed, many are ridden and looked after by women, and some are even shown and ridden by young teenagers, and are also hunted and show-jumped.

If it has been badly handled and spoilt, a stallion can be difficult, and even dangerous, to manage.

By its nature, it is prone to rear up, and may then come down on top of the person leading or holding it. This rearing is used in fighting; stallions rear up and strike out with their forelegs. They also attack with teeth. In the herd a stallion fights at the beginning of the mating season for possession of his mares, or if another challenges his supremacy. Each stallion keeps his own group of mares separately. And woe betide any other stallion that may cast covetous glances, or try to interfere with any of them. On the other hand, if the challenger wins he takes over the mares and assumes leadership of the group, as their lord and master, and protector.

Out of the breeding season, from the end of July to February, there is no difficulty and a stallion can be ridden and handled quite normally. It can be ridden in company with mares without any trouble. But during the breeding season, he should not be ridden near a mare, as she may be coming into season. Then, look out for trouble!

The stallion's paddock should be strongly fenced, the top rail being high enough, so that he could not possibly jump it. Otherwise if there is a mare anywhere near, in a neighbouring field, he will be off, and out of his paddock. No mares of course should be grazed in any adjoining fields.

A mare can either be covered in a covering barn, or, the more natural way, she may be allowed to run out with the stallion during the breeding season. A large percentage of mares can be got safely in foal by this natural mating.

If a mare is to be serviced in the covering barn, it needs three people, for safety, one to hold the mare, another to hold the stallion, with the third to guide the stallion and keep the mare's tail out of the way, and generally help to hold the mare if she becomes violent, as some do. Some will even try to throw themselves onto the ground. One also runs the risk of being kicked as some stallions, after covering the mare, will kick out violently.

A stallion is limited to a maximum of twenty to twenty-five mares in his first season, while afterwards the maximum is thirty to forty. He may be allowed to cover a few mares at three years old, but four is the usual age for commencing stud duties. He may continue up to the end of his life, even twenty-five to thirty years.

If he covers forty mares in a season the minimum number of services is eighty as each mare has two to each heat; but it may amount to considerably more as many mares do not hold and must be re-served each time they 'break'.

It is essential to 'try' the mares first with a 'teaser', to prevent the stallion being needlessly wasted. A 'trying gate' is used, well-padded in case the mare kicks. If an ordinary gate is used a mare may be injured by catching her hindlegs in its bars.

When the mare is in season she should not be served when in full heat, but just after as she is going off. She must be hobbled or she may injure the stallion, or put him right off service.

After being served keep the mare moving about briskly for about twenty minutes before returning her to her field or loose-box. Do not put her straight back, or let her stand and stale or she may reject the results of the service.

When a mare and teaser are allowed to touch noses over the trying gate they will make a great deal of noise, roaring and squealing, and will strike at each other in quite an alarming way. A good teaser will soon make it apparent whether a mare is in season, or not.

The majority of stallions are bold and eager, but a few take some time to show an interest and great patience is needed in persuading them to cover the mare. If over eager a stallion may be crooked and over-reach and waste the service, or may even injure the mare. Having a mare covered is not to be undertaken lightly by an amateur but is best left to an expert stud-groom, with years of experience. Each one will have his own individual methods and from experience has learnt many valuable tips, which he keeps secret and will not impart to any stranger. He naturally hates having any onlookers, especially women.

31 The Dual Purpose Horse or Pony

Where only one animal is kept for use by the whole family, the owner may at some time wish to try his hand at driving as well. Indeed driving is also growing annually in popularity. It is as well therefore

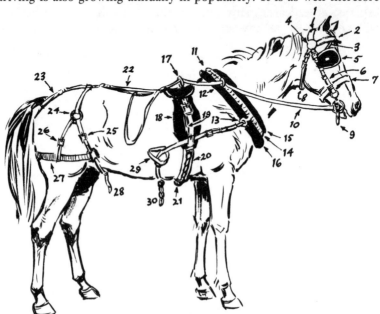

Parts of harness
1. Crown-Piece
2. Brow-Band
3. V-strap
4. Rosette
5. Winker (or Blinker)
6. Cheek-Piece
7. Nose-band
8. Throat-lash
9. Bit
10. Reins
11. Hames Strap
12. Driving Rein Ring
13. Trace Bar
14. Hames
15. Forewale of Collar
16. Afterwale of Collar
17. Rein Terret
18. Back-Band
19. Shaft-Tug
20. Girth
21. Belly-band
22. Crupper Strap (Back Strap)
23. Crupper
24. Split Cross Strap
25. Loin Strap (Hip Strap)
26. Quarter Strap
27. Web of Breeching
28. Breeching Strap
29. Trace
30. Hooking-in Chain

to choose an animal which is a good general purpose ride-and-drive horse or pony. For this purpose something about 14·2 hands in height is recommended, and no bigger. If of the rather cobby type it will not only be up to weight for the adult members, yet not too big to be ridden by the youngsters, and will also be suitable for driving.

Buy one with a medium shoulder, neither too laid back nor too upright and with an action which is not too high-stepping, nor yet too much of a 'daisy-cutter'. As the points which make a good riding horse do not make a good draught horse, and vice versa, one must compromise and try to have something mid-way between the two.

The parts of a single driving harness are shown in the accompanying illustration. Note the winker (or blinker); it is illegal to drive a horse or pony without these. The usual type of bit used is what is known as a Liverpool driving bit.

There are two kinds of collars, the neck and breast. The neck-collar is generally used, but the breast-collar is excellent for light work; its lining must be absolutely clean, smooth and supple; there is a metal shield on the neck over which the supporting strap runs, to prevent any rubbing. The breast-collar was used by the Army for artillery and transport.

Collar injuries are caused by rubbing owing to the movement of the shoulder blades; also pressure of the collar can gall the top of the neck, in front of the wither. The best way to relieve any injury is by using a wider or narrower collar. Do not use pads, or remove the stuffing over a galled part.

Owing to its shape the collar is put on upside down over the pony's head, and then reversed when past its ears. One frequently sees a beginner trying vainly to put on a collar the wrong way up. To watch his bewilderment is one of the simple joys of life!

The hames carry the trace bar and driving rings for the reins. They are collar-shaped metal branches between the forewale and afterwale of the collar.

The hame or housing strap brings together the sides of the collar at the top. If it stretches the collar can open slightly and may pinch the pony's neck. It should be regularly examined to prevent this happening.

The pad is really a small saddle; it must not press on the backbone and is held in position by the girth. The latter must not be too tight; it should be possible to insert one's finger between the girth and the

S

pony's belly.

The back-band supports the shaft-tugs and the belly-band is a continuation of it; it should be fastened loosely enough to allow two hands' breadth between it and the pony's belly.

The back or crupper strap fastens the crupper to the saddle to prevent the latter slipping forward, and its length is adjusted accordingly.

The breeching is slightly higher than the level of the shafts and hangs horizontally. It is adjusted by the loin and quarter straps. It must fit so that the saddle cannot be pushed forward when the pony is going downhill, or is backing; also it must not prevent the pony's quarters from moving freely. When the pony is throwing its weight into the collar there should be about four inches between its buttocks and the breeching.

The traces must be long enough to keep the pony always clear of the vehicle's footboard and are hooked into the trace attachments.

Bits most frequently used are single bits, such as the familiar double-ringed snaffle, or the Liverpool driving bit. Winkers (or blinkers) must not be loose, or flap, and their width is adjusted by the V-strap on the forehead so that they allow the pony free forward vision. The original reason for wearing blinkers was to prevent the pony seeing the wheels following it. They also of course help to prevent it from shying at anything imperfectly seen from the side. This is probably their most important function, especially with modern road conditions and traffic, although one does not use them— and their use is not compulsory—on a ridden horse, which is just as likely to shy at anything imperfectly seen sideways. The Army did not use them at all. If a horse or pony is properly schooled to harness work it should not need blinkers any more than a ridden animal.

When harnessing up, put the collar on first; hames and traces are usually attached to the collar, with the traces loosely looped up to keep them out of the way. If the collar needs widening it is first stretched on a bracket, or on one's knee, before putting it on. It goes on upside down until past the pony's ears. The right way up is for the narrowest part to be at the top; so it is put on with the widest part uppermost, and is then turned round, once over the pony's ears.

Keep the housing strap as tight as possible.

The saddle is put on slightly further back than its correct position, which should be the same as that of an ordinary riding saddle, until the pony's tail has been put through the crupper and the latter is in place. The crupper is then fastened to the saddle and adjusted to allow the saddle to be in its proper place. The pony is then girthed up, with the belly-band left unbuckled. The breeching is put on next.

The bridle then follows and the reins are passed through the terrets on the saddle and fastened to the bit; the spare end of the reins is folded through the nearside terret.

To put the pony to, stand it in front of the vehicle. The shafts are raised above the pony's back and the vehicle is pulled forward. The shafts are then lowered and run through the tugs up to the stops. The traces are hooked in and the breeching is buckled round them to the slots on the shafts. The belly-band is then adjusted. Unless one has a very quiet pony which can be depended upon to stand still, putting it to really requires two people: one to hold the pony while the other raises the shafts, pulls the vehicle forward 'and lowers them in their correct position, on each side of the pony. If one tries to do it single-handed the pony may decide to wander off while one is handling the vehicle; if it does move out of position there is the danger of one of the shafts coming down onto the pony, and possibly frightening it.

Undo the traces last when taking the pony out from the shafts, in case it decides to rush forward directly the traces are undone. Having got the pony out from between the shafts leave the rest of the harness on until it is in the stable, or safely tied up, if it is going to be unharnessed outside.

There are various vehicles from which one can choose. One may fancy a sporting dog-cart—and with a good pony between the shafts it can make a very smart looking turn-out. Or one can have a gig, or a governess cart (with a door at the back). This makes a good safe family vehicle, especially if there are children. There is also the ralli car. In addition there is the phaeton, though this is usually for a pair, and the chaise. But the dog-cart, governess cart, gig or ralli car are probably the most suitable.

When driving any two-wheeled vehicle one must be careful to keep it balanced, in order to ease the load on the pony. The sliding seat helps one to do this. If there is too much weight in front the shafts are forced down and weight is thrown onto the pony through the saddle. When there is too much weight at the back, the shafts pull upwards onto the pony. When the balance is even the shafts have a slight amount of play, while the buckle of the shaft-tug moves gently up and down when the pony is trotting. When going up an incline the driver (and any passenger), should lean slightly forward, and they should lean back slightly when going downhill. If the hill is steep a considerate passenger will alight and walk up it. Obey the same rule as when riding and do not trot down a hill, as there is the danger of the pony slipping and coming down on its knees, particularly with modern road surfaces.

Harness is cleaned in the same way as riding tackle, except for any patent leather-work on the harness, which should be kept well polished. Use a good shoe cream on patent leather.

Special harness polish can be bought for black harness. Frequently examine buckles and holes in all straps for signs of wear. Driving harness has perhaps more strain put upon it, consequently with more wear and tear, than riding tack. So frequent examination is most important, to prevent the risk of accidents.

The art of driving, like riding, is a special subject in itself and a lifetime study, and does not come within the scope of a book on stable management.

In these days of constant rush and noise there is something very pleasant and restful in sitting behind a good pony, and going peacefully along a quiet country lane on a fine spring or summer day, with no noise save the clop of the pony's hooves and the song of the birds—which one never has a chance of hearing in a car, or on a motor-cycle. Our forefathers had a great deal that we have lost in this modern age. For strict utility, a car—yes. But for sheer pleasure, a pony and trap—every time.